FILM AND SOCIETY

SCRIBNER
RESEARCH
ANTHOLOGIES

Martin Steinmann, Jr., GENERAL EDITOR

RICHARD DYER MacCANN

FILM AND SOCIETY

SCRIBNER
RESEARCH
ANTHOLOGIES

CHARLES SCRIBNER'S SONS   New York

Printed in the United States of America
Library of Congress Catalog Card Number 64-23525

To JOHN GRIERSON

Preface

Each Scribner Research Anthology is a collection of written sources upon a single historical, political, literary, or scientific topic or problem—the Hungarian Revolt, Shakespeare's *Julius Cæsar,* or extrasensory perception, for example. In addition to these sources, it contains (1) "Guide to Research," an account of the rationale and the methods of research and of research-paper writing, (2) an introduction to the topic of the anthology, (3) suggested topics for controlled research, and (4) suggested sources and topics for library research.

Each anthology is designed to serve two purposes. First, each gives the student access to important sources—texts, documents, letters, diaries, essays, articles, reports, transcripts of hearings, for instance—on a given topic. Some of these sources are otherwise available in only a few libraries, some (manuscripts and historical and government documents) in only one. In any case, the collection as a whole is not otherwise available in one volume. Second, each anthology gives the student either all his sources for a controlled-research paper or some of them for a library-research paper. Each anthology can be valuable either for readings in courses in history, literature, science, or humanities or as the basis for a research paper in these or in other courses.

A controlled-research paper—a paper in which the student's search for sources is limited to, and in certain ways controlled by, those sources contained in one anthology—is not so noble an undertaking as a library-research paper. But it is often more successful—more rewarding for the student and easier for his instructor to teach effectively and judge fairly. Its advantages for both student and instructor are often considerable.

For the student, it sometimes provides sources unavailable in his school library. And it enables him to learn a good deal about research (selection, interpretation, and evaluation of sources; quotation and paraphrase; and documentation) without prior instruction in use of the library (and, incidentally, without overtaxing the facilities and the resources of his library and without loss of, or damage to, sources either irreplaceable or difficult and expensive to replace).

For the instructor, it permits focus of class discussion upon a limited set of topics. It enables him to track down the student's sources conveniently. And—perhaps the greatest advantage of all—it enables him to judge both conveniently and exactly how well the student has selected, interpreted, and evaluated his sources and how well he has quoted and paraphrased them.

In many schools, a controlled-research paper is either a preliminary to or a part of a library-research paper. A library-research paper is probably the most difficult paper that the student can be assigned to write. The problems that confront him are not simply those common to any paper—organization, paragraphing, and transitions, for instance—and those (already mentioned) common to all research papers. He has, in addition, the problem of using the library well—of, for example, using the card catalogue, periodical indexes, and other reference works. But, if the instructor assigns a controlled-research paper as a preliminary to or, as it were, an early part of a library-research paper, the student need not come to grips with all these problems at once.

Each Scribner Research Anthology is compiled according to the following editorial principles. Each source that is not anonymous is prefaced by a biographical note on its author. At the foot of the same page is a bibliographical note. Each source is reprinted exactly as it appears in the original except for (1) some typographical peculiarities, (2) explanatory notes, given in brackets, and (3) omissions, indicated by ellipses (". . ."). And, finally, for each source that has pagination in the original, page numbers are given in brackets within the source itself—thus: "[**320/321**]," where everything before the slash (and after the preceding slash, if any) is from page 320, and everything after the slash (and before the next slash, if any) is from page 321. For a source hitherto unpublished, no page numbers are given; and the student who uses it should cite the page numbers of the Scribner Research Anthology. Footnotes to a source are given as in the original. Where the original pagination of a footnote is not evident, its page number precedes it in brackets.

MARTIN STEINMANN, JR.

Bingham Bay
Lake Gogebic
August, 1960

Guide to Research

THE IDEA OF RESEARCH

Research is the organized, disciplined search for truth; the aim of all research is to discover the truth about something. That thing may be a historical object like the Stonehenge monuments or a historical event like the Hungarian Revolt or the Battle of Waterloo. It may be a work of literature like Shakespeare's *Julius Cæsar* or Miller's *Death of a Salesman.* It may be a recurring event like the motions of the planets or the circulation of the blood. It may be an experimentally repeatable phenomenon like behavior of rats in a maze or perception apparently unaccounted for by the five senses. Or it may be a political problem like the decision to use the atomic bomb in World War II. Archeology, history, political science, literary criticism and scholarship, astronomy, physiology, and psychology—these are some of the many divisions of research. Indeed, all the sciences—physical, biological, and social—and all other scholarly disciplines share this organized, disciplined search for truth.

The search for truth has often been confused with such aims as confirming prejudice, instilling patriotism, and praising friends and blaming enemies. The attempt to prove the preconceived conclusion *that* one college is superior to another, for example, is not research (though the attempt to discover *whether* one college is so superior is). Research is hostile to prejudice.

General Methods of Research. The best general method of research is first-hand observation. But this method is not always possible and, when it is possible, not always practical.

The best method to begin discovering the truth about something is to observe that thing and the circumstances surrounding it. To discover the truth about *Julius Cæsar* or *Death of a Salesman,* get the play and read it, or go to the theatre and watch a performance. To discover the truth about the planets, observe them through your telescope. To discover the truth about the intelligence of rats, build a maze and run some rats through it.

This first-hand observation is not always possible, however. To discover the truth about the Battle of Waterloo, you can't observe the battle. The best that you or anyone else can do is to observe other persons' observations, the recorded observations of eye-witnesses: diaries, letters, and memoirs, for instance, of soldiers and generals who were in the battle. With more recent historical events—for example, the Hungarian Revolt—you are better off. You can watch films and listen to tape recordings. You may be able to interview people who were there. But these observations are still second-hand; and, on the whole, history can be observed only at second-hand. The sole exception is history that you have been part of. You may have fought in the Hungarian Revolt—though, if you did, you may be prejudiced.

Even when first-hand observation is possible, it is not always practical. You may have a copy of or tickets to *Julius Cæsar* or *Death of a Salesman* but not know enough about the principles of dramatic criticism to interpret the play unaided. You may have a telescope but not know how to use it or, if you do, not know what to make of what you observe through it. You may have some rats but not know how to build a maze or, if you do, not know enough about animal psychology to run your rats through it properly. The best that *you* can do under these circumstances is to supplement whatever first-hand observations you can make with observations of the first-hand observations of other people better-trained or better-equipped than you. Read *Julius Cæsar* or *Death of a Salesman* and also critics' interpretations of the play. Observe the planets, if you can, and read treatises on astronomy. Do what you can with your rats, and read reports of experiments with rats. After all, no one can master the special methods and come by the special equipment of all scholarly disciplines. Indeed, few people can do this with more than one discipline, and then not before they're thirty. But all people who want a liberal education should try to discover as much of the truth about as many scholarly disciplines as their abilities and their circumstances permit. Indeed, the achievement of this is what is meant by "a liberal education."

Primary and Secondary Sources. As the foregoing account of the general methods of research suggests, there is, ultimately, only one source of the truth about something—the thing, the event, or the phenomenon itself: the Stonehenge monuments, the Hungarian Revolt, or the Battle of Waterloo; the text of *Julius Cæsar* or *Death of a Salesman;* Robert Oppenheimer's testimony on the use of the atomic bomb against Japan; the motions of the planets or the circulation of blood; extrasensory perceptions or rats running in a maze. Such a source is a *primary* source. And, in historical research, where the thing itself (the Hungarian Revolt or the Battle of Waterloo) cannot be observed at first hand, a report of an eyewitness or a film or a tape recording is also counted as a *primary* source. But any other second-hand source (an interpretation of *Julius Cæsar* or *Death of a Salesman,* a treatise on astronomy, a report of an experiment with rats) is a *secondary* source.

A primary source is, of course, better. But, if a primary source is unavailable to you (if it is a book, perhaps your school library does not have it) or if you are not trained or equipped to use it (you don't know how to run rats through a maze or you have no telescope), then a secondary source must do. In any case, except for the most mature scientists and scholars, a good

secondary source is useful and often indispensable.

It is worth noticing that being primary or being secondary is not an intrinsic characteristic of the source itself. It is, rather, a relationship that either exists or does not exist between a given source and a given topic of research. Consequently, a given source may be primary in relation to one given topic but secondary in relation to another. Two examples may serve to make this important point clear. Edward Gibbon's *The Decline and Fall of the Roman Empire* (1776-1788) is a secondary source in relation to the topic of the Roman Empire but a primary source in relation to that of eighteenth-century English prose style or that of eighteenth-century historiography. Samuel Taylor Coleridge's *Lectures on Shakespeare* (1811-1812) is a secondary source in relation to the topic of Shakespeare's plays but a primary source in relation to that of nineteenth-century principles of dramatic criticism or that of Shakespeare's reputation.

It is worth noticing also that a given source may be primary or secondary in relationship to more than one topic. James Joyce's novel *A Portrait of the Artist as a Young Man* is a primary source in relation not only to the topic of the structure of *A Portrait of the Artist as a Young Man* (and dozens of other topics on the novel itself) but also to the topic of use of the stream-of-consciousness technique in twentieth-century fiction.

THE RESEARCH PAPER

A research paper is a paper giving the results of research, the methods by which they were reached, and the sources, primary or secondary, which were used. A research paper attempts to tell the truth about a topic, and also tells how and where this truth was discovered. As we have seen, the sources of a research paper may be either written sources (literary texts and historical documents, for example) or sources of other kinds (experiments, for example). Since a research paper written in school is almost always based upon written (printed) sources, we shall here discuss only that kind. A research paper based upon written sources may be either a library-research paper or a controlled-research paper. A library-research paper is a research paper for which your search for sources is limited to those sources contained in the libraries available to you; a controlled-research paper, to those sources contained in one anthology —to those contained in this volume, for example. Here we shall emphasize the latter kind.

Finding Your Topic. The first step in writing a research paper based upon written sources, whether a library-research or a controlled-research paper, is finding a topic. We say "finding a topic" rather than "choosing a topic" because the process is more like finding a job than choosing a sandwich from a menu. Unless your instructor assigns you a topic, which he may do, you must look for one; and the one you find may not be just what you want but the best one that you can find. But, if you look long and carefully, you may find a topic that so well suits your interests, your capacities, and the time and the space at your disposal that your paper will almost surely be a success.

Finding a topic is the most important single step in writing a research paper, and the things that you should have in mind when looking for a topic are (1) your interests, (2) your capacities, and (3) the time and the space at your disposal. If you are interested in a topic, if you know something about the special methods of research that the topic requires, and if your topic is narrow enough to require no more time than you have for research and no greater development than you can give it in a paper of the length assigned you, then the paper that results will probably be satisfactory. For example, the topic of figures of speech in *Julius Cæsar* may interest you greatly. But, if it does, you must ask yourself whether you know enough about figures of speech to do research on them

and, if you do, whether this topic is narrow enough. Even the topic of metaphors in the play would be too broad for most papers; metaphors in Brutus' soliloquies might be about right. In any case, before you take a topic for a paper, you should do some reading on that topic; otherwise, you won't know whether it is interesting, within your ability to handle, and within the scope of your assigned paper.

Once you think that you've found a topic, take great care in phrasing it. The best phrasing is a question or a series of closely related questions. Better than "The character of Brutus" is "To what extent is Brutus motivated by self-interest and to what extent by the public interest?" The latter is not only more narrow and more precise; it provides you with a criterion of relevance in selecting your sources. At the end of this volume, you will find a list of suggested topics, intended to call your attention to topics that might not occur to you. But these topics are suggestive rather than definitive or precise.

Finding Your Sources. Finding sources for a library-research paper and finding ones for a controlled-research paper, though different in several respects, are alike in certain others. Finding sources in the library requires knowledge of how to use the card catalogue, periodical indexes, special bibliographies, reserve shelves, and encyclopedias. Finding sources in this volume or a similar one does not. But, in either case, you must have a clear idea of what you are looking for; and you must be prepared to put up with a high ratio of looking to finding. In other words, you must have not only criteria of relevance but also a willingness to do a good deal of skimming and a good deal more of careful reading, some of it fruitless.

The basic criterion of relevance you provide by careful phrasing of your topic, a problem discussed in the preceding section. The other criteria you provide by making a preliminary or tentative outline —perhaps in the form of subtopics, perhaps in the form of questions. Such an outline is not to be used for your paper. The outline for your paper will probably be quite different and, in any event, cannot be made until after you find your sources and take your notes. This preliminary outline guides your research and, as we shall see, provides you with the subtopic headings necessary for your note-cards (see "Taking Your Notes," page xiii).

Making Your Working Bibliography. Once you have found a promising source ("promising" because, though it seems to be relevant, it may turn out not to be) you want to make some record of it so that, once you have completed your search for sources, you can turn back to it, read it, and, if it turns out to be relevant, take notes on it. This record of promising sources is your *working* bibliography. It is so called for two reasons: first, because you work with it as you proceed with your research and the writing of your paper, adding promising sources to it and discarding irrelevant ones; and, second, because this designation distinguishes it from your final bibliography, which appears at the very end of your research paper and contains only sources actually used in the paper. For a controlled-research paper, your working bibliography may be nothing more elaborate than a series of check marks in the table of contents of your research anthology or a list of page numbers. For a library-research paper, however, you need something quite different.

A working bibliography for a library-research paper is a collection of three-by-five cards each representing a promising source and each containing full information about that source. Once you have completed your research, written your paper, and discarded all promising but (as they turned out) irrelevant sources, this bibliography is identical with your final bibliography. Having a separate card for each source enables you to add and to discard sources easily and to sort and arrange them easily in any order you please. Eventually, when this bibliography becomes identical with your final bibliography, you will arrange sources alphabetically by au-thors' last names. Having full information about each source on its card enables you to turn back to it easily—to locate it in the library without first looking it up again. You find this information in the card catalogue, periodical indexes, or other bibliographical aids; or, when browsing through the shelves or the stacks of the library and coming upon a promising source, you find it in or on the source itself—for example, on the spine and the title page of a book.

If the source is a *book,* you should put the following information on the three-by-five working-bibliography card:

(1) the library call number,
(2) the author's (or authors') full name (or names), last name first for the first author,
(3) the title of the book,
(4) the name of the city of publication,
(5) the name of the publisher (*not* the printer), and
(6) the year of publication (often found on the other side of the title page).

See the example of such a card on the opposite page (note the punctuation carefully).

If the source is a *periodical article,* you should put the following information on the three-by-five working-bibliography card:

(1) the author's (or authors') full name (or names),
(2) the title of the article,
(3) the name of the periodical,
(4) the volume number,
(5) the week, the month, or the season of publication, together with the year, and
(6) the page numbers covered by the article.

See the example of such a card on the opposite page (note the punctuation carefully).

These two forms take care of the two standard cases. For special cases—such things as books with editors or translators as well as authors, books published in several editions or in several volumes, and daily newspapers—see any good handbook of composition.

860.3
J23

Jones, John A., and William C.
Brown. A History of
Serbia. New York: The
Rowland Press, Inc., 1934.

WORKING-BIBLIOGRAPHY CARD FOR A BOOK

Smith, Harold B. "Fishing
in Serbian Waters." Journal
of Balkan Sports, VII
(May, 1936), 26-32.

WORKING-BIBLIOGRAPHY CARD FOR A PERIODICAL ARTICLE

Taking Your Notes. Once you have found sources, entered them in your working bibliography, read them, and found them relevant, taking notes requires your exactly following a standard procedure if your notes are going to be useful to you when you come to write your paper. An extra five minutes given to taking a note correctly can save you a half hour in writing your paper. Here is the standard procedure:

(1) Take all notes on four-by-six cards. Never use notebooks, loose sheets of paper, or backs of old envelopes.

(2) Limit each note to information on a single subtopic of your preliminary outline *and* from a single source. It follows from this that you may have many cards on the same subtopic and many cards from the same source but that you may never have one card on more than one subtopic or from more than one source.

(3) On each card, in addition to the note itself, put

   (a) the appropriate subtopic heading in the upper left-hand corner,

   (b) the name of the source (usually the author's last name will do) in the upper right-hand corner, and

   (c) the page number (or numbers) of that part (or those parts) of the source that you have used in taking your note. If you have used more than one page, indicate your page numbers in such a way that, when you come to write your paper, you can tell what page each part of the note comes from, for you may not use the whole note.

(If you follow these first three rules, you will be able, when you come to outline and to organize your paper, to sort your notes in any way you please—by subtopic, for example—and to arrange them in any order you please. Such flexibility is impossible if you take your notes in a notebook. If you follow the third rule, you will also be able to document your paper— write footnotes, for example—without again referring to the sources themselves.)

(4) In taking the note itself, paraphrase or quote your source or do both; but do only one at a time, and use quotation very sparingly.

Paraphrase and quotation require special care. Anything between paraphrase and quotation is not acceptable to good writers: you either paraphrase or quote, but do nothing in between. To paraphrase a source (or part of a source) is to reproduce it in words and word orders substantially different from the original. When you paraphrase well, you keep the sense of the original but change the language,

retaining some key words, of course, but otherwise using your own words and your own sentence patterns. To quote a source (or part of a source) is to reproduce it exactly. When you quote well, you keep both the sense and the language of the original, retaining its punctuation, its capitalization, its type face (roman or italic), and its spelling (indeed, even its misspelling).

Omissions and additions require special care. If, when quoting, you wish to omit some of the original, you may do so only if the omission does not change the sense of the original (never leave out a "not," for example!) *and* if it is indicated by ellipses (three spaced periods: ". . ."). If you wish to add something to the original, you may do so only if the addition does not change the sense of the original (never add a "not"!) *and* it is indicated by square brackets. The most usual additions are explanations ("They [i.e., the people of Paris] were alarmed") and disclaimers of errors in the original, indicated by the Latin *"sic,"* meaning "thus" ("Colombis [*sic*] discovered America in 1592 [*sic*]"). You must, of course, carry these ellipses and square brackets from your note-cards to your paper. And, if you type your paper, brackets may be a problem, for most typewriter keyboards do not include them. If your keyboard does not, you may do one of two things—either use the slash ("/") and underlining ("__" and "—") in such a way as to produce a bracket ("⌐" and "⌐") or draw brackets in with a pen. In any event, don't substitute parentheses for brackets.

In your paper, quotations no longer than three or four lines are to be enclosed within a set of quotation marks and run into your text; longer ones are to be set off from the text, without quotation marks, by indention from the left-hand margin and, especially in typewritten copy, by single-spacing. But never use either of these devices unless the language is exactly that of the original.

Your usual treatment of a source should be paraphrase; use quotation only if the

Fly - fishing   *Smith*

  Smith says that fly-fishing is a method of fishing used chiefly by wealthy Serbians and foreign tourists, that the flies used are generally imported from Scotland, and that "Serbian trout are so snobbish that they won't glance [27/28] at a domestic fly."

  [Query: How reliable is the information in this rather facetious article?]

NOTE-CARD

language of the original is striking (strikingly good or strikingly bad), if it is the very topic of your research (as in a paper on Shakespeare's style), or if it is so complex (as it might be in a legal document) that you don't want to risk paraphrasing it.

Let us look at the sample note-card above. The topic of research is methods of fishing in Serbia; the subtopic that the note deals with is fly-fishing in Serbia; the source is Harold B. Smith's article "Fishing in Serbian Waters," from the *Journal of Balkan Sports* (see the second of the two working-bibliography cards on page xiii).

Note the subtopic heading ("Fly-fishing") in the upper left-hand corner; the name of the source, abbreviated to the author's last name ("Smith"), in the upper right-hand corner; the page numbers ("[27/28]"), indicating that everything, both paraphrase and quotation, up

through the word "glance" is from page 27 and that everything after that word is from page 28; the sparing and appropriate use of quotation; and the bracketed query, to remind the note-taker that he must use this source with caution.

Writing Your Paper. Many of the problems of writing a research paper based upon written sources—organization, the outline, the thesis paragraph, topic sentences, transitions, and the like—are problems of expository writing generally. Here we shall discuss only those problems peculiar to such a paper. Two of these problems —paraphrase and quotation—we discussed in the preceding section. Two others remain: reaching conclusions and avoiding the scissors-and-paste organization.

When you come to make the outline for your paper and to write your paper, you will have before you three things: (1) your *preliminary* outline, containing ordered subtopics of your topic; (2) your working bibliography; and (3) your note-cards. These are the *immediate* results of your research; they are not the *final* results. They are only the raw material out of which you must fashion your paper. At best, they are an intermediate stage between finding your topic and making your final outline. The preliminary outline will not do for the final outline. The working bibliography will almost certainly require further pruning. And the note-cards will require sorting, evaluation, organization, pruning, and exercise of logic and common sense. All this needs to be done, preferably before you make your final outline and begin to write your paper, though almost inevitably some of it will remain to bedevil you while you are writing it. To put the matter in another way, you are, with these things before you, a Sherlock Holmes who has gathered all his clues but who has reached no conclusions from them, who has not come to the end of his search for truth. You must discard irrelevant clues, ones that have no bearing on the questions that you want answered. You must arbitrate the claims of conflicting or contradictory clues. You must decide which one of several probable conclusions is the most probable.

Once you have reached your conclusions, you must organize your paper and set forth this organization in your final outline. Organization and the outline are, of course, problems common to all expository writing. But a problem peculiar to the research paper is avoiding the scissors-and-paste organization—avoiding a paper that looks as though you had cut paraphrases and quotations out of your note-cards, pasted them in columns on paper, and connected them only with such phrases as "Jones says" and "On the other hand, Brown says." Such an organization is the result of a failure to reach conclusions (with the consequence that there is nothing but "Jones says" to put in between paraphrases and quotations); or it is a failure to see the necessity of giving the conclusions reached *and* the reasoning by

which they were reached (with the consequence that, though there is something to put between paraphrases and quotations, nothing is put there, and the reader is left to write the paper for himself).

Documenting Your Paper. To document your paper is to give the source of each paraphrase and quotation that it contains, so that your reader can, if he wishes to, check each of your sources and judge for himself what use you have made of it. To give the source is usually to give (1) either the information that you have about that source in your working bibliography (except that the name of the publisher of a book is usually not given) or the information that accompanies each source in a research anthology *and* (2) the information about page numbers that you have in your notes. This information you may give either formally or informally, as your instructor decides.

Formal documentation is given in footnotes. For a full discussion of footnotes, see any good handbook (one cheap and widely accepted one is *The MLA Style Sheet*). The form of footnotes is similar to, but not identical with, the form of bibliographical entries. With these three sample footnotes, compare the two sample working-bibliography cards on page xiii:

[1] John A. Jones and William C. Brown, *A History of Serbia* (New York, 1934), p. 211.
[2] Harold B. Smith, "Fishing in Serbian Waters," *Journal of Balkan Sports*, VII (May, 1936), 27.
[3] Smith, pp. 27-28.

Informal documentation is given in the text of the paper, usually parenthetically, as in this example:

> Fly-fishing in Serbia is chiefly a sport of wealthy Serbians and foreign tourists (Harold B. Smith, "Fishing in Serbian Waters," *Journal of Balkan Sports*, VII [May, 1936], 27), though in some mountain districts it is popular among the peasants (John A. Jones and William C. Brown, *A History of Serbia* [New York, 1934], p. 211). The flies used are generally imported from Scotland; indeed, Smith facetiously adds, "Serbian trout are so snobbish that they won't glance at a domestic fly" (pp. 27-28).

As this example suggests, however, informal documentation can be an annoying distraction. It probably works out best in papers that use only a few sources. In such papers, there are few occasions for long first-references to sources: for example, "(Harold B. Smith, "Fishing in Serbian Waters," *Journal of Balkan Sports,* VII [May, 1936], 27)." But there are many occasions for short succeeding-references: for example, "(Smith, pp. 27-28)" or "(pp. 27-28)." Occasionally, informal documentation may be profitably combined with formal, as in a paper about Shakespeare's *Julius Cæsar.* In such a paper, references to the play might well be given informally —for example, "(III.ii.2-7)"—but references to critics formally.

How many footnotes (or parenthetical documentations) do you need in your paper? The answer is, of course, that you need as many footnotes as you have paraphrases or quotations of sources, unless you group several paraphrases or quotations *from the same page or consecutive pages of a given source* in such a way that one footnote will do for all. One way to do this grouping—almost the only way— is to introduce the group with such a sentence as "Smith's views on fly-fishing are quite different from Brown's" and to conclude it with the raised numeral referring to the footnote. Your reader will understand that everything between the intro-

ductory sentence and the numeral comes from the page or the successive pages of the source indicated in the footnote.

Making Your Final Bibliography. Your paper concludes with your final bibliography, which is simply a list of all the sources—and only those sources—that you actually paraphrase or quote in your paper. In other words, every source that you give in a footnote (or a parenthetical documentation) you include in your final bibliography; and you include no other sources (inclusion of others results in what is unfavorably known as "a padded bibliography"). The form for entries in your final bibliography is identical with that for ones in your working bibliography, given above. You should list these sources alphabetically by authors' last names or, if a source is anonymous, by the first word of its title, but not by "a," "an," or "the." For example:

BIBLIOGRAPHY

Jones, John A., and William C. Brown. *A History of Serbia.* New York: The Rowland Press, Inc., 1934.
"Serbian Pastimes." *Sports Gazette,* XCI (October 26, 1952), 18-19, 38, 40-42.
Smith, Harold B. "Fishing in Serbian Waters," *Journal of Balkan Sports,* VII (May, 1936), 26-32.

MARTIN STEINMANN, JR.

Contents

FILM AND SOCIETY

Introduction

Public concern about the arts, like so many other basic concerns in human life, can be traced at least as far back as the Athenian philosophers Plato and Aristotle.

Plato's *Republic* is the description of a society in which everything would be arranged to provide for justice and excellence. Through wise organization and planning the right kind of men would be brought forth and trained. Once trained and put in their places, however, these men might be misled by the wrong kind of music, drama, or literary art. The dramatist, in Plato's view, might make the people and their leaders afraid and excited—or soft and ineffective—or at least desirous of what was not proper for them. There could be only a limited role in the ideal republic for the "poet"—that is, the man of ideas, the interpreter of history. A public censor must watch over him.[1]

And therefore when any one of these panto-mimic gentlemen, who are so clever that they can imitate anything, comes to us, and makes a proposal to exhibit himself and his poetry, we will fall down and worship him as a sweet and holy and wonderful being; but we must also inform him that in our State such as he are not permitted to exist; the law will not allow them. And so when we have anointed him with myrrh, and set a garland of wool upon his head, we shall send him away to another city. For we mean to employ for our souls' health the rougher and severer poet or story-teller, who will imitate the style of the virtuous only. . . .[2]

Aristotle, on the other hand, always the practical observer, disagreed with Plato, who was his teacher. He could not get upset about the dangers of drama. In his view, epic and tragic poetry might help to work off the fears and excitements and imaginations most people already had. His theory of public purification through pity and fear, presented as an incidental comment in the *Poetics,* was a most generous view of the advantages to be gained from the artist's imagination of life. It allowed considerable freedom for the man of ideas. Yet it was also a conservative view, in that Aristotle accepted drama the way it was— or at least the way it had been presented by Sophocles or Euripides—insisting that at its best it was socially useful, psychologically sound, and sometimes aesthetically inspiring.[3]

The communication arts still find themselves attacked and defended from the same opposite poles. Conservative critics and men in public life who become disturbed about the arts often find themselves agreeing, whether they know it or not, with Plato, the utopian visionary. Artists, in rebuttal, often use arguments first put forth by that cautious scientist Aristotle.

In American history, the Puritan tradition has long been hostile to the theater just as in English history. The film censorship laws in many cities and in a few states have been the natural development of an attitude that looks on the imitation of life as sinful in itself and sees the themes of certain plays as leading to sin in the spectator. The Puritans did not agree with Plato on most subjects; but, in his assumption that the state should impose religious observances and censor theatrical excesses, the New England divines and the Greek idealist had something in common.

For many years (as Bosley Crowther points out in his summary of the history of censorship, p. 108) American advocates of freedom of speech have sought to over-

---

[1] Plato, The Republic, trans. Benjamin Jowett, Modern Library ed. (New York: Random House, n.d.), Bks. II, III, X, *passim.*

[2] The Republic, Bk. III, pp. 99-100. The main argument is presented in the first half of Bk. III.

[3] Aristotle, De Poetica, trans. Ingram Bywater, The Basic Works of Aristotle, ed. Richard McKeon (New York: Random House, 1941), VI, 1460.

1

throw the Puritanical approach of motion-picture censor boards. Helped by an increasing emphasis by the Supreme Court on the key importance of free speech in making democracy work, this pressure has been successful. It has brought movie-makers today to a point of almost total freedom of expression. Apart from restraints on obscenity, defined by the Supreme Court as that which is "totally without redeeming social importance,"[4] judicial restraints on communication have almost ceased to exist. Only occasional tides of public wrath seem to be able to roll back, for example, the excesses of brutality sometimes exhibited in films or on TV.

Having passed through a period of freeing ourselves from questionable restrictions, it may be that we are entering a period of questionable freedoms. The subject matter of some recent plays and films suggests that this may be the case. Are there new methods of social self-control—new ways of restricting the audience or labeling the communication—that a democracy may wish to impose in order to protect its citizens from false, misleading, overwhelming, or degrading messages?

The Federal Trade Commission enforces rules against misleading advertising claims. But interference with other kinds of messages is not something to be undertaken lightly. As John Stuart Mill said in his essay "On Liberty": "The peculiar evil of silencing the expression of an opinion is, that it is robbing the human race. . . . There must be discussion, to show how experience is to be interpreted. Wrong opinions and practices gradually yield to fact and argument; but facts and arguments, to produce any effect on the mind, must be brought before it."[5] The modern communicator would add: The dramatist must be just as free to bring arguments before the mind as the stump speaker or editorial writer.

From the beginning, the social critics of the motion picture have stressed its wide appeal and its great power to excite. The appeal and the power are much greater, they say, than those of plays or novels. Yet this assumption, while it might have been true when movies were new, has never been subject to much proof. In fact, the whole question of proof about the influence of motion pictures is still up in the air, and perhaps always will be. There are hundreds of studies by educators which tend to show that students pick up certain kinds of facts rather more quickly from films than from books and that they may remember the facts longer. But it is hard to prove that basic social attitudes—and, after that, basic behavior—can be changed by the magic of a single film.

Perhaps the most serious attempt so far to examine the effect of films on attitudes is the 1933 Thurstone-Peterson study (described by Mortimer Adler in "Research: The Immature," p. 85). This study went pretty far toward proving the power to shift social attitudes—for children, at least. It was based on "attitude scales," statements ranging from one extreme to another, relating to issues raised by themes of the films. When the same children checked stronger statements after seeing the film, presumably this showed a change in attitude.[6]

Further studies of this puzzling question would be immensely valuable to society. Yet such studies are not at all in the interest of the entertainment industries. If another independent study were to be made

---

[4] *U.S.* v. *Roth*, 354 U.S. 476 (1957).

[5] John Stuart Mill, "On Liberty," *Utilitarianism, Liberty, and Representative Government.* Everyman Library ed. (London: J. M. Dent, 1947), pp. 79, 82. Much of Chapter II, "On the Liberty of Thought and Discussion," pp. 78-113, would be of interest to readers concerned with this issue.

[6] L. L. Thurstone and R. C. Peterson, *Motion Pictures and the Social Attitudes of Children* (New York: The Macmillan Company, 1933). The Payne Fund series, of which this study was a part, is described as "the best-financed research approach to the question of children's relation to films" in a recent study by Wilbur Schramm, Jack Lyle, and Edwin B. Parker, *Television in the Lives of Our Children* (Stanford, California: Stanford University Press, 1961), p. 312.

today, using attitude scales similar to the Thurstone-Peterson investigators', to find out if the easy flow of violence on TV shows actually influences specific young people—picture by picture, in a cumulative way—the people who make their living from such shows would naturally be up in arms. They would find their own witnesses to testify, as certain psychiatrists testified before the Kefauver subcommittee, that Aristotle had said the last word —that violence on the screen is really good for us because watching it purges us of our aggressions. Yet there are also psychiatrists on the other side of this question, as the subcommittee demonstrated.[7] Thus, though its issues change from age to age, public concern about the arts remains very much alive.

Here, then, are the largest of the controversies swirling around the moving image today: Does it have a marked influence? If so, can that influence be measured? Should the moving image be controlled in some way? If so, by what standards or rules? By what agencies? Is self-control by the producers of communication enough to satisfy the public need? What, after all, is the public need? How is it different from what the public wants?

Motion-picture producers, for sixty years or more, have quarreled among themselves about the question "What does the public want?" In the broadest sense, they will agree, perhaps, that the public wants entertainment. But one producer (especially if he happens to be working on a musical production at the moment) will assert that entertainment means something light and happy, with songs, dancing, and lots of stars, while another producer (especially if he happens to be filming a hard-hitting story about some new twist in crime) will hold that entertainment can also come from tough dramas about modern prob-

lems. Here, too, audience research is sketchy, at best. People seem to go to both kinds of movies, as well as to a good many other kinds. Sometimes they want one kind more than the other, and film producers find themselves in what they call a cycle or trend.

Of course this argument about what the public will buy at the box office is quite different from the question "What does the public need?" The public may need to see documentaries about the dangers of atomic annihilation or the decline of party organization in Congress; but what happens instead is that people flock to see long, gory spectacles on wide screens or dizzy comedies starring Rock Hudson and Doris Day. Actually, what the public wants for relaxation may often be good for it—a better choice than the solemn subjects thought up by educators or censors (see the selection by Allardyce Nicoll, p. 29). But, apart from that, we should realize that there has always been a fundamental conflict in human nature between wants and needs, between appetite and wisdom. Dessert always seems more immediately attractive than vegetables. Profit-making story salesmen—like candy salesmen—are usually eager to cater to childish wants. Social agencies, educators, and government—like parents—are likely to think only of long-term needs.

What about the film-maker, then? What should he think about first of all, the story or the audience? Is it better for him to start with a subject or theme (which may correspond to what we have called an audience "need") and then sell it to the audience as hard as he can? Or is it better for him to ask what the audience seems to be wanting at the moment and simply supply it to them? This has always been a matter of much dispute among movie people. The dispute usually winds up in a draw, like the argument about what the

---

[7] Dr. Eleanor Maccoby, then lecturer in the department of social relations at Harvard University, told the Kefauver committee: "I expect when we do the research that we will find that aggressive feelings are sometimes increased rather than reduced by aggressive scenes on television or in the movies" (*Hearings Before the Subcommittee to Investigate Juvenile Delinquency of the Senate Committee on the Judiciary, Juvenile Delinquency* [Television Programs], 84th Congress, 1st Session 9-10 [1955]).

audience should get, because the film-maker, too, is human. He is just as likely to get excited about a theme and then try to get the audience to respond to it as he is to fling himself into a new cycle of audience enthusiasm and try to find a story to go with it.

"The public doesn't know what it wants until we give it to them." This Hollywood proverb, sometimes attributed to Samuel Goldwyn, is probably a perfectly sound basis for dividing up the responsibilities of mass communication. The artist's role is to try something out, and he does it (1) because he loves the idea and (2) because he has made a guess that the audience will want it. He certainly has to care about the public's response if he is spending $3,000,-000 on a film. The audience responds by either buying the idea or not, depending on the temper of the times, the skill of the artist, and—we must add—the trumpeting of the publicity men. Afterward, of course, there is a great temptation for the artist to take the credit if he succeeds and to blame the public if he fails.

This book is divided into sections that reflect these major issues.

After Part One briefly traces a little of the business history of motion pictures, Part Two offers some observations from critics and a film-maker on what the audience wants in films. The opinion of Mervyn LeRoy, a leading Hollywood producer-director, on what films are likely to be popular is opposed, for example, to that of Harold Hobson, a distinguished British critic. In a related article, the American critic Arthur Knight takes a skeptical look at the new popularity of the art film.

Part Three, in a sense, is broadly opposed to Part Two because it presupposes that the film-maker may often start with a concern about a subject rather than a concern about what the audience wants. But there is some controversy within this part too. Irving Thalberg, the first production chief at M-G-M, turns out rather unexpectedly to lean toward the first

theory, or perhaps a compromise between the two theories; and Ernie Pyle, the columnist and war correspondent, offers a succinct and persuasive statement in favor of films that help the audience escape. Hortense Powdermaker, in a general statement, and James Agee, in a specific review, question the methods by which film stories set up the claim to be "real," or a reflection of the problems of their time, while Gilbert Seldes reminds us of the pleasures of the Western myth.

In Part Four can be seen various views of the film's possibilities as a political instrument. The critical description by Siegfried Kracauer of a Nazi film contrasts with the eloquent defense by John Grierson of democratic propaganda, while Leo Rosten, coming to grips with the problem of definition, also points out how difficult it is for theatrical films that deal at all with social problems to avoid the tag of propaganda.

Part Five is an extensive analysis of the problems of censorship and self-restraint that arise when the power and the influence of the film are feared or deemed serious enough to require control. Bosley Crowther and Joe Hyams particularly disagree on the current advisability of some form of audience classification for films.

Part Six and Part Seven, the last two sections of the book, call special attention to aspects of film distribution that are changing fast before our eyes.

Hollywood has always found the extra income from foreign rentals an important part of its box office. But in recent years the rise of television in America has cut into the domestic market for theatrical films. This has made world trade proportionately far more important: over fifty per cent of the distributor's gross income now comes from abroad. At the same time, of course, receipts from film-making for American television have become an essential part of the budget for most of the old-line studios. These two trends have quickly combined, as John Tebbel reports, in the newest trend of all: overseas sale of American TV films.

The world arena magnifies the old issues of audience, content, propaganda, and censorship. The arguments of national advantage in the cold war (Norman Cousins vs. Eric Johnston) add special overtones, but we can still see Plato vs. Aristotle in the background. On the other hand, there is a real artistic disadvantage in trying to please everybody in the world, even without trying to conform to national policy. The acid predictions of George Bernard Shaw and the more hopeful view of Jean Benoit-Levy both point to the dangers of blandness and sameness if a stereotype of the worldwide audience dominates the thinking of film-makers. Even with a flood of such films, the result may merely be a state of noncommunication.

When films are shown on television, another factor comes into focus—the role of direct government supervision. In the United States, there is a limited number of very high frequency channels in each geographical area. The federal government owns these channels and licenses them for three years at a time to private companies. This situation presents for the first time in the history of American motion pictures the prospect of federal regulation. Laws affecting Hollywood have been threatened by Congress in the past, but tighter "self-controls" have prevented any such action. What will be the relationship of the Federal Communications Commission and Hollywood in the future? The beginning of the argument is before you. It is certain to become more controversial and more important in the years to come.

As consumers of communication, we are living in an era of quantity and speed. The mass media bring us more and more to read and look at, faster than ever before. We must realize that there is a strong profit motive on the part of huge corporate interests—advertisers, networks, publishers, film companies—to get and hold our attention. They are very polite and friendly about it, but that is what they want. And they will use, for commercial purposes, whatever will amuse, hypnotize, shock.

The content, the style, and the effectiveness of these fast, furious, friendly communications are increasingly matters of the greatest social concern. It seems likely that the controversy over censorship and control, for example, will grow louder for some years to come. Perhaps it will be the long-run decision of this country to leave control of words and images entirely to individual citizens—to "let the consumer of communication beware." In any case, serious study of the mass media, including the moving image, is becoming a matter of central importance for the health of any free nation.

PART ONE

FILMS PAST, PRESENT, AND FUTURE

The Rise and Place of the Motion Picture*

TERRY RAMSAYE (1885-1954) was editor of the weekly trade magazine *Motion Picture Herald* from 1931 until his death. Before 1931, he had
been a newspaper reporter in Kansas City and Chicago, an advertising and
publicity man for films, and a producer of newsreels and travel films. He wrote
the first important history of the motion-picture business, a two-volume work
that still stands as a major source for the silent days: *A Million and One
Nights* (1926).

. . . .
After more than a century of conscious
striving toward the motion picture, it was
achieved in October of 1889. The machine
was the peep-show Kinetoscope, invented
by Thomas A. Edison, building on the en-
deavors of the prior workers, and empow-
ered especially by George Eastman's film
for [1/2] "roller photography," made available in September of that year.

The world was not consciously waiting
for the motion picture. Mr. Edison was not
much concerned about it, either. He had
supervised it into being with desultory attention across two years, apparently mostly
because of an assignment to himself to
make a machine to do for the eye what his
phonograph did for the ear. He was of the
pioneer culture of the Middle West, concerned with work—not play, not entertainment. The phonograph had been evolved
to be a robot stenographer, and was developing as an entertainment device, with
problems and commercial headaches. He
let the kinetoscope stand in a corner of his
laboratory at West Orange, gathering dust.
He did not trouble to patent it in Europe.

By the enterprise of promoters impelled
by showmanship, the kinetoscope presented
the first film pictures to the public the
night of April 14, 1894, after five years, at
the Kinetoscope Parlor, 1155 Broadway,
New York, with a battery of machines. The
pictures were brief snatches and shards of
vaudeville acts, boxers in fractional rounds,
trivia which had challenged the interest of
the shop mechanics who had custody of the
new mechanism. One customer at a time
could peek into each machine. The little
show in Broadway was a moderate success.
The invention drew a ripple of Sunday
supplement attention. Meanwhile, the machine went into export sales and carried
the seeds of film technology to the capitals
of the Old World.

THE SCREEN

Within months the pressures of showmanship demanded a union of the kinetoscope's moving pictures with the magic
lantern, so that a screen could entertain a
whole audience at once. In less than two
years that was achieved, and by the spring
of 1896 the career of the film in the theater
had begun. The pictures immediately and
automatically found their place as a com-
ponent of the variety shows, just then beginning to reach for the pretentious name
of "vaudeville." Also black tent theaters
became attractions with traveling carnivals
and at the amusement parks with which
electric traction companies were creating

* Terry Ramsaye, from "The Rise and Place of the Motion Picture," *The Motion Picture Industry*, ed. Gordon
S. Watkins, in *Annals of the American Academy of Political and Social Science*, CCLIV (November, 1947), 1-11.
Reprinted by permission of The American Academy of Political and Social Science.

car-ride traffic. The screen was certainly starting at the bottom of the ladder.

The production function continued in the hands of the tinkerers and mechanics and the flotsam of the backwaters of showmanship. The screen was not finding anything to say beyond the level of the dime museum interest.

The screen sensation of 1898 in London was a subject in Charles Urban's endeavor at a scientific series in which he presented some microscopic studies of life in a Stilton cheese, thereby bestirring the British cheese industry into a demand for censorship. Indicative of the cultural status of the art, the American Mutoscope and Biograph Company of New York, competing with the Edison enterprise, made a brave step by interesting the famed Joseph Jefferson and presenting some excerpts from his Rip van Winkle performances. That classic material aroused no interest, but the Biograph subject entitled "Girl Climbing Apple Tree" became a hit and keynoted a policy.

The industry was beset by patent wars, infringements, piracies, and all the devices of chicane the pitchmen vendors of movies could invent. The business was at low tide. In the vaudeville theaters the pictures had been moved to the end of the bill, to tell the audience the show was over and to clear the house. The films had come to be called "chasers." The Battle of Santiago was pictured with models in a Brooklyn bathtub, and the Boer War [2/3] was fought for the screen in Flatbush with glimpses of the metropolis in the background.

Here and there appeared some timid steps toward giving the screen a story to tell. For instance, Edwin S. Porter, Edison cameraman, experimented with a bit of a tale to give excuse for that perennial picture of the fire engine making a run. It was a race for life in which the fire chief saved his own child, and then fell from his chair and found it was a dream. The title was "The Life of an American Fireman." Enough interest and print sales resulted to encourage the production of "The Great Train Robbery," that now historic classic known as "the first story picture." It was made in 1903. Moving through the tedious, unorganized distribution of the time, this primitive drama of bandits, bravery, fast riding, and excitement was two years becoming a hit. It also incidentally highlighted the program of the Nickelodeon, a little house casually opened to a film program for the lack of other entertainment, by John P. Harris in Pittsburgh about Thanksgiving time in 1905. With a five-cent admission the theater played to standing room for weeks on end.

THE EARLY AUDIENCE

The five-cent theater of the movies had arrived. In a wildfire wave, imitative nickelodeons rose across the land, all of them in centers, like Pittsburgh, with a high content of foreign-born polyglottic population. Immigration was at high tide. American industry was bringing in labor for mines and mills. Steamship and labor agents were plastering the ports of the Mediterranean with posters of the United States as a land of golden promise, with life made gay with buffaloes, Indians, excitement, and natural wonders.

The workers came over, high of hope, poor in pocket, and finding workaday life dull and demanding. They brought none of their native arts, and they were not literate enough to enjoy their feeble foreign-language press. As for American amusements, there was the language barrier, besides the price. The motion picture's new theater, with a five-cent admission and the silent films of the big open places and excitement, romance, thrills, and success on the spot, made good in a fashion on the promises they had read in Trieste.

Meanwhile, the petty tradesmen of the foreign-labor quarters, shrewd, nimble, anxious, behind the counters of their candy shops, soda fountains, banana stands, and pawnshops, saw the new interest of their customers. They became vendors of the new entertainment. Within a year of that opening in Pittsburgh, there were nearly five thousand of the little five-cent shows.

Demand took production off the roofs and out of the back yards of Manhattan into studios on Long Island, in the Bronx, at Fort Lee over in New Jersey, in the suburbs of Chicago and Philadelphia. Cameramen and some of Broadway's idle actors became directors of the "story pictures." Also, the demand for "story suggestions" rose to the point that $15 was a standard price for "a suggestion." A typical story sale was a plot summary of "Enoch Arden" which one author sold repeatedly. That went on until the Kalem company was required by court order to pay $25,000 for making "Ben Hur" without consulting either the estate of General Lew Wallace or Harper's, the publishers.

In that period the budding industry had everything to learn. It had no recognizable precedents, and its accidentally acquired personnel brought little knowledge of any other businesses. Procedure was on the general assumption that anything could be done until forbidden, specifically, positively by law [3/4]—and thereafter only in the cover of the Jersey highlands.

Somewhat marginally, as the pictures reached up into middle-class levels of consciousness, some eyebrows were raised at the Mediterranean tastes manifest on the screen. The protest began with the peep show "Dolorita in the Passion Dance" in Atlantic City in 1894, and got really articulate in the New York papers about 1906 when the Children's Society went to court about exhibition of pictures on the Thaw case. Regulations of sorts, including censorships by various cities, resulted.

. . . .

It began to be apparent that the audience was developing selectivity. Each of the major contributors to the General Film program had for awhile a designated day. When the little one-sheet poster out in front said "Biograph Day," the attendance was better. That was presently traced to story and picture quality, and that in turn

traced to the work of one "Larry" Griffith, ex-actor, who had left the stage in 1906 in a "resting" period to essay a job in the humble art of the films. He was due presently to come to fame as D. W. Griffith, later David Wark Griffith. Some of those rather able but anonymous persons in his little Biograph dramas had names like Walthall, Lawrence, Pickford, and Gish.

The audience was expanding. The screen was seeping up into the middle class with neighborhood houses of considerably more comfort and pretense than the little nickelodeons of the labor districts. A ten-cent admission price became a commonplace. "Nickelodeon" began to give way to fancies like "Bijou Dream" and such invitations as "The Family" and "The Cozy."

The old stage institution of the road show, with its "direct from Broadway" melodramas—remember "Sag Harbor," "Way Down East," "East Lynne," "Under Southern Skies," "Cameo [4/5] Kirby"—was feeling competition. Also the town opera house was venturing a try at movies. The motion picture was bringing drama within walking distance of most of urban America; and the stage was trying to live from the carriage trade. At the peak of this development, in the period 1913–16, there were probably twenty-eight thousand motion picture theaters of all sorts in the United States.

Meanwhile, the art of story telling on the screen was acquiring skill, quality, and fluidity. The principal influence was Griffith, who with his cameraman extraordinary, William Bitzer, was first to explore the narrative uses of the close-up, the cut-back, and the development of parallel lines of action—invaluable to the Griffith suspense technique of "relief on the way." The dramas were still in single reels.

. . . .

By 1912 the American motion picture was close to a ceiling. Its horizontal development across the land and its audiences had neared a saturation. The next move had to be a break-through. Again, as ever, the situation found its instrument— in this instance Adolph Zukor, born in Hungary, educated in the American industrial scene, beginning as a furrier's apprentice, and becoming incidentally an investor in a penny arcade enterprise which he had to take over to save the investment. So he came to the amusement world with evolving interests in exhibition. By 1912 he had come to a parting of the ways in his associations. He found inspiration and opportunity in the availability of the American rights to a foreign-made four-reel picture entitled "Queen Elizabeth" with Sarah Bernhardt in the title role. The time had come, considered Mr. Zukor, for the screen to take its place along with the stage in offering a whole evening's entertainment. He also arrived at the line "famous players in famous plays" to keynote a policy. Thereby the "feature" era was born, meaning the rise of the hour-long picture taking over against the established program of short pictures.

The public gave encouragement by patronage of the longer pictures and responding to the promotion which presented them. A signal success was had from roadshow type presentations of "Quo Vadis," a long spectacle production made in Rome and vastly more successful in America than in Europe. D. W. Griffith, irked by Biograph's reactionary adherence to the short-picture policy with which it had risen, went off into an independent project which delivered "The Birth of a Nation" which by its success gave powerful impetus to the feature movement in 1915.

A new and ever growing public was becoming aware of the screen. There were growing pains and problems. The exhibition plant was not adequate for [5/6] the delivery of the expanding pictures. A new order of more pretentious screen theater was initiated in 1914 with the opening of the Strand Theater on Broadway, soon to be followed by others equally ambitious in the larger centers. [6/7]

. . . .

GROWTH OF THE INDUSTRY

. . . .

A minor statistical indication of the swiftness of the upturn was afforded in the case of Charles Chaplin. In 1913 he left a vaudeville act to take employment in Keystone's slapstick comedies at $150 a week. In the autumn of 1915 he signed a contract to appear in twelve two-reel comedies in one year at a salary of $10,000 a week, plus a bonus of $150,000. In turn The Lone Star concern sold the British Empire rights to the comedies for the total of Chaplin's salary, $670,000. The deals all made money. By 1916 the patrons of the lowly cinema were willing to pay real millions at the box office for one comedian.

The motion picture made its own order of fame. When Adolph Zukor had launched his Famous Players company, he presented a schedule of attractions in three classes— A, B, and C. Class C was to present famous *picture* players in famous plays. Bernhardt was typical of Class A. Mary Pickford was Class C. Brief experience showed that the public which the screen had assembled knew nothing about and cared nothing for the great ones of stage and opera, and cared very much for their own people, the stars of the movies. The older arts obviously were without status in melting-pot America. [7/8]

. . . .

The prosperity of the pictures in World War I, as through World War II, was lavishly supported by the eager buying of the free-spending workers temporarily rich on war wages. The box-office-admissions curve inevitably follows the pay-roll graphs. And sometimes the doles, too. The only exception in history was the onsweep of the nickelodeon wave through the "stringency" of 1907, when the industry was too small to figure in national reactions. The people's art lives out of the people's pocket.

The American industry continued to fortify its world position by the acquisition of the outstanding talent of production abroad as rapidly as it appeared, adding continually to the great talent pool of Hollywood. This enhanced and enriched the product for the markets both at home and abroad, and incidentally reduced competitive development. Britain contributed able players, and from Germany and France came notably skilled technicians and directors.

ENTER THE TALKING PICTURES

In 1926 the art of the motion picture came to revolutionary change with the arrival of electronic sound recording and reproduction, a by-product of telephone and radio. The personal instrument was the late Sam Warner, one of the four sons of Benjamin Warner who had come to these shores and the land of opportunity nearly a generation before. Contemporaries in the industry of the screen looked askance and doubtingly on the talking picture, but demonstration by Warner Brothers prevailed. The silent esperanto of pantomime of nickelodeon days was no longer an asset. By 1926 the audiences all spoke American. So in the next three years the industry was made over with pictures laced with words and music. Importantly, the American talking picture was still to be dominant on the screens of the great market of the English-speaking lands. In fact, the English understood American perfectly, despite the fact that there has been found to be a lot of English that most Americans cannot understand.

When the screen acquired its voice, a new order of material was required. The silent picture had become a hybrid art of mingled pantomime and printed word presented in the subtitles. Some pictures, incidentally, required a capacity for swift reading. They did not do so well.

Seeking talking picture play material, the screen turned to the stage and its playwrights, and thereby reaped a reaction in direct retribution for what it had done to the stage when it swept the road shows out of the hinterlands. The stage, driven back

from that contact with the larger public, had taken refuge in the service of sophisticated metropolitan minorities. In direct consequence came sometimes painfully sophisticated drama and dialogue of candor that would never be tolerated by Dubuque, Bad Axe, or Abeline. Translated to the screen and taken out to the provinces, and even a few squares from Broadway, this material gave rise to protests, threats and acts of censorship, and movements toward Federal regulative legislation.

Back in 1922 the industry, confronted [8/9] with a wave of public disapproval pertaining mostly to conduct of players and other more official figures in the public eye, had organized the Motion Picture Producers and Distributors of America, Inc., and installed Will H. Hays as president and titular "czar of the movies." He became in effect a super public relations counsel. By 1928-29 it was not personnel but product that was out of hand.

REGULATION

Now to the rescue came Martin Quigley, publisher of journals of the industry since 1915, a Catholic layman of prominence, with the device of self-regulation entitled the Production Code, a document of guidance to picture makers calculated to help keep the pictures in line with common decency and American mores. It began and continues essentially as a formula intended to apply the principles of the rather nonsectarian and accepted Ten Commandments to picture production. It is convenient, and accurate enough for the moment, to say that the code requires that a picture, while portraying sin for dramatic purposes, shall not become the Devil's advocate. It was formally adopted by the organized industry in March 1930—forty-six years after "Dolorita in the Passion Dance" got the pictures into trouble on the Boardwalk in Atlantic City. [9/10]

. . . .

When World War II swept across the global scene the American industry sustained important invasions of foreign revenue and there were piercing cries. However, the war-enriched masses at home so besieged the box office that it entered into a period of unprecedented prosperity.

In sequel to the end of the shooting aspects of World War II, sometimes called the peace, the walls of nationalism and the issues of nationalism became even more sharply defined. Additionally the fringes of the Russian iron curtain were extending over the screen in lands of Soviet influence. Every nation, great and small, strove for a motion picture industry of its own, mainly for propaganda reasons of its own. [10/11]

. . . .

MASS SUPPORT NECESSARY

Clearly, the motion picture, in coming of full estate, seeks to serve all peoples and all classes. That is a wide straddle. Its costs are such that it can be generally supported only by the massed buying power of majorities. Inevitably, many minorities cannot be served as they are by the less expensive stage or the relatively inexpensive printed word. Some of those minorities include the most erudite, critical, and articulate persons. From that condition of limitation arises much of the impatient, often militant, criticism of the screen. Some censorship requirements and many projected movements actually represent only areas of unsatisfied demand. Few indeed of the militants who would influence the course of screen development are aware of anything beyond superficial aspects and casual observation. The screen has done little and continues to do little to tell its own story. Few are interested. The people who pay for the pictures want to see them as emotional experience, not as subjects of study.

A Religion of Film*

HENRY BRADFORD ("BRAD") DARRACH, JR. (1921-   ), associate editor of *Time* magazine, has been principal cinema reviewer for the magazine since the early fifties. Before joining the staff of *Time* in 1945, he was a school teacher and a newspaper reporter for the Providence *Journal* and the Baltimore *Sun*. This selection, which is of interest because it attempts to embrace the whole contemporary range of foreign film-making in one article, was the "cover story" in the September 20, 1963, issue of *Time*.

It wasn't the sort of place people usually see a movie in. No boorish Moorish architecture, no chewing gum under the seats. Instead, the hall was a deep blue nave, immensely high and still, looped gracefully with golden galleries. And the images on the screen were not the sort one sees at the average alhambra. No Tammy, no Debbie, no winning of the West. Instead, a bear roamed and roared in a Mexican mansion and a regiment of French actors fought the American Civil War and a samurai disemboweled himself right there in front of everybody.

The first New York Film Festival, now at Lincoln Center's Philharmonic Hall, must confess its infancy compared to Cannes and to Venice, which had its first film festival in 1932. But by its taste and high excitement, by the quality of its films and the intelligence of its sellout crowds, it may well mark for Americans a redefinition of what movies are and who it is that sees them. For in the decade since Hollywood came unstuck and television became the reigning medium of mass entertainment, the movies have suddenly and powerfully emerged as a new and brilliant international art, indeed as perhaps the central and characteristic art of the age.

ALL THE WORLD'S . . . The new status of cinema has largely been achieved by movies from abroad, by an array of vigorous and original creators who live and work in every quarter of the globe. At the heart of the new movement is a hardy little band of inspired pioneers: Japan's Akira Kurosawa (*Rashomon*); Sweden's Ingmar Bergman (*Wild Strawberries*); France's Alain Resnais (*Hiroshima, Mon Amour*) and François Truffaut (*The 400 Blows*); Italy's Federico Fellini (*La Dolce Vita*), Michelangelo Antonioni (*L'Avventura*) and Luchino Visconti (*Rocco and His Brothers*); England's Tony Richardson (*Look Back in Anger*); Poland's Andrzej Wajda (*Kanal*) and Roman Polanski (*Two Men and a Wardrobe*); Argentina's Leopoldo Torre Nilsson (*Summerskin*); India's Satyajit Ray (*Pather Panchali*).

Their imitators are legion. All over the world—in Canada, Greece, Brazil, Japan, Israel, Hungary and both Germanys, even in Moscow and immoderately in Manhattan—cinemania has descended upon the rising generation. Young men at all hours of the day and night stalk through the streets clutching fleaweight cameras and proclaiming prophetically a new religion of cinema. Its creed has been passionately enunciated by Director Truffaut.

"It is necessary," he once cried, "to film

* Henry Bradford Darrach, Jr., "A Religion of Film," *Time*, LXXXII (September 20, 1963), 78-82. Reprinted by permission from *Time* The Weekly Newsmagazine; copyright Time Inc. 1963.

another thing in another spirit. It is necessary to abandon these expensive, disorderly, insalubrious studios. The sun costs less than a battery of lights. A borrowed camera, some cheap film, a friend's apartment, friends to play the parts, and above all the faith, the rage of the cinema—the rage to storm the barricade, to use this way of expression—the way of the future, the art of the future. A revolution of intentions is beginning. No longer do we trust in the old labels, the established themes. To express ourselves! To be free, free of prejudice, free of the old cult of technique, free of everything, to be madly ambitious and madly sincere!"

. . . A SOUND STAGE. In France, where the movement is called the New Wave, 60 young directors made their first full-length films in less than two years (1959-60). In Poland, 22 films both long and short are now in production. In Brazil, nine new directors have made their film debuts in the last two years, and two dozen more will do the same in the next twelve months. The rage and the revolution are rising everywhere, and everywhere the new movements are really one movement, a new international cinema in which all the world's a sound stage and the screen emblazons a microcosm of mankind.

With startling speed, the new international cinema has created a new international audience. It is a young audience; exhibitors in a dozen countries report that eight out of ten foreign-film buffs are under 30. It is a vehement audience; it applauds what it likes and hisses what it doesn't. It is an expert audience; the new generation of moviegoers believes that an educated man must be cinemate as well as literate. And it is a mass audience; financially, the new cinema is a going concern.

Not that foreign films have seriously challenged the commercial hegemony of American movies, which still capture two out of every three dollars the world spends on cinema. But in the last ten years they have doubled their take in the international market (*La Dolce Vita* alone grossed $10 million), and in the U.S., where in 1953 they grossed $5,200,000, they have in recent years grossed as much as $69,000,000.

Public support and their own technical economies have given a great measure of artistic independence to the men of the new cinema. More and more they have been able to say what they want to say and not what some banker thinks the public wants to be told. The results have not always been happy. The new men, in particular the very young [78/79] new men, have turned out miles of absolutely asinine acetate, and whoever wirtes thos subtitlse ouhgt to be shto. Nevertheless, with stunning consistency, with the fire and *élan* of spirits snatched out of themselves and whirled away in the tremendous whirlwind of the spirit of the age they have wrung out of their hearts remarkable efforts of film. They have evolved through the last decade a vast pageant of heroic drama and gentle eclogue, of delectable gaiety and dispirited lust, of mordant wit, glittering intellect, grey despair, apocalyptic spectacle and somber religious depth. They have held the camera up to life and shown humanity a true and terrifying and yet somehow heartbreakingly beautiful image of itself. They have created a golden age of cinema.

Strong words? Perhaps. But consider the carat of the films displayed at the first New York Film Festival. The program was restricted to new pictures never before seen in the U.S., but the festival's director found a score of excellent shorts and half a dozen top-chop features. Among them:

The Exterminating Angel, one of the strongest of Buñuel's many strong films, relates a harrowing parable of salvation and damnation in which the grand old anarchist pours all the vials of his wrath upon the idle rich and the mother church and in the process disports a religious imagination seldom paralleled in its demonian ferocity since the visions of Hieronymus Bosch.

In the Midst of Life, the first full-length film by a 32-year-old Frenchman named Robert Enrico, is an adaptation of three stories by Ambrose Bierce, all treating of the U.S. Civil War. Though the picture was made in France with a French cast, the American atmosphere of the period is exquisitely interfused. The story is told in a sure and subtle flow of images, and Jean Boffety's photography makes a grave and lovely homage to Mathew Brady.

Knife in the Water is a Polish thriller as sharp as a knife and as smooth as water. Director Roman Polanski, 30, puts two lusty men and one lusty busty woman aboard a small sailboat, throws them a knife, and for the next 90 minutes lets the tension build, build, build *(see cover picture)*.

Hallelujah the Hills, the work of America's Adolfas Mekas, is a gloriously funny and far-out farce about two great big overgrown boy scouts who pratfall in love with the same girl.

The Fiancés, the second movie made by a 32-year-old Italian named Ermanno Olmi, will probably become a cinema classic. Director Olmi tells an almost too simple story of how absence makes two hearts grow fonder, but he tells it with total mastery of his means.

The Servant plays morbid variations on the theme of *Othello*. Directed in Britain by Joseph Losey, an American who lives and works in Europe, the film tells how a sinister servant destroys his master by playing to his weakness for women—and for men.

SHADOW OF THE BOMB. The historians of the new cinema, searching out its origins, go back to another festival, the one at Venice in 1951. That year the least promising item on the cinemenu was a Japanese picture called *Rashomon*. Japanese pictures, as all film experts knew, were just a bunch of rubber chrysanthemums. So the judges sat down yawning. They got up dazed. *Rashomon* was a cinematic thunderbolt that violently ripped open the dark heart of man to prove that the truth was not in it. In technique the picture was traumatically original; in spirit it was big, strong, male. It was obviously the work of a genius, and that genius was Akira Kurosawa, the earliest herald of the new era in cinema.

Trained as a painter, Kurosawa got interested in the movies because they seemed to him unnecessarily stupid. *Rashomon* was his tenth picture, and since *Rashomon* he has produced a relentless succession of masterpieces. *Seven Samurai* (1954), considered by many the best action movie ever made, is a military idyl with a social moral: the meek shall inherit the earth—when they learn to fight for their rights. *Ikiru* (1952), Kurosawa's greatest work, describes the tragedy and transfiguration of a hopelessly ordinary man, a grubby little bookkeeper who does not dare to live until he learns he is going to die. *Yojimbo* (1962), conceived as a parody of the usual Hollywood western, mingles blood and belly laughs in a ferocious satire on the manners, morals and politics of the 20th century. *I Live in Fear* (1955), an eerie and comminatory meditation on the life of man in the shadow of the Bomb, was shown last week as a special treat for festival fans but it may never be shown commercially in the U.S.—the exhibitors think it's too hot to handle.

Kurosawa in the raw is not everybody's meat. Not since Sergei Eisenstein has a moviemaker set loose such a bedlam of elemental energies. He works with three cameras at once, makes telling use of telescopic lenses that drill deep into a scene, suck up all the action in sight and then spew it violently into the viewer's face. But Kurosawa is far more than a master of movement. He is an ironist who knows how to pity. He is a moralist with a sense of humor. He is a realist who curses the darkness—and then lights a blowtorch.

DEATH OF THE HEART. Kurosawa made moviegoers sit up and take notice, and the next thing they noticed was Ingmar Bergman. As a man he didn't look like much —just a gangling, green-eyed, snaggletoothed son of a Swedish parson. But as an artist he was something unprecedented in cinema: a metaphysical poet whose pictures are chapters in a continuing allegory of the progress of his own soul in its tortured and solitary search for the meaning of life, for the experience of God. In his early films *(Illicit Interlude, Naked Night)*, Bergman struggles to free himself from the fascination of the mother, the incestuous longing for innocence, safety, death. In the dazzling comedies of his second period (*A Lesson in Love, Smiles of a Summer Night*), he fights the inevitable war between men and women. In *The Seventh Seal,* he plunges straight down into the abyss of God and wanders there among the gnarled and leering roots of living religion. In his recent films (*The Virgin Spring, Through a Glass Darkly, Winter Light*), God is present again and again but always in dreadful or ambiguous wise: as a spring of water, as a giant spider, as a silence. Never as love, never in the heart's core.

And so the search goes on. It is conducted with intelligence and irony, with a beauty that endlessly inveigles the eye, with a sense of form that is subtle but perhaps more theatrical than cinematic, with a gift of intuition so intense it sometimes seems insane. But Bergman is not a sick man; he is a sick genius. His sickness is the sickness of the times: the death of the heart, the **[79/80]** separation from the source. His genius is the genius to say what all men suffer.

Bergman hit Paris like a wild north wind. In 1957, when a cycle of his films was first shown at *La Cinémathèque Française,* the main film library in Paris, hundreds of *cinémanes* stood in line night after night for three nights to get seats. "We were absolutely overthrown," says Director Truffaut. "Here was a man who had done all we dreamed of doing. He had written films as a novelist writes books. Instead of a pen he had used a camera. He was an author of cinema."

THE WAVE HITS. Stimulated by Bergman and encouraged by a charming American feature, *The Little Fugitive,* that had cost only $100,000, Truffaut got a loan from his father-in-law and one fine day in 1958 got cracking on a film called *The 400 Blows.* About the same time Claude Chabrol, who worked with Truffaut as a reviewer for *Cahiers du Cinéma,* blew his wife's inheritance on a picture called *Le Beau Serge.* Meanwhile Marcel Camus, an assistant to some top French directors, popped off to Brazil to make a film in color called *Black*

Orpheus. And Alain Resnais, an obscure documentarist, buttonholed some businessmen for money and flew off to Japan to shoot a picture called *Hiroshima, Mon Amour.*

Suddenly all the films arrived in Paris. Suddenly the press and the public were buzzing about them. Suddenly they carried off the top prizes at Cannes. Suddenly there was a New Wave.

Four years and several shoals later, the New Wave is still rolling strong. It has thrown up a dozen films of first quality and new actors of international note (Jeanne Moreau, Jean-Paul Belmondo, Jean-Pierre Cassel). It has also produced two dozen talented young directors. Philippe de Broca has created two of the funniest films (*The Love Game, The Five-Day Lover*) made in France since René Clair was clicking. Jean-Luc Godard has done an astonishing cubistic melodrama (*Breathless*). Pierre Etaix, Louis Malle, Roger Vadim, Henri Colpi, and Agnes Varda have all done exciting work. But the world fame of the new French cinema derives largely from the labors of two men.

COLD ONE, WARM ONE. Alain Resnais, 41, the more famous of the two, is the supreme theorist and technician, the Schoenberg of the new cinema. *Hiroshima* startled the critics with its methodic modulations and harmonic structures. *Last Year at Marienbad* made *Hiroshima* look like casual noodling. In it four kinds of time, five points of view and innumerable frames of symbolic reference were assembled in an infinitely intricate structure that seemed more like a puzzle than a picture, that might more suitably have been fed to an electronic computer than shown to a human being. And when the puzzle at last was solved, what did it signify? Everything —and nothing.

Resnais, in short, has the skill to say whatever he wants to say on the screen. Unhappily he has nothing, or almost nothing, to say. As an artist he lacks humanity, lacks blood. He is out of this world, a man of air. Nevertheless, his work is important. He has shattered the public image of what a film is. He has freed all film creators to remold the cinema nearer to their art's desire.

François Truffaut, 31, perhaps the most richly talented of the new French directors, is as warm as Resnais is cold. His films are about real people with real feelings: a boy who runs away from home, a husband whose wife runs away with his best friend. His films are heavy because real life is heavy, but at the same time they are gay and somehow lucky. They are natural things, and like natural things they are full of false starts and irrelevant twists. But they grow and go on growing in the mind long after the film says *fin*. Truffaut goes on growing too. *Shoot the Piano Player* is much more skillful than *The 400 Blows*, and *Jules and Jim* in its bittersweet worldly wisdom makes the other two seem like child's play.

CINEMA BREASTERNS. Meanwhile, the cinema in Italy had suddenly taken a new lease on life. After the sudden death of postwar neorealism *(Open City, The Bicycle Thief)*—stabbed in the back by politicians persuaded that seamy movies were hurting the tourist trade—the Italians produced almost nothing but mythological monstrosities and what are known in the trade as "breasterns." Only the great Vittorio De Sica achieved a faint infrequent toot *(The Roof)* on the clarion of reform. But around the turn of the decade Pietro Germi, who later made a wickedly wacky comedy called *Divorce—Italian* **[80/81]** *Style,* came into view. And about the same time three major Italian talents rose vigorously to their full height.

Luchino Visconti, 56, is an Italian nobleman—Count of Modrone and a direct descendant of Charlemagne's father-in-law—whose friends say he "votes left and lives right." By the same token, his movies look left but are made right. In *Rocco and His Brothers* (1960), a bruising revival of neorealism, he followed a family of peasants as they moved from the country to the city and saw them grated away like cheese in the big mindless mechanism of Milan. In *The Leopard* (1963), adapted from Giuseppe di Lampedusa's touching elegy for feudalism, he summons from the grave a way of life and the valiant dust of a proud but kindly man who lived that life and leaves the vivid air signed with his honor.

Visconti's films are sometimes laborious and doctrinaire, but they have the solidity and urgency of living bodies. At times they seem to lack direction, but actually they are borne on a slow, irrefutable current doomward. On the tiny raft of hope his heroes glide toward the cataract of fate.

IMAGINATION MINUS TASTE. Federico Fellini, 43, is the most inventive, versatile and popular of the new Italians. In *I Vitelloni* (1953) he put together a conventional but faultless social satire. In *La Strada* (1954), a poetic comedy, he followed in Chaplin's footsteps but couldn't quite fill the little fellow's shoes. In *La Dolce Vita* (1960), the film that made him and Actor Marcello Mastroianni famous around the world, he constructed a spectacular travesty of the Apocalypse in which the prophecy is luridly fulfilled and Rome, the Great Whore of *Revelation,* wallows gorgeously through seven nights of destruction. In *8½* (1963), his most daring film to date, he aimed his camera into his own psyche and let it record his fears and fantasies, desires and despairs in a cinematic language that owes more to Joyce than it does to D. W. Griffith.

All these movies were executed with tremendous verve; Fellini is unquestionably one of the most imaginative fellows who ever had his name on a canvas chair. Unfortunately, his imagination is not controlled by taste; he panders incessantly and shamelessly to the public letch for sensations. But there is nothing petty in his pandering. He is a vulgarian in the grand manner, the Barnum of the avant-garde.

TASTE MINUS VARIATION. Michelangelo Antonioni, 49, is the temperamental antithesis of Fellini—a sensitive esthete who could hardly make an error of taste if he tried. He has done only three pictures *(L'Avventura, La Notte, Eclipse)* that really matter, but they matter a lot; any one of them would suffice to establish him as one of the finest stylists in the history of cinema. His style is slow and spacious. His scenes begin a little while before they begin and end a little while after they end. His camera usually sits still, and his actors move like figures in a funeral procession —as indeed they are. Each of Antonioni's films is a somber and ceremonious wake for the living dead. His characters have lost all sense of the meaning of life, of the reason for being. They wander through a weary series of loveless loves, hoping vaguely that mere amorous friction will rekindle the fire of life in hearts gone cold.

The theme is a great and timely one, and Antonioni states it in grave and noble measures. The trouble is that he states it again and again and again. He seems to have nothing else to say. If that's a fact, the eclipse he envisions may very well be his own.

In the work of all the important new Italians, and no less in the films of the rising young Frenchman, the attitudes toward sex have much agitated the critics. There are several attitudes, none of them new and most of them sick but all of them more serious and significant than Hollywood's. In Hollywood movies, sex is a daydream for people who are scared of the real thing. In the new French movies, sex is a sort of physiological religion, a mystical experience almost as profound as, well, eating. In the new Italian movies, sex is what one feels bad after, as good a way as any to get lost. In any case, people in the new European movies do not moon around like people in Hollywood movies and wonder what sex is like. If they want to do it they do it, and in some films they do it pretty often. But when they have done it they forget about it till the next time. Sex is explicit in the new European pictures and often it is exploited. But at least it is real.

ANGRY YOUNG TONY. Men like the French and Italian directors simply assume that cinema is an important art in its own right. Most British moviemen are not so sure; British movies are traditionally regarded as subsidiary to drama and to literature.

Most of the new British movies have in fact been adapted from plays and novels, and the new cinema in England has rather tamely taken its direction from the ingroup in the allied arts. But since the ingroup happened to be the Angry Young Men, the direction has been vehemently taken. Politically the direction has been left; geographically it has been north. Almost all the good British movies of the last five years have been films of social protest, and in general the protest has been leveled at living conditions in the industrial slums of Yorkshire.

Director Jack Clayton instituted the trend with a cruel little monograph on class warfare called *Room at the Top* (1958), but before long an angrier and younger man moved in on the movement and pretty well took it over. In rapid succession Tony Richardson directed *Look Back in Anger, The Entertainer, A Taste of Honey,* and *The Loneliness of the Long Distance Runner.*

In cinematic terms, Richardson is not a great director—not by a long chalk. By temperament and training he is a stage director, and sometimes he is a very good one. He is clever at casting and knows how to make the most of a strong player. Under his tutelage Albert Finney, Rita Tushingham, Tom Courte-[81/82] nay and Rachel Roberts have become international cinema attractions. But moviegoers are getting a bit bugged by that same scummy old roofscape and the eternal kitchen-sinkdrome. They sometimes find it a bit hard to believe that things are really all that bad in Merry England. Yet at their best, the British protest pictures have served up great juicy chunks of local color, and they have handsomely displayed six or eight of the most talented young cinemactors in the world.

OUTSIDE THE EPICENTER. Britain, Italy, France: Western Europe is currently at the epicenter of the new cinema. But can the center hold? Secondary concentrations of film production are forming rapidly all over the world—some of them behind the Iron Curtain. In Poland there is a small but fiercely active cell of film fiends. Director Polanski is obviously a completely prepared professional, and Andrzej Wajda, the Polish Kurosawa, is even more accomplished. When his two tragedies of battle *(Ashes and Diamonds, Kanal)* were released in the U.S. in 1961, they startled moviegoers with their black intensity. Hungarian production has doubled in the last ten years, and in the last three years the quality of the movies that come out of Moscow *(The Cranes Are Flying, Ballad of a Soldier, My Name Is Ivan)* has steeply improved.

In the free world outside Europe, cinematic creation is even more gingery.

In India there is Satyajit Ray, 42, a one-time commercial artist in Calcutta who has proved himself one of cinema's greatest natural talents. In the last five years, six of Ray's films have been released in the U.S., and every one of the six swells with the fullness of life and glows with the light of the spirit. His first three pictures *(Pather Panchali, Aparajito, The World of Apu)* made up a trilogy that speaks a thousand volumes about life in India and stands as the supreme masterpiece of the Asian cinema. The films that follow it *(Devi, Two Daughters, The Music Room)* are even more accomplished. They are beautiful to look at and musical to be with. They are quiet films, as all deep things are quiet. They are not in a hurry to happen, they take time to live. They experience life, they experience death. Nothing human is alien to them. They are works of love.

In Argentina there is Leopoldo Torre Nilsson, 39, the Bergman of the Antipodes. He is by no means a great artist, but his films *(The End of Innocence, Hand in the Trap)* are intelligent, tasteful, passionate and relentlessly true to life in Argentina. And they get better year by year.

In the U.S., when most people think of movies they still think of Hollywood. But the new American cinema is not coming out of Hollywood—it is springing up in New York. There are art houses, film libraries and terribly strange little film groups that meet at midnight in Green-wich Village garrets and show movies about nail biting and things. It is all wonderfully stimulating, and since the late '50s several hundred people have been running all over town trying to make independent pictures.

Quite a few have succeeded. In 1957 Morris Engel made *Weddings and Babies*. In 1959 Robert Frank shot *Pull My Daisy*, and Sidney Meyers directed *The Savage Eye*. In 1961 John Cassavetes released *Shadows*, and Shirley Clarke did a movie version of Jack Gelber's play *The Connection*. The same year Jonas Mekas fired off *Guns of the Trees*, and two years later his brother gave out with *Hallelujah*. In 1962 Herbert Danska filmed *The Gift*, and Frank Perry came in with *David and Lisa*, the best U.S. film of the year. And in 1963 Robert Drew, Greg Shuker and Ricky Leacock produced *The Chair*. Some of these films were heavily haired-over and a few were downright funky, but most of them looked new and alive and original, and when they were shown in Europe the men of the new cinema were mightily impressed.

NEW TECHNIQUES. More than many others, U.S. moviemakers have taken advantage of new techniques: light weight, hand-held cameras; directional microphones that spot the right voices in crowds; transistorized sound equipment. Such devices have been used with striking effect—particularly in the "living camera" pictures of Drew and Leacock. This or similar equipment is now available in most major centers of moviemaking, and so are a number of extremely sensitive and rapid varieties of film that can just about see in the dark.

The men of the new cinema know these new tools and use them. As a result, the craft of film is changing rapidly and so is the art of film. The new tools have enlarged its language and enriched its spirit. They have set the camera free as a bird. They have put in its head the eyes of a cat. Anywhere a man can go a camera now can go, and anything a man can see a camera can see better. Such an instrument is sure to make the art of film more supple, more various, to put within its reach a larger share of life.

THE WAY LIES OPEN. Such an instrument indeed may do something even more important. It may free the movies from the gilded cage in which they have so long languished; it may free the creator from the grip of the financier. The new equipment is absurdly inexpensive to own and to operate. A standard motion picture camera, for instance, costs $25,000; an Arriflex costs $3,500. Eleven standard studio lamps cost $2,100; eight of the new portable lamps do the same job and cost only $566. With such reduced expenses, the new international cinema can quite comfortably be supported by the new international audience.

For the first time since Edison cranked up his Kinetograph and recorded Fred Ott's Sneeze, the way lies open to a free exploration of the full possibilities of cinema as an art. The possibilities are clearly immense. No other art can so powerfully exploit the dimensions of time and space. No other art has so many ways of involving a human being. It involves his eyes, ears, mind, heart, appetites all at once. It is drama, music, poetry, novel, painting at the same time. It is the whole of art in one art, and it demands the whole of man in every man. It seizes him and spirits him away into a dark cave; it envelops him in silence, in night. His inner eye begins to see, his secret ear begins to hear. Suddenly a vast mouth in the darkness opens and begins to utter visions. People. Cities. Rivers. Mountains. A whole world pours out of the mouth of the enraptured medium, and this world becomes the world of the man in the darkness watching.

A tremendous power, a great magic has been given to the men of the new cinema. What will they do with it? Will Resnais really be able to renovate the esthetic of cinema? Will Bergman at last kindle the fire in the heart and light his gloomy world with love? Will Ray redeem his prodigious promise and become the Shakespeare of the screen? Or will new men emerge and surpass them all? Whatever happens, the pioneers have broken through. The world is on its way to a great cinema culture. The art of the future has become the art of the present.

Epilogue*

RICHARD GRIFFITH (1912-   ) and ARTHUR MAYER (1888-
) are coauthors of *The Movies,* a big book of pictures and text covering
60 years of American film history; this selection is the Epilogue from their
book. Both men have written many magazine articles about motion-picture
trends. Mr. Griffith is a film critic and has been associated with the Film Library of the Museum of Modern Art in New York since 1949; he was appointed
its curator in 1951. Mr. Mayer became manager in 1933 of the Rialto Theater
on Times Square in New York City; from 1937 to 1950 he was the partner of
Joseph Burstyn in a company that pioneered in the distribution of foreign
films, including *Open City* and *The Bicycle Thief.*

Sixty years have passed since Mr. Edison
said, "Let there be light" and, in less clarion tones, "Let there be pictures that
move, or at least seem to move"—sixty
years in which the plaything he regarded
with so little paternal pride became an art
and an industry, in which shabby, indom-
itable little men blossomed over night into
financial giants, and photogenic boys and
girls into world-wide idols. Mr. Edison's
plaything helped to mold the manners and
mores of our times. Above all it has
brought joy to millions who had little
interest in its commercial or aesthetic
achievements.

The certainty of the late nineties that
science would fertilize a brave new world
devoid of disease, poverty and brutality
has been transformed into the dread that
it might annihilate our not too bad old
world. White magic has turned to black
and the vision of Mr. Edison bearing gifts
to mankind has been replaced by the spec-
ter of Dr. Einstein speaking in equations
and logarithms, incomprehensible but terrifying. The age of electricity which we
welcomed so rapturously is about to be replaced by the era of atomic energy which
may turn our earth into a paradise or into
a wasteland.

But though man's faith has become
man's fear, and his naïveté has been replaced by what he regards as sophistication, he is not greatly changed—not at
least that aspect of him with which this
book has been concerned. Theatrical entertainment, of which he formerly had so
little, is now running out of his eyes and
his ears. But what makes him laugh or cry,
what he finds endearing, exciting or exalt-
ing remains substantially unaltered. The
grandchildren of those adventurous souls
who shuddered so pleasurably in their col-
lapsible wooden chairs as the Empire State
Express bore down upon them now shrink
in their plush divan seats with similar de-
licious apprehension as Cinerama's shoot-
the-shoots impel them downward at break-
neck speed. It was as much fun to hold
hands in a nickelodeon while the hero
and heroine exchanged less chaste embraces as it is now in a picture palace. And
recently it has been discovered that it is
equally agreeable in the living room.

If there's a story to be told—and that's
what movies are made for—it will grip

* Richard Griffith and Arthur Mayer, "Epilogue," *The Movies* (New York: Simon and Schuster, 1957), pp.
435-436. Reprinted by permission of the authors.

you on the little old flat screen with the same compelling intensity as on Cinema-Scope, VistaVision, Todd A-O, or any other of the wide-screen processes which engulfed us in the early 1950s and which will in turn be engulfed by something equally novel and sensational in the 1960s. The more things change, the more they remain the same! Grandpa did not think it ludicrous when Theda Bara hissed, by means of a printed caption, "Kiss me, my fool." Papa and Mama gave each other a fond reminiscent glance when boy whispered to girl, "Listen, darling, they're playing Our Song." It is inevitable that words and situations we today accept without misgiving will be the laughingstock of tomorrow. The pendulum of taste swings backward and forward, but the fundamentals of entertainment remain static.

Cinematic prophets, commentators and tycoons alike, have been wrong with a rare consistency. They discouraged films running longer than twenty minutes, they disparaged sound, they discounted television. One prediction, however, requires no clairvoyance. The fans of the future, like those of the past, will have and hold dear Westerns and comedies, melodrama and romance, spectacles and musicals. The Westerns may well be more psychological, the comedies less slapstick, the melodrama more credible, the romance less sentimental, the spectacles more spectacular, and the musicals less formalized. Our guess—and it is only a guess—is that tomorrow's movies will be more flexible and experimental in style and substance than the movies of the past. They will turn increasingly, as source material, to the great classics of fiction and drama. Occasionally they will flirt with fantasy, occasionally they will even dare to face the honest realities of daily life.

Regardless, however, of subject matter, moviegoers will continue to insist on glamorous personalities to identify with and to idolize—stars like Garbo and Monroe, Valentino and Brando. There will be sweethearts and vamps (though of course they will be called something smart and snappy), girls with curls or with impressive mammary developments, Latin lovers or taciturn he-men. Their impact on the dreams of young people—and plenty of old ones for that matter—will not differ greatly from one generation to another. If we cannot share the current teen-age passion for Elvis Presley, let us recall that our parents could not see what we saw about Frank Sinatra that was so wonderful. And also there will be the men who will make fans of the future laugh, the successors to Keaton, Langdon, Lloyd and Lewis. And if God is very, very kind, there may come another Chaplin to make them cry as they laugh.

But these gods and goddesses are not the sum or even the greatest part of the hold the movies have had, or will have, on us. Our true allegiance lies elsewhere. "Even little children," wrote Gilbert Seldes, "know that the thing which seems to be real [435/436] on the screen is not real, and the riddle of appearance and reality enchants them, although not in the same degree as it enchanted Berkeley and Hegel and Kant. The appeal of the moving picture, to the subconscious, touches those regions in which we are still little children, puzzled by the question of where the light goes when it goes out." Our true allegiance, then, is as it has always been, to illusion—in the case of the movie, the most literal and therefore the most satisfying illusion ever devised. Now this illusion, in its familiar form, is being mortally challenged by a newer form of itself. Will television kill the movies? Of course not, for television is movies too. All that can happen is the death of a system of production and exhibition which we have identified so long with the movies that we cannot imagine them produced and distributed otherwise. But it is time to stretch our imaginations. Whether the movies of the future will come to us via the big screen, the small box, or some as yet unknown channel will depend on which of them best serves illusion.

We cannot guess now which of them

that will be. We are living in days of heart-breaking uncertainty for picture-makers and delightful fluidity for picturegoers. Independent production is replacing the forty-year reign of the mass-producing factories. The major companies may well, in the coming years, become primarily bankers, landlords and distributors, rather than picture producers. They will merge and consolidate into vast entertainment empires, producing plays and television shows, making records, owning television stations and music-publishing concerns.

Meanwhile, many of the old hard-top film houses will disappear. But as they grow fewer in number they will grow more varied in character. There will be theaters specializing in long runs, in reserved seats, in unique types of projection such as Cinerama, Todd A-O, and their successful successors. There will be small art houses, drive-ins, and, for all we know, fly-ins. Above all there will be a theater in practically every American home. What was formerly man's castle will have become his picture palace. Even in the home, however, there will be diversity: movies on old-fashioned television but with larger screens, stereophonic sound, and—who knows—maybe 3-D minus polaroid glasses, toll TV so that first-run pictures can be shown to those prepared to pay for the privilege, films transmitted via closed-circuit wire relayed for a fixed annual fee from the local movie house.

One thing is certain: more Americans will see pictures every hour of the day than ever saw them before. Their importance in our daily life not only for purposes of entertainment but for education and propaganda will be greater than ever before achieved by any medium of communication. Will they be better, will they be worse than the movies of yesterday and today? It is a foolish question. To those of us who have lived through the wonders of the past sixty years there can be no misgivings about the glories of the future. The authors of this book are jealous of the men who will write its sequel in 2017!

PART TWO

WHAT DOES THE AUDIENCE WANT?

Shakespeare and the Cinema*

ALLARDYCE NICOLL (1894-   ), teacher and authority on drama, is a former director of the Shakespeare Institute, located at Stratford-on-Avon. From 1933 to 1945, he was professor of the history of drama and chairman of the department of drama at Yale University. It was during this time that he wrote *Film and Theatre*, from which this selection is taken. He is the author of many books on the Elizabethan theater, as well as six volumes of *A History of English Drama*, which spans the period from 1660 to 1900.

. . . .

For the late sixteenth century, the Elizabethan stage occupied a position by no means dissimilar to that taken in our own times by the cinema.

A realisation of this fact gives us to pause. So familiar have we become with the complaint that the composite authorship practised in the studios denies any possibility of individual expression and of artistic growth; the film itself has become so common and so cheap a form of entertainment; and the records, true or false, of managerial incompetence and illiteracy have been so bruited abroad in current gossip, in newspaper paragraphs and in satirical farces; that the cinema, where it has not been completely [5/6] condemned and despised, has been accepted merely as a thing which might make an hour pass easily, with no thought of its artistic possibilities. Lovers of the theatre are constantly seeing in it the cause of the drama's decline, and, noting the way in which the film has filched stage successes from every land, have denominated it fundamentally parasitic in its aims and in its methods. . . .

. . . .

. . . Allowing for the disappearance of that stern [6/7] religious enthusiasm which fired the hearts and made bitter the tongues of the Elizabethan sermonisers, we may perhaps see a fairly close connection between the opponents of the stage in the sixteenth century and the twentieth-century opponents of the film. Of hard words and of what is more galling than hard words—contempt, both have accorded much. Even if we neglect those who, for religious and moral reasons, seek to deflect their charges from doors that, in their opinion, open the way to the underworld (of gangsters or of devils), we realise that, although the film has become one of the most familiar and potent forces in modern life, comparatively little attention has been paid to its aims, its positive achievements and its potentialities by those more serious spectators from whose aid it might most have profited. [7/8]

. . . .

. . . In 1595, when Shakespeare was reaching his maturity, there were two groups which attacked the public theatres —first, the religious enthusiasts and the civic authorities who would, had the power been granted them, have banished all the players and sternly closed their houses of entertainment, and second, the literary exquisites. The former, with their insistence upon the "corruption of youth with incontinence and lewdness" and upon the "great wasting both of the time and thrift of many poor people," sound a note familiar enough today; Shakespeare's Cleopatra,

* Allardyce Nicoll, from "Shakespeare and the Cinema," *Film and Theatre* (New York: Thomas Crowell, 1936), pp. 5-11, 15-16. Reprinted by permission of Thomas Y. Crowell Company.

now become an examination question for school-children, once was regarded as more recent moralists regard the Cleopatra of De Mille. These, however, need not greatly concern us: more important are the littérateurs. For Sir Philip Sidney and those who thought with him, the drama was a fine thing and fit to be prized, but the contemporary play was not. In the grip of rude forces, the popular stage, they [8/9] opined, was degrading the muses Thalia and Melpomene. Loving them in spite of their degradation, these men sought to encourage a purer form of artistic expression in dramatic terms. The chill, but regularly faultless and conventional, academic dramas, acted by students and gentlemen, not for hire but for their own amusement and edification, were their ideal. They esteemed the historically interesting but lifeless *Gorboduc* beyond any of the successful plays presented in the public theatres and ever aimed at stripping the stage of those meretricious ornaments which appealed to the idle and uncritical fancies of the crowd. [9/10]

.   .   .   .

. . . the theatre has ever discovered its true strength in the addressing of large and representative audiences. Sophocles gained power from the vast body of Athenian citizens who filled the theatre of Dionysus for his *Oedipus Rex,* and to Shakespeare came vigor and vitality from the crowds of London citizens who flocked to the Globe playhouse, there to witness and to welcome a *Hamlet* and a *Twelfth Night.* The cinema in this may be regarded in a light no different from that in which we view the stage. The crowd's judgments, it is true, are often fickle and erratic; but that is a condition which all who practice these arts must accept. No doubt it is disturbing to find the same people hailing *Emperor Jones* and *Abie's Irish Rose* with kindred enthusiasm; no doubt we shudder and marvel to think that a profound [10/11] *Hamlet* and a dull *Mucedorus* tied for pride of place about the year 1600; but so the theatre is made and in such conditions

we must rest content. After all, in every art form there are essential premises which must be agreed to before anything of creative value is produced. If you wish to be a dramatist you must be prepared to write for the established theatres of your day; and if you esteem the cinema and believe it to be an art you must be prepared to discover that art among the commercial films of Elstree and of Hollywood, calculated to appeal to the public at large. [11/15]

.   .   .   .

. . . The average film of the day is trivial in theme and often vulgar in expression; that we cannot deny. Yet again a doubt enters. Exactly in this way did Sidney speak a few years before Shakespeare entered the service of the Lord Chamberlain's players; and his error teaches us caution. In Sidney's time a new theatre had barely been born. Dependent though the Elizabethan stage may be on medieval achievements in the realm of the mystery play and the comic interlude, fundamentally it started afresh and discovered its own life-force with the first regular comedies and tragedies written shortly after the middle of the sixteenth century. Within thirty years Shakespeare had arrived, but Sidney, penning his words immediately before his advent, was impatient, expected too much and failed to appreciate the signs already apparent in his time.

Nor was it that external conditions improved out of all recognition within the intervening space of twenty or thirty years. Shakespeare wrote for the same audience —a general and many-headed audience— for the stinkards in the yard as well as for the gentlemen in the sixpenny boxes. The public was avid of novelty and sensationalism, delighting mightily in the gory horrors of a *Titus Andronicus;* the theatrical managers exploited freely whatever [15/16] came uppermost at the moment, heaping ghosts upon the stage while the going of ghosts was good and mad ladies in white linen when ghosts began to pall; stars ruled the boards and a clownish

Kemp or a bombastic Burbage demanded fat parts for the proper portrayal of his personality; considerations of art were left to the universities and little was aimed at on the public stage save immediate success; and over all stood the iron censor with his bowl of ink. Yet Shakespeare wrote.

. . . .

What Makes a Good Screen Story?*

MERVYN LeROY (1900-   ) began his theatrical career as an actor in vaudeville and became a motion-picture director in 1927. He has directed such socially-conscious films as *I Am a Fugitive from a Chain Gang, Little Caesar,* and *Madame Curie,* as well as such contributions to entertainment as *Gold Diggers of 1933, Anthony Adverse, Three Men on a Horse, Thirty Seconds over Tokyo, Quo Vadis, No Time for Sergeants,* and *A Majority of One.*

. . . .

What baffles the makers of movies and the writers of stories is that public taste is not so lofty and cosmopolitan as is generally believed. This is a fact that has long since failed to surprise the pollsters. What the average person says he likes and what he really pays his money to see are two different things.

Question: What kind of movies do you like?

Answer: Good, meaty pictures with dramatic impact, such as *Death of a Salesman.*

Question: Did you see *Death of a Salesman?*

Answer: I just happened to miss that one, but I heard it was great.

Question: What pictures *did* you see last month?

Answer: Well, just for laughs, you know, *Ma and Pa Kettle.* And a Betty Grable picture—I forget the name.

Question: Did you ever see *The Heiress,* the picture that won Olivia de Havilland the Academy Award for the best performance of 1949?

Answer: I never got around to that one; but that's the kind I mean—dramatic.

It's like the boy who *says* he wants to marry a good, strong person, like his mother, but who really marries the blonde who swings her hips when she walks down the street.

It's a matter of public record by now that *The Heiress* [38/39] was not a big financial success. Yet everyone kept telling the industry that we should make more pictures just like it. We can't make more pictures like *The Heiress* if they don't justify their cost. It's like the book-publishing business. A well-written, artistic success can be a commercial failure. The publisher who doesn't pay for his artistic flops with commercially successful books that will pay the printer's bill isn't going to be publishing *any* books, great or small, very long. Of course, in the book world the biggest artistic successes often do very well. It's the little artistic successes that are commercial flops. The same is true of motion pictures.

As for movies just for the intelligentsia, these so-called critics' pictures rarely make money, and I'll tell you why. Anyone who makes a picture for a critic is out of his mind. A critic isn't representative. I have never found a bad picture any critic could help and I've never found a good one any critic could hurt. *Another Part of the Forest,* for instance, was a critics' picture. It was beautifully done, *but it was not a picture most people wanted to see.*

If you saw *Francis,* the movie about the talking mule, you saw a really enjoyable picture. The people in it were great and the people who made it were great, *and it*

* Mervyn LeRoy, from "What Makes a Good Screen Story?" *It Takes More Than Talent* (New York: Knopf, 1953), pp. 38-41. Reprinted from *It Takes More Than Talent* by Mervyn LeRoy, by permission of Alfred A. Knopf, Inc. Copyright 1953 by Alfred A. Knopf, Inc.

was a picture everyone wanted to see. They needed a talking mule in *Another Part of the Forest*. Because it's this way: *The Blue Boy* is a beautiful picture, but comparatively few people have seen it. The *Mona Lisa* is one of the greatest pictures the world has ever known, but more people have seen Lana Turner. My answer to that is: people want entertainment. If The Blue Boy sang like Jolson, they'd go to see him. Or if Mona Lisa looked like Hedy Lamarr, more people would go to the Louvre. Hollywood was crazy to have made a picture like *Mourning Becomes Electra*. [**39/40**] That was a great play and beautifully written, but who the devil wants to see it as a picture? You might want to see *Quo Vadis*. Or *Ivanhoe*. Or *Bend of the River*. But who wants to see a movie whose basic theme is incest? There is nothing inspirational about such a story. At best, its appeal is to a limited sophisticated, cosmopolitan audience. Owing to Breen Office restrictions, the same honesty of characterization and motivation as was shown on the stage could not be shown in the picture. Therefore it didn't come off. There were a lot of heavy dramatics over a theme that was never brought out or clarified.

This isn't to say that we ever set out to make a bad movie. We all set our sights on the highest goal. But the fact is that the would-be motion-picture writer cannot begin his writing career with too arty an ap-

proach. There has to be the perfect blend. Maybe your story is it. Maybe it falls short. The point is that you'll be more successful in cracking a brand-new field if you will remember certain basic box-office-proved points.

You have to remember that the majority of people who go to movies go because they want to forget their worries for a while. Movies are escape. In the main, people don't want to go to be reminded of the troubles and tragedies they must face the next day unless the story is extremely inspirational. They want to leave the theater happier than when they went in. For example, though musicals may be only fantasy, they also take us away from life as it is lived from day to day.

The cynics are always with us—those who say Hollywood cannot face reality, that everything must be glossed over and made unreal. What the cynics do not realize is that dreams are often more real than reality. There is a reality beyond that which we see and touch and feel. There [**40/41**] exists within man a groping toward an idealistic extension of himself: an undefeatable belief that life can be pleasanter than it may be at the moment, a stanch conviction that there are possibilities beyond his own narrow horizons. The movie with the fairytale, Cinderella, happy-ending plot brings joy because it also brings hope.

Secret of Success*

HAROLD HOBSON (1904-   ), a graduate of Oriel College, Oxford University, became English dramatic critic for the *Christian Science Monitor* in 1932 and its London literary editor in 1946. From 1942 to 1948 he was assistant literary editor for the *Sunday Times* of London as well; he has been that newspaper's drama critic since 1947. He also reviews films for both newspapers. He is the author of several books, including *Verdict at Midnight* (1952), *The French Theatre of Today* (1953), and *Ralph Richardson* (1958).

In Paris this season the situation in the cinema seems to be analogous to that of the theater in Britain. The most successful films have been those produced for small, specialized, cultivated audiences.

They have been shown, of course, in cinemas built on a less grand scale than the palatial houses in the Champs Elysées, where the great commercial ventures are exhibited. But these smaller houses, when I have visited them, have been comfortably full, while several of the vast saloons of the popular cinema have been, lamentably, empty. The life and conviction seem to have gone out of the big entertainment film on the Continent, as they have gone out of the London drawing room comedy.

I do not mean to go so far as to say that no new continental commercial films are successful. Robert Dhéry, for example, has used his experience of the United States, gained during the long run of "La Plume de ma Tante," to make a comedy called "La Belle Américaine," which is highly thought of; and René Clair has produced another comedy, "Tout l'Or du Monde," which if not up to the standard of "Le Million" and "Sous les Toits de Paris," is certainly not to be despised.

Nevertheless, neither of these films, nor yet the big spectacular color film, "Amours Célèbres," with its almost unbelievably opulent cast of Edwige Feuillère, Dany Robin, Brigitte Bardot, Suzanne Flon, Pierre Dux, Alain Delon, Pierre Brasseur, Jean-Pierre Belmondo, Jacques Dumesnil, Simone Signoret, and Jean Desailly, has aroused anything like the discussion and the interest of Michelangelo Antonioni's "La Notte," Alain Resnais's and Alain Robbe-Grillet's "L'Année Dernière à Marienbad," or Marguerite Duras's "Une Aussi Longue Absence."

Why is this? There was a time when the popular film really was popular, and when it had artistic value. The most obvious examples of this, of course, are the early Chaplin pictures; but there are others, too. Despite a racialism which is abhorrent to British audiences, D. W. Griffith's "The Birth of a Nation" was an outstanding work; and the same director's "Intolerance," though it delighted in violence, was packed with intelligence, vitality, and imagination.

But now, in the making of big commercial films, there is too much of the spirit of consumer research. There is too strong a desire to give the public what it wants.

Now it is impossible deliberately and successfully to give the public what it

* Harold Hobson, "Secret of Success," *Christian Science Monitor*, December 7, 1961, Sec. 2, p. 1. Reprinted by permission of the Christian Science Publishing Society.

wants; for what the public wants is passionate conviction and belief underlying what is being given to it. Such things cannot be achieved by specific determination. They are present only when the artist or director is giving the public what *he* wants. This was the case with Chaplin and Griffith—and the public responded.

But now the efficiency expert in public taste is called in, and he gives all the wrong answers. He is convinced that what the public wants is brutality and sex. But to offer these coldly and by calculation is to court disaster.

"Amours Célèbres," for example, consists of four stories based on a strip cartoon in a Paris evening paper. It has no compelling motive behind it. There is no feeling in it and [*sic*] the director had to make it, or he would have burst. Its frigidity repels. It is significant that the only story of the four to succeed, that in which Mme Feuillère appears as a star of the Comédie Française at the debut of the dazzling Mlle Georges, is the only one that has no sex motif.

But Signor Antonioni in "La Notte" really did feel profoundly about declining love; Mme Duras in "Une Aussi Longue Absence" felt profoundly about the peril of disturbing a fragile happiness; and M. Robbe-Grillet in "L'Année Dernière à Marienbad" felt profoundly about his peculiar method of telling a story. They thought not of what the public would like, but of what they had to say.

That is the reason for their success. [1]

For Eggheads Only?*

ARTHUR KNIGHT (1916-   ) has been motion-picture critic for the *Saturday Review* since 1949. Active also in other areas relating to motion pictures, he has been a film consultant for CBS-TV, has taught film history at the College of the City of New York and at the University of Southern California, and is curator of film for the Hollywood Museum. He has published many articles and *The Liveliest Art* (1957), a world history of motion pictures.

There is in all probability no more egregious misnomer in an industry scarcely noted for the accuracy of its terminology than that elegant soubriquet, "art house." With its connotations of eggheadism, snobbism and Continental sophistication, "art house" has so much more style, so much more *chic* than *Variety*'s show-biz-like "sure-seater." Nor do art house operators like to be confused with (or even compared to) the managers of "exploitation houses," those dingy palaces dedicated to sex, sadism, and the fast buck. Often, however, the chief distinction would seem to lie in the demitasse of black coffee served in the lobby of the snootier establishments. For make no mistake about it, the art house operators—may their tribe increase—are in business just as surely as their competitors who feature *Mr. Rock and Roll, I Was a Teen-age Werewolf,* or *The Garden of Eden.* They too must find a product that will bring in the customers. They too must find means of exploiting their pictures that will pay off at the box office. And the sad truth is that art, by any of its traditional definitions, seems to be one of the last of the desiderata that bring patrons to the art house ticket windows.

Consider, for example, the saddening experience of one of the canniest and most successful importers of foreign films for the art house market. Early in 1957 Ilya Lopert released Henri-Georges Clouzot's *La Mystère Picasso,* one of the most ambitious, ingenious and exciting pictures ever made on a specifically art [24/25] subject. It had all the elements that one might expect would win it fervent support throughout the art house circuit: a controversial artist, a world-famous director, a new way of revealing the creative process, Technicolor, CinemaScope. . . . *Picasso* lasted a scant two weeks in the very same New York theater that had played Clouzot's sensation-jammed *Diabolique* to crowded houses for almost a year. Consider the no less disheartening experience of a New York art house operator who reluctantly consented to book a shoddy Brigitte Bardot picture in the hope of proving once and for all that it took more than sex to sell a picture to art house audiences—and promptly found the theater doing bigger business than the Roxy!

Both the managers of art theaters and the distributors of art films are notoriously careful people. They have to be. Mistakes in their field can be costly. The exhibitor must be prepared to pay thousands of dollars for the advertising and publicity that go out before a new picture opens. To get a particular film, he may even have to guarantee the distributor a certain amount

* Arthur Knight, "For Eggheads Only?" in *Film: Book 1,* ed. Robert Hughes (New York: Grove Press, 1959), pp. 24-32. Reprinted by permission of the author and the editor.

of money or number of weeks of playing time—regardless of its eventual acceptance by the public. The distributor, on the other hand, in addition to the not inconsiderable sums he must pay to acquire his films in the first place (anywhere from $10,000 to $100,000, and occasionally more), must also stand the expenses of titling or dubbing them for American distribution, as well as some part of the initial advertising costs.

And yet, as such *flops d'estime* as *The Diary of a Country Priest, Umberto D, Day of Wrath,* and *La Mystère Picasso* remind us, both the art film distributors and the art house exhibitors are often more willing to gamble on the attractiveness of a good picture than are their patrons. Indeed, in many instances their taking a film for distribution in itself must be considered as less a gamble than an act of love. A number of the distributors are men of genuine taste and discrimination who are so devoted to the art of the film that they will risk financial loss in order to bring to American audiences the outstanding works of European directors. Being businessmen as well, they generally find it necessary to hedge their investments in art with more patently profitable [25/26] investments in European pin-ups, salving their consciences—and they *do* have consciences— with the knowledge that the income from their Bardots, Lollobrigidas, and Martine Carols will help pay for their next Bressons, deSicas, and Michael Cacoyannises. Occasionally, of course, these distributors have the pleasant surprise of finding a picture they had imported out of sheer altruism—an *Open City,* a *Bicycle Thief,* a *Young and the Damned*—paying off in good round sums at the box office. The franker ones among them, however, will point out that the reasons for this unanticipated success probably lie outside the artistic merits of the picture itself—a *Life* display hinting at sexual perversion in *Open City,* a glimpse of a shapely leg in the ads for *Bicycle Thief,* the savage undercurrents of sadism that pervaded *Young and the Damned.*

All of which suggests that while the patronage of art theaters is unquestionably growing in this country, the number of patrons for genuinely artistic films is actually lamentably small. The eggheaded core, that section of the art house audience with the intellectual curiosity to search out the works of Bardem, Bresson, Mizoguchi, Cacoyannis or Satyajit Ray, is still not enough to make such films a safe commercial investment — unless, adventitiously, they include elements that happen to appeal to the critics of *The New York Times, The New Yorker,* and a handful of other opinion makers who can help swell the lines at the box office. For good or ill, it is in this field of the art film that the critical confraternity swings the most appreciable weight. And the distributors and exhibitors of such films, unfortunately, seem to ponder their reviews with a far greater intensity than the audience for which they were written. A favorable notice from Bosley Crowther or John McCarten, they know, will bring in the crowds; if the notices are unfavorable, they realize that they might just as well bring in another picture.

What too many intellectuals ignore is the fact that Crowther, McCarten, and indeed most critics in the mass circulation dailies and weeklies are writing for a wide audience, for hundreds of thousands of readers. If a film like *Ordet* or *The Girl in Black* is likely to prove caviar to the general, it is their duty to [26/27] say so (although not necessarily in terms of utter disparagement). But this does not mean that their readers, particularly those who are forever calling for "better films," should accept these critics uncritically. Rather, it becomes the duty of truly intelligent film enthusiasts to read between the lines—or elsewhere, in specialized publications like *Sight and Sound* or *Film Quarterly*—and make their own decision as to the films that *they* want to support at the box office. More than that, it is their duty to support these films, if they can possibly afford to, during the early days and weeks of their run.

It is a matter of simple film economics.

The greatest effort to popularize and sell a new picture is expended during the initial weeks of its engagement. If the returns warrant it during that period, the picture stays on and is publicized further. If not, the film is dropped and another booked in its place. A truncated run, moreover, not only means less income for the distributor from his most lucrative booking, the downtown art house. It also means that when he tries to move his picture into a second-run theater, or to book it in other parts of the country, he will meet with stolid opposition. "What did your picture do at the Paris?" he will be asked—and be forced to accept play-dates at unfavorable terms, at unfavorable times or even be refused any additional bookings whatsoever. The film enthusiast who, learning of a picture that he very much wants to see, decides to favor his pocketbook and wait until it goes to the second-runs not only risks not seeing the picture at all, but he also makes it just a little less likely that the manager of the first-run house will play another such film in the near future. Not with Brigitte Bardot standing them in the aisles whenever her pictures are shown.

Beyond any doubt, the art house audience is growing. In an era that saw the aggregate movie attendance shrink from a peak of approximately 85 million customers per week in 1946 to something under 45 million per week in 1958, the number of art houses—or, to define a bit more precisely, the number of theaters that will book foreign films—has shot up from about a dozen just after the war to around 450 today. For a phenom-[**27/28**]enal success, like *Rififi* or *Diabolique,* the bookings may go to more than 2000. But not only is it the sheerest snobbism to equate European films with art; it is also, alas, quite impossible to equate commercial success with artistic values. The audience that now supports the art house type of operation has certainly been won over through an impatience with the standardized Hollywood product. It patronizes them, in the main, anticipating a kind of titilation [*sic*] or sensation that censorship and mass pro-

duction methods have combined to eliminate from American pictures. Relatively few go in search of art as well.

As new forms of production emerge in Hollywood, however, as independent, individualized picture making supplants the vast film factories of the past, the distinction between Europe and Hollywood as a proper source for art house product is rapidly disappearing. *Love in the Afternoon, The Happy Road,* and *The Matchmaker* are all recent independents that had their premieres on the art house circuit, films that might have been lost in the fast shuffling of product in and out of the larger showcases. Indeed, *Love in the Afternoon* affords an especially clear illustration of the particular advantages of art house distribution for certain pictures. Opening the same day in New York at both the mammoth Paramount on Broadway and the small, off-Broadway Plaza, it remained at the Plaza for seventeen profitable weeks while its Broadway run was a slim four. More and more, the independent producers are finding it expedient to play their less costly items in the art theaters, where lower overhead makes it possible for a film to run longer and build its audience.

Thus, the new Hollywood's "off-beat" productions are already hotly competing with the Europeans for art house screen time—and finding support from the same art house audience that had, for one reason or another, been patronizing foreign films almost exclusively. It seems safe to predict that in a few years the art theaters will no longer be thought of as the special province of French, Italian, or British pictures, but rather of a film *type*—pictures (even American) whose appeal is based on unconventional ideas, values or characters rather than on stars [**28/29**] and spectacle. If such films happen to be artistic as well, so much the better.

The years since the war have also seen in the United States the birth—or rather, the renaissance—of a film society movement of considerable proportions. There are today some 300 organizations that call themselves either film societies, film clubs, or film study groups; and probably at least another 500 meeting informally and irregularly in schools, museums, and private homes that carry out some of the functions of such organizations. They show film classics or simply old films; they run documentaries, science films and experimentals; they may even, on occasion, supply their members with program notes or invite guest speakers to introduce the pictures. It is a movement that has grown to such an extent within the past ten years that there has recently been formed an American Federation of Film Societies, the equivalent of the *ciné-club* organizations that have existed for decades on the Continent and in England.

Superficially, one would expect that the small, highly selective, highly specialized film society would be the true domain of any eggheads devoted to *cinéma pur*. Unfortunately, this is only partially true. Amos Vogel, the director of Cinema 16, America's largest and most successful film society, has divided his own audience into "eggheads, middle-brows, and pseudo-eggheads," and he has discovered from repeated polling of his membership that the true eggheads are by no means in the majority. Experimental films and films on the arts invariably trail far behind the number of requests for revivals of popular features, Museum of Modern Art classics and certain documentaries, he has found. Some societies have been organized by "Foofs" (Friends Of Old Films); [1] they will look at anything, good, bad, or indifferent, so long as it was produced before 1928. Others dignify with the title of "film society" a passion for old Garbos, Barrymores, or W. C. Fields movies. And Elodie Osborn, who organized a perfectly respectable society in Salis- [29/30] bury, Conn., almost lost the main part of her membership by including in her series one year a screening of Akira Kurosawa's *Rashomon*. Her eggheads preferred more conventional forms of film art.[2]

In other words the film societies, far

from forming a homogeneous group wholeheartedly supporting the finest in film art, in fact fall into at least three main categories. One would be the specialist film groups, whether "Foofs," experimentalists, or Garbo fans. Membership in these is almost Masonic, the innermost circles being reserved for those who have collected the greatest amount of esoterica on their particular enthusiasms. There is about these clubs an intensity, a passion to be found nowhere else in the film world. It smacks, rather, of the devotion of the stamp collector, where rarity is virtually the sole test for quality. It is a twilight world of special values and associations, a world notably, even intentionally, apart from the mainstreams of film creativity. Such groups tend to be small and, so long as costs of film rentals are covered, prefer to remain so.

Cinema 16 has become the prototype of another form of film society that is being widely emulated today, particularly in clubs affiliated with colleges and universities. These are groups that offer their membership a mixed package of what Mr. Vogel describes in his annual prospectus as "outstanding social documentaries, controversial adult screen fare, advanced experimental films, classics of the international cinema and medical-psychiatric studies." Such organizations are performing a real service, both to their communities and to films, by building audiences for types of pictures that could never hope for commercial exposure, pictures that— either for reasons of censorship, economics or both—would never be shown in ordinary moviehouses. To be successful, however, the organizers of these societies have had to learn that their own tastes can never be the final criterion. They have had to throw into their programs cartoons, old features, pictures of monkeys and children. They have had to [30/31] make, each in

---

[1] A species first identified by Christopher Bishop; the word takes care of the kind of antiquarians called "moldy figs" in jazz parlance. (Ed.)

[2] Mrs. Osborn has since let the main part go its own way—back to their TV sets and/or the local moviehouse. A few stalwarts from the old society comprise what her husband calls the "reel" society. (Ed.)

his own way, the commercial compromise —the extent of that compromise being directly related to and in proportion with the size of the audience they hope to enroll, or need to retain in order to stay in business next season.

The remaining contingent is, in effect, an extension of the art house via 16mm into those communities where European films are rarely exhibited. Often such societies are formed in college towns, frequently on the campus itself. Invariably they arise out of the interest and hard work of a single individual and consequently have a tendency to disappear either when that individual's enthusiasm has spent itself or he leaves the institution. Or if the society should prove outstandingly successful, as was the case with the Gothic Film Society at Ann Arbor, Mich., there is always the possibility that the local theater manager, stimulated by the success of the film society, will begin a program of art films himself. But while the longevity of these organizations is often disappointing, during their life span they do tend to offer intelligent programming and superior films drawn from the catalogs of the Museum of Modern Art and the leading non-theatrical distributors of features, documentaries, art films, and experimentals. The step from such societies to a full-scale art theater, however, is a fairly short one —with both the advantages and the disadvantages that this implies.

But the big fact, the encouraging fact, is that the number of these groups is on the increase. Thanks to the efforts of the Museum of Modern Art Film Library and distributors like Brandon, Contemporary, Film Images, and Trans-World, more titles of first quality are available to them now than ever before. And thanks to the educational programs that have been going on in schools, colleges, and museums for the past 20 years, more people have come to look upon the film as an art form than ever before. They want to see the best —although neither they nor the film society organizers are always quite certain of what that best consists of. Basically, however, people tend to join film societies for the same reasons that they patronize the art theaters. They are dissatisfied with most of the pictures shown in their neighborhood houses—so dissatisfied that they would sooner [31/32] stay away from the movies altogether than risk the boredom and sterility of the average Hollywood feature. A film society, like an art theater, at least holds out to them the promise of a certain level of quality and interest—and in addition, the psychological satisfaction that comes from being part of an intellectual group.

For today's film society leaders ("foofs" to one side) the challenge is obvious. They must themselves turn critic, learning to recognize the differences between a good film and one that is simply popular. They must also become showmen, learning how to build programs from such pictures that will, at some point or another, give pleasure to the greater portion of their audience—and accepting with cheerful resignation the axiom known to all showmen, "You can't please everybody." Above all, they must learn to combine these qualities of critic and showman to provide their membership with series that will lead them gradually to a greater appreciation of the motion picture. Experience has shown that while these groups can be led, they resent bitterly being hit over the head with culture, no matter how elevating. Movies, some deep-seated instinct tells them, are for entertainment; they are quite properly suspicious of films for which they have not been sufficiently prepared, films shown them simply "because they are good." "Good" means too many things to too many people.

The challenge, then, would seem to lie in creative programming, in balancing the several elements of every screening to take into consideration the emotional and intellectual requirements of the membership. Clearly, variety is the answer: a careful, discriminant selection of cartoons, documentaries, experimentals, and features that will provide something for everybody. Perhaps the greatest single danger in this period of film society expansion is trying to put all eggheads in one basket. As the art houses become increasingly an adjunct of the movie industry's mass distribution facilities, the film societies can provide a sorely needed refuge for the intelligent film enthusiast—provided he knows that his intelligence will be respected in ways not possible either in commercial or art house circles.

PART THREE

DOES THE SCREEN REFLECT SOCIETY?

The Modern Photoplay*

IRVING THALBERG (1899-1936) was the first and greatest executive producer in Hollywood. His name was on only two films, but he was in charge of production at Metro-Goldwyn-Mayer from 1924 until his death; and most of that studio's outstanding pictures in the first years of sound were produced under his supervision. His last films were *The Barretts of Wimpole Street, Mutiny on the Bounty, Romeo and Juliet,* and *The Good Earth.* Beginning as a secretary to Carl Laemmle at Universal Pictures, he was picked at the age of 25 by L. B. Mayer to run the new M-G-M; and his career there has become a proud legend in Hollywood. The following selection is from one of his rare speeches, delivered at the University of Southern California in 1929 under the auspices of the Academy of Motion Picture Arts and Sciences.

In order to understand the modern photoplay, in my opinion, which is based on about twelve years of experience during which time I have made fifty or more pictures in each of those years, one must understand the meaning of the word, entertainment, for entertainment is the purpose and end of the photoplay. The definition of the word, entertainment, as given in the dictionary, is that something which engages and holds the attention agreeably. There seem to be two essential points in this definition—that entertainment engages the attention of people, and that it brings about a pleasing response in them. Entertainment is the objective of the photoplay and we must keep in mind that as entertainment it must appeal to the varied tastes of all people. Other arts generally appeal to a selected group, but the motion picture art, and it is an art, must have universal appeal. This is fundamental, for the motion picture industry, with its investment of hundreds of millions of dollars, is based on the hope that it will appeal to the people of a nation and of a world, and if it did not have this appeal, it could not have reached its present state of development.

We have seen that the foundation upon which the whole motion picture industry is built is the desire to provide entertainment. Therefore, when we are judging or criticizing what we see on the screen, we must first consider it from the standpoint of entertainment value. We can also judge it from an artistic or technical viewpoint as well, but its entertainment value must be the first criterion. [58/60]

. . . .

We have seen that motion picture audiences are interested in pictures, movement, and changes in form, but even more important than these is the necessity of having the subject matter of photoplays correspond closely to current thinking—they must be topical. One of my chief functions is to be an observer and sense and feel the moods of the public. When I am asked to pass on the expenditure of huge sums of money and decide whether one kind of picture should be made or another kind, the greatest problem to be settled is that of judging whether or not the subject matter

* Irving Thalberg, from "The Modern Photoplay," in "Introduction to Photoplay" (mimeographed, Academy of Motion Picture Arts and Sciences and the University of Southern California, 1929), pp. 58, 60-61. Reprinted by permission of the Academy of Motion Picture Arts and Sciences.

of the story is topical. What is accepted by the public today may not be accepted tomorrow. One of the finest examples I can give you of this is that war pictures in one period and another, in order to be successful, have had to be presented in an entirely different flavor.

During the war, various patriotic pictures were produced with success, showing war as a glorified thing in which no sacrifice was too great to make for your country, and having all the various forms of patriotism that could be gotten into a picture, including titles such as "The Kaiser, the Beast of Berlin." The people were stirred up and were thinking along those lines, and war photoplays capitalized on that thought. After the war, however, the war pictures were not successful, at least that was the common belief. However, we produced a picture called "The Big Parade" which to a great extent has made history along the lines of pictures, and the only difference between it and the other war pictures was the different viewpoint taken in the picture. We took a boy whose idea in entering the war was not patriotic. He was swept along by the war spirit around him and entered it but didn't like it. He met a French girl who was intriguing to him, but he wasn't really serious about her. The only time he was interested in fighting was when a friend, who was close to him, was killed. It was a human appeal rather than a patriotic appeal, and when he reached the German trenches and came face to face with the opportunity to kill, he couldn't do it. In other words, a new thought regarding the war was in the minds of most people and that was the basis of its appeal.

. . . Close attention to what the public is thinking about at the moment cannot be applied to the stage because stage audiences are not the normal audiences that the picture ones are. They are a centralized group of people, exotic, as a rule far better educated than the masses, and a different form of psychology and attention must be applied to them than to the picture audiences. The great successful plays never made any attempt to carefully correspond to the current thought of the moment and we find [60/61] some that have run for generations. However, the spirit of modern life, the attitude of modern life, the attitude of children toward parents, the family life or the lack of it, is so quickly and so normally and clearly brought out in pictures. Of course, in each picture of the kind in which one thought is given the predominating position, there is an exaggeration, but nevertheless, there is a resemblance to the current thought of the day.

The motion pictures present our customs and our daily life more distinctly than any other medium and, therefore, if we were to come back a thousand years from today and tried to find some form of expression that would more clearly, more perfectly explain how we live today, it would have to be the motion picture, because there is no medium of today that so universally must please as great a number of people, and to do this it must be current in its thinking and in the processes by which its heroes and heroines do things. It couldn't be the magazines or the newspapers because they only use unusual subjects; and our literature appeals to an exotic or a sentimental group.

Right there is another side to this question. I have often been asked, "Do you think that the modern pictures, the great pictures, will endure forever?" While no one can state with any authority what will happen; in my opinion, the modern picture will not live forever as an artistic production, because one of the most important features of pictures is currency— the immediate fitting in with current thought. Now, of course, there are exceptions and at all times, a great story, a great work of genius will overcome any obstacle. We have the work of a master artist like Emil Jannings. At times he has been successful in overcoming all obstacles of ordinary standards of acceptance by the public. A great director like Ernest [sic]

Lubitsch, through his cleverness and his genius will and has at times overcome the general lack of acceptance of his type of thinking. In short, I believe that although the modern picture will not live forever as a work of art, except in a few instances, it will be the most effective way of showing posterity how we live today.

The American Film: 1929-48*

RICHARD GRIFFITH. For biographical data, see "Epilogue," p. 23.

. . . .
. . . Films dramatising the life and death of machine-age criminals had been familiar since Josef von Sternberg first dealt with the notorieties of Chicago in *Underworld* (1927). This sophisticated film, and Lewis Milestone's *The Racket* (1928), exemplified the subjective treatment of crime towards which silent technique naturally led directors of the period. The coming of sound shifted the emphasis from the criminal mind to criminal behaviour, enhancing the violent elements of the crime saga. The mere addition of recorded sound itself added immensely to the physical effect of the gangster film. The terrifying splutter of the machine-gun, the screaming of brakes and squealing of automobile tyres, were stimulants equal in effect to the head-long suspense developed by the introspective silent technique.

More important still, sound brought to the crime films those corroborative details which identified the underworld as a familiar segment of contemporary American life. The gangster talkies were written by newspapermen and playwrights, veteran observers who knew the metropolitan world and its cesspools at first hand. Maurine Watkins, Bartlett Cormack and Norman Krasna had all written [433/434] gangster plays before going to Hollywood. John Bright and the late Kubec Glasmon had been news-reporters in Chicago. To the gangster himself, these knowing writers added the racketeering night-club proprietors, the gold-digging moll, the 'mouthpiece', the strong-arm henchman, the moronic sycophant. Individual films

began to explore the colourful details of the half-world and to depict unusual and ingenious criminal methods. Melodrama was the staple ingredient of the cycle, but as writers increasingly dominated the gangster films of 1930 and 1931 they formed a documentary mosaic, a panorama of crime and punishment in an unstable society. George Hill's *The Big House* (1930) showed prison as a breeding-ground for crime. *Little Caesar* (1930) traced the rise of a snarling hoodlum to the position of virtual overlord of a modern city, terrorising business and paralysing the police. *The Secret Six* (1931) was equally frank in depicting the vigilante methods used to combat organised crime when the law failed. The last big gangster films of this cycle made explicit the emergent fact that the gangster had become a popular hero because only an outlaw could achieve success in the economic chaos of depression America. Both *Smart Money* (1931) and *Quick Millions* (1931) made their heroes argue that a man was a fool to go into legitimate business when it was obvious that business methods applied to crime yielded much bigger returns.

Most extraordinary of all, *The Public Enemy* (1931) told the now-familiar story of the rise and fall of a gangster in terms of his social environment. The leading character (James Cagney) moved as though propelled by fate, by the inevitable doom of those born to the slums. This biography of a criminal dared the little-used and generally unsuccessful episodic form in order to detail every stage in the formation of the hero's psyche. As a boy, the futile me-

* Richard Griffith, from "The American Film: 1929-48," in *The Film Till Now*, ed. Paul Rotha and Richard Griffith (New York: Funk and Wagnalls, 1949), pp. 433-437. Reprinted by permission of Vision Press Limited.

diocrity of his middle-class family is contrasted with the excitement of city streets where every saloon and poolroom is an invitation to excitement and, incidentally, to virile adulthood. A bar-room piano-player teaches [434/435] adolescent boys dirty songs; in return, they pick pockets and he acts as their 'fence'. The petty crooks and ward heelers of the neighbourhood approvingly watch their progress from minor thievery to the organised robbery of fur warehouses and, finally, to the biggest bonanza of all, the liquor racket. It is as though they had gone to school and after rigorous training passed their examinations to general approbation. Their lives as adults are detailed with a realism new to the screen. In danger more from rival gangsters than from the police, they move uneasily from apartment to apartment, their surroundings at once luxurious and sordid, their women women and nothing more. Towards the end of the film, Cagney indicates his boredom with his current mistress by pushing a grapefruit in her face. A few minutes later, his befouled corpse is delivered to his mother's doorstep as though it were the day's supply of meat.

The intentions of Bright and Glasmon in this film were undoubtedly sociological; the reactions of audiences were frequently romantic. Young girls longed to have grapefruit pushed in *their* faces, and the tough, not to say sadistic heroes in the persons of Cagney and Clark Gable became the beau ideal of men and women alike. The gangster cycle, growing more harrowing with each picture, was box-office throughout the early years of the talkies. But though audiences in general did not recoil from the opened cesspool, its stench offended more delicate nostrils. The Daughters of the American Revolution, the American Legion, and that greater legion of women's clubs and business men's clubs which run the machinery of community life in the United States, disliked this focussing upon 'America's shame'. They pointed out, truly enough, that audiences sentimentalised the gang-

ster and envied his life of unrestrained violence and excitement. Useless for the Hays Office to reply that the gangster films were grim object lessons against crime, and that their moralising was nearly always vocal and specific. To small-town civic leaders, the films seemed morbid, unpleasant, and somehow unpatriotic. The [435/436] major portion of American film revenue comes from small towns. Hollywood gave in. In the spring of 1931 the gangster film was a staple product; before the beginning of the next year it had vanished from the screen.

Its disappearance marked the first instance of a paradox which has plagued the Motion Picture Industry ever since. A story 'theme' becomes popular enough with general audiences to warrant a cycle of films to be built around it. But the 'theme' itself is repugnant to the upper middle class who, though they form only a small percentage of total motion picture patronage, are organised and articulate. Then, although the cycle's box-office warrants its continuance, it is abandoned in deference to the pressure groups. Yet these attempts to curb or guide public taste are seldom wholly successful if they are in opposition to the time-spirit. The gangster as stencil disappeared, but his influences remained. The crime films had brought the habit of a naturalistic approach to the screen. Their best-known contribution was a new swiftness of continuity which lifted the movies out of the dialogue doldrums of the photographed play. In pictures which revolved round the events of murder, pursuit and capture, speech became speedy and succinct. This brief dialogue blended with the staccato rhythm of films based on action to produce vivid impact. In 1931 Norbert Lusk said of *Smart Money*: 'Every word has the force of a newspaper headline.'

Once they learned that speech need not carry the story, directors and writers began to use it as an atmospheric adjunct. Edward G. Robinson's famous 'So you can dish it out but you can't take it', was one of the many phrases the gangster film brought into general circulation. Screen dialogue took on an idiomatic crispness in the mouths of Robinson, Cagney, Joan Blondell, Ruth Donnelly, Marjorie Rambeau, Chester Morris, Allen Jenkins, and Warren Hymer, very able players brought from Broadway.

The end of the gangster era found the screen equipped with a corps of efficient actors whose brilliant thumbnail characterisations gave audiences a sense of acquaintance [436/437] with the background of events ordinarily remote from their lives. The cycle had given jobs to writers whose knowledge of the seamy side of American life was drawn from experience and was articulate and controlled. Above all, it had accustomed audiences to seeing contemporary life dealt with from a critical point of view. Except in *The*

Public Enemy, the gangster films had avoided tracing the social backgrounds of crime. Yet the exhaustiveness of their naturalistic detail was in effect a tacit statement that the slum, and therefore society, was responsible for uncontrolled twentieth-century crime. It was this unpleasant implication, perhaps, more than the danger that the crime film itself might breed criminals, that lay at the bottom of the boycott of the gangster film by the small-town civic clubs.

But it was too late to turn back the clock. The new critical attitude, along with speedy continuity, idiomatic dialogue and naturalistic acting remained a characteristic of the sound film. . . .

.   .   .   .

The Problem Film in America

RICHARD DYER MacCANN (1920-   ) completed a Ph.D. in government at Harvard with a dissertation on the history of motion-picture production by the U.S. government. For nine years he was Hollywood correspondent for the *Christian Science Monitor*, and from 1957 to 1962 he taught film writing and documentary film at the University of Southern California. He is the author of *Hollywood in Transition* (1962). A portion of the present article appeared in a series of news features, "The American Film," distributed to foreign editors by the U.S. Information Agency in 1957 and 1961. The present version is published here for the first time.

"This is an entertainment industry." So goes the most treasured proverb in Hollywood. "If you have a message, send it by Western Union."

This proverb assumes that a movie house is a place for dreaming, not learning. There is a great deal of truth in such an assumption. It is both reasonable and provable that average men and women would rather not look at the tribulations of everyday life on the screen. And so it is natural, in theory, for a film producer to cast into outer darkness any proposal for a "message picture," since such a subject is likely to have a limited audience.

Yet in actual practice movie-makers have been unable to resist the temptation to tell stories of social significance. This is partly because the motion picture has always seemed especially comfortable with realism and with the kind of photography which explores the dark alleys of human experience. It is also because conflict between man and his environment frequently provides the elements of excitement needed for successful drama. Furthermore, it can be argued that greatness in drama requires concern with large issues of good and evil in the real world: the top Academy Awards sometimes seem to reflect this value judgment.

There are other, less dependable, reasons for the vitality of the problem film. Motion-picture producers are as different from each other as most human beings are. Some producers are interested mainly in profits. They will catch a trend of public concern and swing with it, turning out "quickie" pictures about gangsters, narcotics, juvenile delinquency, or mental health—stories with "built-in exploitation values" of violence, sex, and shock. Other producers are particularly proud of the influence of the screen and its power to induce learning even when learning is not intended. Such men know they have power and are eager to use it to benefit mankind.

There have been times of retreat—the depression of the early 1930's, for example, or the period of fear and perplexity following the Communist investigations of the Un-American Activities Committee of the House of Representatives in 1947-52. There have been periods of excessive zeal —induced for the most part by the inflammations of wartime. But Hollywood movie-makers, and movie-makers around the world, have always turned part of their attention to the contemporary social scene.

The biggest problem about problem films is not persuading producers to make them. The problem is quality—and after that, timing. It is not easy to construct with taste and conscience a thoughtful film which can contribute to public awareness at the time of greatest need. It is much easier to make a formula film, full of shock techniques, long after the issue has become obvious, nagging, and overheated.

Some of these questions of taste and timing can be illustrated by tracing the history of the problem film in America. They have become increasingly complicated questions as audiences have grown more sophisticated and as films from a wide variety of foreign sources have entered the American cultural experience.

Before tracing these historical developments down to their latest puzzling trend, a more direct effort at definition may be helpful.

What is a "problem film"? If it is defined simply as a film in which people are in trouble, then such a film would include most of the basic conflicts in dramas since the beginning of time—all the romances that did not run smooth, all the triangles and murders and fate-driven tragedies, even the peculiar trail of obstacles which seem to have beset all those struggling musicians honored by what are called biographies. But if the problem film is defined as a film concerned with contemporary human situations as they are affected by sociological or technological change, the term becomes a more useful one.

"Sociological or technological change" suggests the problems caused by man-made environment, rather than by the broader influences of geography or regionalism. This limitation also tends to rule out individual psychological problems. The latter is a difficult line to draw, since society is agreed to be responsible for a good many individual traumas. The line might fall somewhere between *Days of Wine and Roses*, which is an individual story but is concerned primarily with the problem of alcoholism, and *Long Day's Journey Into Night*, which circles about a central character who is a narcotics addict but is primarily the story of a particular family's destructive relationships.

"Contemporary human situations" restricts the problem film to present-day themes. A fascinating subgroup of historical films gets lopped off by this limitation, and it may be objected that the problems of dictatorship and assassination in *Julius Caesar* are fully as valid now as in the time of Shakespeare or the Roman Empire. It may be added that such films as *The Crucible* and *The Friendly Persuasion* presented the issues of false accusation in early New England and of pacifism among Quakers in the Civil War primarily because the film-makers wanted to bring these issues to the public consciousness today. This separation is a difficult one to make, and not everyone may wish to make it. It leaves out such widely differing achievements as *Potemkin,* a famous Soviet reenactment of an abortive Russian rebellion in 1905, and *The Life of Émile Zola,* which spends much of its time attacking anti-Semitism during the Dreyfus case in France. It leaves out all those morality plays set in the American West, of which *High Noon* is one of the most ambitious and effective examples.

Technically speaking, such historical dramas depend on "asides" to the audience in the form of situations or philosophical speeches, if they are to be reinterpreted as having modern implications. Poverty, war, and man's inhumanity to man are subjects available to the dramatist in every age. It is today's kind of poverty, the most recent war, and the latest tools of oppression and cruelty which are the burden of the problem film. It is the modern episode of *Intolerance,* D. W. Griffith's four-part historical extravaganza, which carries the crux of his purpose and his message. If *Julius Caesar* or *High Noon* are to be put in modern dress, then the difficulties of adaptation become obvious—the key difficulties of linking closely with the established plot outline those objects and backgrounds and events and expectations of the way of life within which we live.

The same objection applies to the science fiction film, often an opportunity to "say something" about current problems within a fantasy world of the future. Although *Things to Come* and *The Day the Earth Stood Still* have messages for us, the messages come in the context of a special film genre. The writer's task is not the same when the audience releases him from the limitations of the present.[1]

It is impossible, of course, to draw completely clear distinctions. What is the line between a murder melodrama and a crime picture of social significance? How shall we separate simple stories of marital strife from those which shed important light on the problem of divorce? Distinctions can certainly be made, but critics will differ when it comes to labeling specific films. They will also disagree on artistic questions: the permissible extremes of preaching and the acceptable proportions between fiction and fact.

Labeling was easier in the early days. Many of the Hollywood one-reelers (1903-11) had strong social and economic themes and often were obvious preachments. Their style reflected in part the long tradition of moral melodramas, going at least as far back as *East Lynne* or *Uncle Tom's Cabin*. At the same time they reflected the excitement of the exposures in newspapers and magazines of political and business corruption around the turn of the century.

Along with comedies and cowboys, train robberies and beautiful girls, the silent screen offered such titles as *The Ex-Convict, The Eviction, The Grafters, The Money Lender.* Later there was inevitable sensationalizing in such pictures as *Traffic in Souls, The Inside of the White Slave Traffic, Damaged Goods.*[2] One of the early films directed by D. W. Griffith was called *The Life of the Tenement.* Another was *A Corner in Wheat,* in which the monopolistic activity of a "wheat king" is punished in a manner that will never go out of style: he gasps his last as he falls into one of his own huge grain bins.

Selfish slum landlords (*The Awakening of John Bond*), mill owners who used unpaid prison labor (*The Fight for Right*), and hypocritical politicians (*The Reform Candidate*) all came in for their share of condemnation in these early screen subjects. Labor problems got a going-over from almost every company, though rarely with sympathy for unionism. The workingman's hero might be a minister (*The Better Man*), a railroad engineer (*The Strike at Coaldale*), or the son of a manufacturer (*How the Cause Was Won*).[3]

As the audience for films became larger and more respectable, the stories were more likely to stress themes of private morality (*A Change of Heart*) and the status quo (*The Best Man Wins*). The labor movement was roundly condemned in *The Strike* and *The Anarchist.* War in Europe presented an unprecedented dilemma, but the early pleas for neutrality and even pacifism in *War Brides* and *Civilization* soon became instead *The Battle Cry of Peace, Patria,* and *The Kaiser: Beast of Berlin.*[4]

The postwar, predepression period was notable mainly for loosening morality and exploration of sex, a Freudian freedom lavishly reflected on the screen, sometimes with doubts, more often with approval. The decade was dominated by Cecil B. DeMille and to a lesser extent by the German director Ernst Lubitsch. Yet there were landmarks in social realism, the more prominent because they were so rare— Erich von Stroheim's *Greed* (1923), King Vidor's *The Crowd* (1928), Lewis Milestone's *All Quiet on the Western Front* (1930).

By the very nature of the silent film, its personalities were often seen as symbolic. The sweet young girl and the villainous man expressed themselves through heightened gestures that went beyond the momentary story to a universal meaning. Sound brought the opportunity to say more clearly what that meaning was. It also brought more specific ways to identify individuals as separate, untypical, and

1 For a good evaluation and list of science fiction films, see the unpublished master's thesis (Department of Cinema, University of Southern California, 1959) by Douglas Menville, "A Historical and Critical Survey of the Science Fiction Film."
2 See the comprehensive and perceptive study of American motion pictures up to 1939 by Lewis Jacobs, *The Rise of the American Film* (New York, 1939), pp. 67-77, 136-156.
3 *The Film Index: Film as Art*, ed. Harold Leonard (New York, 1941), pp. 66 ff.
4 Jacobs, pp. 248-263.

therefore not necessarily representative of social problems. Eventually, it brought the opportunity for a drama more mature and more complex than the simple good and evil of many silent films.

More important, sound brought the noises of violence.[5] Mervyn LeRoy's *Little Caesar* (1930), drawing story material from the headlines of the day, started a new cycle in the first years of sound. As the cycle roared on, it became harder and harder to tell whether the gangster films (*Quick Millions, The Public Enemy, Smart Money, Scarface,* and many others) were concerned with problems or with excitement for its own sake. After an interval of public disapproval, during which it was argued that such films might influence real life as well as reflect it, film producers came back with stories of violence which emphasized lawmen rather than lawbreakers—*The Petrified Forest, The Wrong Road, Public Hero No. 1.* There were even attempts to explore the causes of crime in *They Gave Him a Gun, Dead End,* and *Angels With Dirty Faces* (1937-38).

Headline hunters throughout the industry began to take apart public problems in every direction. Prisons were exposed in *The Big House, The Last Mile,* and that extraordinary indictment of Georgia penal colonies *I Am a Fugitive From a Chain Gang.* Newspapers were scored in *Five Star Final, The Front Page,* and *Scandal Sheet.* Lawyers were scrutinized in *State's Attorney* and *The Mouthpiece;* and doctors, in *Arrowsmith* and *The Citadel.* Politics got rough treatment in *The President Vanishes, Gabriel Over the White House,* and *The Phantom President.* And among the finest achievements of this breathless, busy era were three anti-lynching films—*Fury, They Won't Forget,* and *The Ox-Bow Incident.*[6]

The economic problems of the great depression were harder to explain. Hollywood was particularly reluctant to examine the mistakes of bankers or businessmen. *Heroes for Sale* and *Cabin in the Cotton* were early attempts to portray unemployment and tenant farming. King Vidor, who had already directed *Street Scene,* reached most deeply, perhaps, into the inarticulate longings of common people when he succeeded in making *Our Daily Bread,* which went beyond the presentation of the problem of unemployment to become a "solution film," an appeal to return to cooperative effort and to the soil. Not until 1940, when the dust bowl crisis was all but over, did *The Grapes of Wrath,* directed by John Ford, become a symbol of Hollywood's ability to take a great economic and social issue and make it come alive on film.

Dore Schary, who produced a good many "message pictures" at Metro-Goldwyn-Mayer (*The Next Voice You Hear, Go for Broke, It's a Big Country*), has insisted that "movies seldom lead opinion; they merely reflect public opinion and perhaps occasionally accelerate it. . . . No motion picture ever started a trend of public opinion or thinking. Pictures merely dramatize these trends and keep them going."[7]

By and large, his analysis is supported by the history of the sound film in America. With rare exceptions—the anti-lynching films, perhaps, and the race-relations films of the late 1940's—Hollywood producers have been slow to call attention to public issues until those issues had already become familiar and obvious, or until a public attitude toward the issue was beginning to take form on one side or the other.

The era of neutrality before World War

[5] See Richard Griffith, "The American Film, 1929-48," pp. 48-50 in this anthology.
[6] Roger Manvell reports that *The Ox-Bow Incident* was refused exhibition by the major circuits in England (*Film*, [London, 1944], p. 132). It is worth noting that certain directors who developed new skills in the sound era with gangster pictures went on to do important work with problem films —William Wellman's *The Public Enemy* (1931) was followed eventually by *The Ox-Bow Incident* (1943). Mervyn LeRoy's *Little Caesar* (1930) preceded *They Won't Forget* (1937), the story of the lynching of a Negro. In his different style, Fritz Lang moved from the criminal manipulations of *The Testament of Dr. Mabuse* (1934)—a veiled attack on Nazism that already had broader social implications than his earlier crime film *M* (1931)—to the analysis of mob psychology in *Fury* (1936), his first American film.
[7] Dore Schary, "Motion Pictures and Their Influence on the Modern World," speech to National Conference of Controllers in Los Angeles, 1955.

II revealed the same irresolution that characterized the silent films before 1917. Even *The Confessions of a Nazi Spy* (1939) was not much ahead of events, and most of the anti-fascist films came late. The pro-Russian wartime pictures (*North Star, Mission to Moscow*) and the postwar anti-Communist pictures (*Walk East on Beacon, My Son John, I Was a Communist for the FBI*) marched hand in hand with public opinion.[8]

Certainly anti-war films must wait for peacetime. Like crime stories, war stories on the screen are usually tempted to glorify the evil they portray. The camera has a natural appetite for the spectacular conflicts of battle. Most war films focus on a combination of carnage and heroism, or on problems of leadership and human relations within the crew or squad. The overwhelming problem of our century has not been handled with notable perception by American film-makers. Since the time of *All Quiet on the Western Front* (1930), it is a rare film that plumbs to any depth the theme of war as its own punishment. John Huston's army documentary, *The Battle of San Pietro* (1944), stands out like a landmark, together with its fictional counterpart, William Wellman's *The Story of G. I. Joe* (1945). For the most part, the American approach to war films suggests that power, guts, and brains inevitably bring success. There are traces of a different approach in dealing with postwar problems —Fred Zinnemann's *The Men* (about paraplegic victims of war) and William Wyler's *The Best Years of Our Lives* (which followed the fortunes of three veterans returning home.)[9]

The most notable effect of World War II on Hollywood film-makers was their experience of making documentaries for the U.S. government or the armed services. John Huston, John Ford, William Wyler, George Stevens, Frank Capra, Garson Kanin, Robert Riskin, Darryl Zanuck, and many others were shaken by facts, touched by actual experience, and influenced by the documentary way of working, a style well known to the rest of the world through the work of three Americans—Robert Flaherty, Pare Lorentz, and Louis de Rochemont. It was De Rochemont who symbolized the postwar awareness of documentary by moving from reenactments of news events in his *March of Time* short subjects to semi-documentary features. *The House on 92d Street* was a spy thriller based on an FBI anti-Nazi case history. *Boomerang* was the fictionalized biography of a U.S. attorney general who had fought against corruption in politics.

Another more indirect influence on postwar Hollywood was the Italian film renaissance. Having begun with stories of the war by Roberto Rossellini in *Open City* and *Paisan,* the neorealist movement came to be identified particularly with the director Vittorio de Sica and his collaborating screenwriter Cesare Zavattini, who later spoke eloquently of the film-maker's mission "to excavate reality." The method must not be, he declared, a "dead formula" but an attempt "to work out the largest possible number of human, moral, social, economic, poetic values from the bare documentary fact. . . . The true function of the cinema is not to tell fables. . . . I go out into the street—catch words, sentences, discussions. . . . I am interested in the drama of things we happen to encounter, not those we plan." In *Shoeshine, The Bicycle Thief,* and *Umberto D,* not only the events but the actors were often taken from life itself.[10]

The echoes of these films went around the world, profoundly influencing Akira Kurosawa in Japan and Satyajit Ray in

[8] See Arthur Knight, *The Liveliest Art* (New York, 1957), pp. 262 ff. This remarkable and readable book, a selective history of the best periods of film-making throughout the world, also has a helpful index to film titles which includes dates of production and the sources from which each film may be rented.

[9] For a stimulating group of critical essays and directors' notes on war and anti-war films, see Robert Hughes, *Film: Book 2* (New York, 1963). For a further list of war films, with some annotation, see the unpublished master's thesis (University of Southern California, 1952) by Donald Fernow, "The Treatment of Social Problems in the Entertainment Film," pp. 9-46.

[10] Cesare Zavattini, "Some Ideas on the Cinema," *Sight and Sound* (October, 1953), pp. 64-69; trans. by Pier Luigi Lanza from an interview in *La Revista del Cinema Italiano* (December, 1952).

India, and stirring respect among American directors. The Italian emphasis on poverty did not seem adaptable in this country. Yet some cross-fertilization of social concern, if not of style, became apparent as the cycle of films on race relations ran its course. The problem of anti-Semitism was presented with shock technique in *Crossfire* and as an obstacle for a love story in *Gentleman's Agreement.* De Rochemont's *Lost Boundaries,* a fact-based story of a Negro who passed for white, was the most gentle and genuine of the Negro series (1949-50). Others were *Home of the Brave, Pinky, Intruder in the Dust,* and *No Way Out.* The cycle was over as soon as the box office began to decline.

Not till 1955 was there another cycle of such identifiable intensity; it lasted for about three years. Like the gangster films of the 1930's, the juvenile delinquency pictures reflected newspaper headlines. They began with *Blackboard Jungle,* a story of violent conflict between a teacher and a high school student, based on some factual incidents in New York City. *Rebel Without a Cause,* less powerful cinematically, was more believable in its best moments; but its ending, too, was irrelevant in its violence, as if to say, "Parents, who are really to blame, will pay attention only if they are terrified." After that came a long parade of shock pictures with titles like *Untamed Youth* and *Dragstrip Riot.*

The problem film is all too often forced into a shotgun wedding with the western formula. The traditional producer is not at ease with factual realism about contemporary themes, the rich detail of daily life Zavattini and De Sica managed to put on the screen. The way to "lick the story," in his view, is to use the familiar pattern of the western—a fistfight in the second reel and a gunfight at the climax. The problem film may try sometimes to substitute ballots for bullets, but the conflicts and tensions are likely to be there in the proper places. In Elia Kazan's *On the Waterfront,* for example, a film of great filmic force and intrinsic meaning descended to an unsatisfying simplification at the end, by de-

pending upon the apparent finality of one fistfight to change the allegiance of union men. In *Storm Center,* a good-hearted but heavy-handed film, the freedom to read is made melodramatic by burning down the library.

In recent years, American studio executives have been increasingly reluctant to film contemporary problems. The rationale for such resistance is buttressed by the growing importance of the world market. The foreign audience is about three times the size of the American audience, contributing, on the average, from 50 to 55 per cent of a picture's gross income. Strictly American stories, therefore, especially those with controversial or "downbeat" themes, seldom find a place on production schedules. The decision-making executives feel that spectacular adventure films are likely to be popular all over the world. Problem pictures, if any, must be prepared to win a profit at the domestic box office alone—now a much more difficult task.

Despite all objections, problem films still get made. *The Ugly American* attempted to show the problems of modern diplomacy in southeast Asia. Southern prejudice against the Negro was effectively attacked in *To Kill a Mockingbird.* An established producer like Stanley Kramer, a man with strong convictions and a backlog of stamina, can find backers and put contemporary issues on the screen. *The Defiant Ones* was a simple parable of a Negro and a prejudiced white man locked together by handcuffs after they escaped from a prison road gang. *On the Beach*—previewed in the Kremlin as well as in Washington— was a story about the world's last survivors of atomic fallout, themselves doomed to extinction. Kramer's *Judgment at Nuremberg* explored the doubtful aspects of the postwar trials of Nazi officials by the victorious nations.

Otto Preminger, too, has offered highly dramatized versions of the judicial process in *Anatomy of a Murder* and of the political process in *Advise and Consent.* His earlier exploration of the grim world of narcotics addiction in *The Man With the Golden Arm* initiated a brief cycle of "dope pictures," including *A Hatful of Rain* and *The Connection.*

The arrival on the screen of Frankenheimer's *The Manchurian Candidate* and Kubrick's *Dr. Strangelove* revealed new tensions between subject matter and style in the problem film. John Frankenheimer's semisurrealistic excursion into delayed hypnotism proposed that an American soldier captured during the Korean war could be brainwashed in such a way as to cause him to assassinate a major political leader after he gets back home. Full of fascinating camera magic, *The Manchurian Candidate* was a film of ideas, but it was more notable for its expert handling of old-fashioned tension.

Dr. Strangelove, or How I Learned to Stop Worrying and Love the Bomb was a palpable burlesque, yet so documentary in its approach, so believable in its mildly laconic dialogue, that some film-goers hardly knew how to react. Stanley Kubrick had earlier dealt harshly with French generals in *Paths of Glory.* In *Dr. Strangelove,* he offered a grim picture of American officialdom caught in the essence of the atomic dilemma—automatic retaliation.

His story—or situation—was based on the notion that an air force general could go berserk enough to order nuclear war against Russia without asking anybody else. This is no easier to accept than long-term hypnotism in these days of bureaucratic committees and consultative conformity. But there is a deep public concern about who pushes the button for a war of annihilation. And it is curious that the first American film to deal with the politics of that problem in its full implications was a film of coarse humor, improbable characterizations, and wildly rocketing action.

The roots of *Dr. Strangelove* are not to be found in any American tradition of political films. That tradition is thin and erratic. The American screen has rarely presented American politics with any depth of understanding. The prevailing tone has usually reflected the feeling of many Americans that politicians are shifty, suspicious characters, but relatively unimportant. The American way of political life was not especially well represented by the manipulated revelations of corruption in *Mr. Smith Goes to Washington* or by the drabness of the well-intentioned *Washington Story*—not even by the sentimentality of *Wilson* or *The Last Hurrah.* *All the King's Men,* the fictionalized story of Huey Long, was perhaps the best of the lot, and it won an Academy Award in 1949. But even this vigorous enactment of a basically familiar story—the conflict between career and personal life—was not followed by other serious films.

Recent attempts to give us political issues on the screen with a one-two punch, combining absurdity and shock, are related more directly to the American fondness for comedy and fantasy—the kind of fantasy that made *King Kong,* the story of a giant gorilla, one of the great hits of film history—the kind of fantasy that has made the "western" the best-loved style of the American film.

The President Vanishes and *Gabriel Over the White House* showed an astonishing ignorance of the American system of government, but these fantastic stories —the first one threatening a military dictatorship, the second turning the Presidency into one—represented the slam-bang frontierism Hollywood producers thought would appeal to an uneasy public. *Mr. Deeds Goes to Town* was Frank Capra's gentler contribution to the restlessness of the 1930's. Its folk hero, giving away his money to help the unemployed—bewildered but strong in his instinctive self-possession—was an inheritor of the Chaplin tradition.

Since the time of Aristophanes, comedy has been a happy and practical vehicle for dealing with public problems. Humor is a characteristically American response to change, upheaval, disappointment, and fear. Charlie Chaplin, the first great comedy star of the screen, touched time and again, in his earliest short films, the basic

conflicts between the individual and society. His feature-length pictures involved
him more deeply in contemporary issues.
The Gold Rush made fun of acquisitive-
ness. *City Lights* was a drama of charity
—the joy that comes with it, the dregs of
disappointment it often brings. With *Modern Times,* Chaplin plunged into a full-
dress attack on the machine-dominated
civilization he saw around him. In *The
Great Dictator,* he found Hitler (and his
mustache) a vulnerable target for scorn.

Comedy is so close to America's heart
that it may even be proposed as a theory
that comedy is the very best way to trans-
mit a message in this country. Preston
Sturges left us a legacy along these lines.
Apart from his repeated satires on politics,
The Great McGinty and *Hail the Conquering Hero,* Sturges gave us in *Sullivan's
Travels* (1941) what is perhaps the most
basic lesson of all for the maker of problem
films. It answers both the hopes and the
fears of those who expect too much from
the dramatization of messages.

In the film, Sullivan is a Hollywood
producer who chooses to go incognito into
the American hinterland in search of social problems to dramatize. By accident he
loses all his proofs of identity, and his last
desperate adventure before being rescued
finds him condemned to a chain gang in
the South. The prisoners are occasionally
allowed to see a movie. He discovers that
what these tortured, pitiful men really
want and need is escape—romance, adventure, slapstick comedy. He returns to his
job determined never in his life to make
another problem film.

These, then, are the familiar troubles of
the producer who wants to show on the
screen contemporary problems of sociological or technological change.

First, he must remember that most people still prefer musicals, spectacles, romantic dramas, and situation comedies most
of the time. Yet there is always a smaller
audience willing to be receptive to new
experiences and new ideas. And there is
always the possibility that a problem film

on the right subject with the right kind of
treatment will touch the hearts of many.

Second, he must realize that a film can
do little good and can make no history at
all if production is held back until the
public crisis is past. The man who would
grapple with today's issues must expect
them to be hot when he touches them. He
should be more than well informed. He
should have time to read deeply and par-
ticipate variously in real life if he is to
know when the timing is right.

Third, he must face the old question of
dramatic treatment. The western formula
is not enough. Violence may be useful in
posing a problem. But violence, at least in
a democratic society, is the opposite of a
solution. It may be said that drama demands conflict and film requires action.
But it is possible to build a slow growth
of honest excitement while believable people talk their way out of their problems,
as they so often do in real life. In Paddy
Chayevsky's play and film *Middle of the
Night,* an older man is searching for the
right thing to do. He knows the dangers
when a man of 56 marries a girl of 24. The
most memorable moments in this film are
full of talk, and they are moments which
reach deep into the drama of human life.
In Robert Sherwood's script for Samuel
Goldwyn's *The Best Years of Our Lives,*
the strains of returning to civilian life are
dealt with by thinking human beings, not
by mythical men of instant action, riding
against the sky.

There is equal danger, of course, in dis-
counting dramatic necessity. The writer of
a problem film may come perilously close
to an academic approach—a plot slowly
plodding toward a nonexistent climax,
with a "moral" reappearing like a billboard along the way. The problem film
is always close to nonfiction—close to that
finest kind of documentary film which
combines emotion with fact, close to the
magazine article or nonfiction book constructed like a story. It is this closeness to
nonfiction and to the dreariness of life itself which tempts the nervous film-maker
to twist truthfulness into dramatic clichés.

Shock versus talk: these are the easy extremes. The film-maker of integrity must steer between them.

Further troubles, however, loom on his horizon. As fewer theatrical films are made, the number of problem films grows proportionately less. As the world market becomes more important, American problems are less likely to be dealt with on the screen. As society itself becomes more complex, the difficulty of presenting contemporary problems on film demands constantly greater literacy and understanding among the men who write and produce motion pictures. As the study of society concerns itself more and more with the individual, with case studies, and with the relationship between a man and his small group loyalties, the notion of speedy persuasion by a mass medium seems more doubtful. As the sources of dramatic material become more sophisticated—as writers for the theater and the novel seek out narrower themes and more intricate techniques—the film-maker may often despair of finding a story that will satisfy anybody.

All these changes and intensifications seem to be pushing the film farther and farther away from the 1930's. Lawmakers and film-makers alike have less hope than they used to have that the stubborn stuff of human nature can be changed by a law or by a film. For the dramatist, then, the immediate object may still be revelation or education, but the believable goal is farther away—the eventual improvement of the quality of life.

Hollywood the Dream Factory*

HORTENSE POWDERMAKER (1901-   ) received her Ph.D. from London University in 1928 and has been professor of anthropology at Queens College, New York City, since 1938. She came to Hollywood in 1946 to study the organization of film production as she would study the organization of a primitive tribe; the resulting book, *Hollywood the Dream Factory* (1950), is characterized by its intelligent reporting of 900 interviews of Hollywood subjects.

. . . .
Movies are successful largely because they meet some of modern man's deepest needs. He has long known increasing insecurity. He is filled with apprehension about the present and the future. The atomic bomb brings fear of destruction, and the struggle between democracy and totalitarianism throughout the world is truly frightening. Even before these two epochal happenings, the anxieties of modern man had increased because of his growing feeling of isolation and consequent loneliness. This feeling occurs not only in big cities with their intensive concentration of people and industry; it has spread even to agricultural areas, where the traditional rural attitudes have been replaced by those usually associated with the city.[3] Anxieties are further deepened by difficulties in understanding national rivalries, the conflicts in ideology, the complex theories of psychoanalysis and of relativity and so on, which whirl about the average man's head. The popularity of any book which attempts to relieve this situation gives further evidence. Joshua Liebman's book, *Peace of Mind,* was on the best-selling list of nonfiction books continuously for several years after its publication, and so also was the latest Dale Carnegie volume, *How to Stop Worrying and Start Living.* But the book-buying public represents only a small fraction of the population; for the masses of people, the reading of books is not the way out of their confusion and apprehension.

In this age of technology and the assembly line, many people wish to escape from their anxieties into movies, collective daydreams themselves manufactured on the assembly line. To some people, the word "escape" connotes a virtue; for others it is derogatory. But escape, *per se,* is neither good nor bad. All forms of art offer some kind of escape, and it may well be that escape is a necessary part of living. The real question is the quality of what one escapes into. One can escape into a world of imagination and come from it refreshed and with new understanding. One can expand limited experiences into broad ones. One can escape into saccharine [12/13] sentimentality or into fantasies which exaggerate existing fears. Hollywood provides ready-made fantasies or daydreams; the problem is whether these are productive or nonproductive, whether the audience is psychologically enriched or impoverished.

Like all drama and literature, movies extend the experiences of the audience vicariously, and translate problems which are common to mankind into specific and

[3] Cf. Carey McWilliams, *Factories in the Field.* Boston: Little, Brown. Also Walter Goldschmidt, *As You Sow:* Harcourt, Brace.

* Hortense Powdermaker, from *Hollywood the Dream Factory* (Boston: Little, Brown, 1950), pp. 12-14. Reprinted by permission of the author.

personal situations, with which identification is easy. Results from some preliminary research with audience reactions provide the hypothesis that audiences tend to accept as true that part of a movie story which is beyond their experience. A low-income group of workers, for instance, were very critical of part of one movie which touched their own experiences, saying, "That's just Hollywood!"—but in the same movie they accepted as completely true the portrayals of a successful girl artist and her two wealthy boy friends, the counterparts of whom they had never met. Those whose associations are restricted to law-abiding respectable members of a community will get their picture of gangsters, thieves, and "bad" women from their movies. This happens even to quite sophisticated people. In a graduate school seminar on case work, a social worker reporting on the case of an unmarried mother said that the mother spoke very casually of being pregnant again. The instructor asked what she had expected, and the student replied: "W—ell, I thought she'd act more like the way they do in the movies!" For people who have never traveled, the movies give them their ideas of what foreigners are like; and the latter may get their pictures of Americans in the same way. The ideas of young people with relatively limited experience about love and marriage may be influenced by what they see in the movies: a young girl in a small Mississippi town complained about the local beaus as compared to the movie heroes.

Almost every movie, even a farce, deals with some problem of human relations, and the manner in which glamorous movie stars solve these problems may affect the thinking of people about their own problems. A middle-aged woman whose husband had recently left her changed her mind three times about how to handle the situation, after seeing three movies in which she could identify her own problem. [13/14]

Movies have a surface realism which tends to disguise fantasy and makes it seem true. This surface realism has steadily grown from the old days of the silent flickers to the modern technicolor talkies, with their increasing use of the documentary approach. If the setting is a New York street, the tendency today is to film an actual New York street. There is, of course, no necessary correlation between surface reality and inner truth of meaning. But if one is true, the other is more likely to be accepted. On the stage, often the inner meaning is accepted and the obviously false settings lose some of their pseudo quality. In the movies, it is frequently the reverse: since the people on the screen seem real and "natural" and the backgrounds and settings honest, the human relationships portrayed must, the spectator feels, be likewise true. It is this quality of realness which makes the escape into the world of movies so powerful, bringing with it conscious and unconscious absorption of the screen play's values and ideas.

. . . .

The Movies*

ERNIE PYLE (1900-1945) was managing editor of the Washington *Daily News* from 1932 to 1935. His syndicated column later appeared in many newspapers. For his war correspondence, he received a Pulitzer Prize in 1944; *Here Is Your War* (1943) and *Brave Men* (1944) are collections of his wartime writings. A motion picture, *The Story of G. I. Joe* (1945), was based on this part of his life. The following brief excerpt is from his American travel stories, collected in book form after he was killed by enemy action on Ie Shima.

. . . .
I believe in the movies. One of my hates is the smart critic who hurls his words at Hollywood's disgraceful commercialism, its insane business extravagances, its illiterate executives, its failure to achieve any approach to real art, its refusal to broadcast a message. But then I'm not a typical movie fan. It seems impossible for me to see more than six or eight pictures a year, and I pick my pictures. The result is that I seldom see a bad movie. So I think the movies are wonderful.

As a matter of fact, instead of the usual "Why can't we make movies more like real life?" I think a more pertinent question is "Why can't real life be more like the movies?" A movie is a series of climaxes —little glimpses of high spots and low spots—and in the end there is the great climax, and the darkness, and no concern for the years of dying embers and the utter monotony ahead.

Why can't human beings too live only in climaxes, in great ecstasy or great despair, with all the long dull stretches left out? Who would mind being blinded in the war, if he could win the girl anyhow, and then have it understood that the rest of his life was to be an idyl and a blessing, with no dreary days or cruel, growing prongs of pity directed at him? And who would mind being the other fellow and losing the girl if in real life he could [265/266] ac-tually come to the end of the reel right there, and never have to brood about it, or hunger?

Of course, characters on the screen are made to suffer, but their suffering is dramatic and romantic, while ours here on the globe is the dull achy kind that embitters and wastes, with no little drama to ennoble it.

It isn't what the movies put in that makes them so wonderful—it's what they leave out. Wouldn't a movie be dull if it ran on for weeks and weeks, showing a man at his work? It's much nicer for the movies to show him working for just thirty seconds.

And in our little tragedies and despairs, and our big ones too, why couldn't we just go stare out a window and bow our heads and look grave and heartbroken for a few seconds, denoting a long period of grief and yearning, and not have to go through the actual months and years of it?

And our happiness too. Maybe you'd like to have happiness strung out, instead of just a flash and a kiss denoting bliss forever. But for me, I think not. Just a moment of happiness is all right, for then there is no dulling. Yes, just wake me up for the peaks and the valleys, and please have the anesthetist ready when we come to the plains, and the long days when nothing happens.

* Ernie Pyle, from "The Movies," *Home Country* (New York: William Sloane, 1947), pp. 265-266. Copyright, 1935, 1936, 1937, 1938, 1939, 1940, by Scripps-Howard Newspaper Alliance. Copyright, 1947, by William Sloane Associates, Inc. Reprinted by permission of William Sloane Associates.

The Lovely Art: Sound*

GILBERT SELDES (1893-   ), who coined a new term in praise of the popular arts in *The Seven Lively Arts* (1924), has become the best-known observer of the mass media. He has been, since his graduation from Harvard in 1914, a music critic, foreign correspondent, managing editor of *The Dial* from 1920 to 1923, dramatic critic and columnist, director of television programs for CBS during the formative period from 1937 to 1945, and dean of the Annenberg School of Communication at the University of Pennsylvania from 1959 to 1963. He is author of *The Great Audience* (1950) and *The Public Arts* (1956), from which this brief sample is taken.

. . . .
. . . fifteen years after the first decade of sound ended, we are still living under the spell of a dozen apparitions created by sound-and-sight. Not only our memories, but our wide-screen movies and our television shows are peopled with the lineal descendants of Cagney and Dietrich and Gary Cooper and Joan Crawford and the Marx Brothers; of Bogart and Boyer, of Stanwyck and Colbert. These are the people who established in our minds the images in action of the gangster and the courtesan, the soft-spoken Western hero, the hoyden and the shopgirl, the bandit and the seducer, the mother, the mistress, and the murderess. Sergeant Friday in *Dragnet* is the child of Sam Spade, and the psychoanalysts of TV in 1956 are graduates from the same school as the movie-analysts of 1940. The Martins and Lewises are trying to create the same phantasmagoria of lunacy as the Marx Brothers—and none too well. [22/23]

. . . .
. . . My instinct is to take the Keystone comedies and the Westerns as the training ground for good players (they were both the best place for a director to start). I think of W. S. Hart: I am not sure whether he was a great mime, a great actor, because I cannot completely separate my- [23/24] self from what I was when I first saw him; I admired him then almost as much as the French critics did who called him "Rio Jim," the incarnation of our national epic (*"le ouild-ouest"*). I like to believe that Hart was really good; he was certainly better than anyone else in his line, and if he wasn't a great actor, he could combine a straight jaw and lackluster eyes into a counterpart of the impassive Indians of Frederic Remington and eventually into *The Virginian*—one of the most enduring images of our time.

I do not know whether this Virginian has any forebears in the actual history of the West. As the sad sheriff who will hang his best friend to uphold the law (with an almost Christlike compassion for the criminal), he has a prodigious family tree in our fiction. Bret Harte's gamblers are his cousins, and his atmosphere is charged with the Teddy Roosevelt legend—the dude with a lion's heart. It was Roosevelt's idolater Owen Wister who gave him his only name, which is not a family name, and Arthur I. Keller his lineaments. In a sense, Bill Hart was playing *The Virginian* all the time, and so, in fact, were dozens of others; the superimposition of Gary Cooper's features or Joel McCrea's doesn't change the image. It continues to our day, and one scene in the creation of the legend is so elemental that it has become the standard bit for parody: the two men stalking each other around the sides of the buildings—the saloon, the feed store, the low-railed porch around the hotel, the hitching-posts—they are always the same. Yet a hundred burlesques leave the effect undiminished. It is always on the stroke of six, the punctual sun is setting, and our hero (sadly) double-checks his gun and goes outdoors, while all the others fall silent, to shoot down the horse-thief whom he loves (and who is checking his gun at the far end of the street)—and as they move toward each other the old magic of the movies reasserts itself and we know that this is one of the things which will not ever vanish from the screen.

It may change. The sheriff may be transformed into the city detective who must track down the killer although the slum or society or the Oedipus complex is really guilty. We may meet the lonely hero again in a meaner West, as in *High Noon,* where the whole community abandons him and he wins his battle and (sadly, proudly) throws the badge of office into the dust. It was, indeed, *High Noon* that provided the clue to the real nature of the Western—it is not only a private myth of the American past and an answer to his demand for freedom ("don't fence [24/25] me in")—it is also a morality play, it is *Everyman.* In an essay as yet unpublished, Joseph Newlin, a student at Columbia University, has traced the parallels between *High Noon* and *Everyman;* they are remarkably close, and they suggest the connection between other Western types and allegories in the historic memories of all the races from which our mythology flows down to us.

Bernard De Voto, who knew and understood the West, had a low opinion of the cowboy, good man or bad, the law or the thief, the Yippee-shooting-riding-pal or the lone-wolf-with-a-past. Our Westerns, he said, are make-believe on a national scale; the period to which they refer was brief (hardly more than twenty years) and unimportant. There were no Robin Hoods— only hired thugs, as repulsive as the hoods of our gangster wars. "The cowboy," he said, "seems an illogical choice as a master symbol of the West. If the symbol is to stand for wilderness skill, the Rocky Mountain trapper . . . would have served better, for his was the most complex skill ever exercised on this continent. If importance for the future makes a culture hero, then it should have been the homesteader. . . . The cowboy image is in great part phony, a counterfeit. . . . Past or present, there is a lot more to the West than a cow outfit." [25/26]

. . . .

No other type of movie could possibly be so important to us. No doubt Mr. De Voto was right about the real cowboy, but the "cowboy" image is shorthand with us for the whole movement of our history from the days of the "liberties" and the Western Reserve, through the brief period when the cowpuncher really was a central figure, down to our own time when, politically, socially, and through the movies themselves, the Westward movement, if not the West itself, dominates our lives. The movies took over a fragment of history, they dramatized the significance of the frontier in American life. . . .

. . . .

[Wilson]*

JAMES AGEE (1909-1955) was a poet, novelist, and film critic. His film reviews for the *Nation* and *Time* magazine are regarded as perhaps the best film criticism by an American; they have been collected in *Agee on Film* (1958), from which the following review of the film *Wilson* was taken. He also wrote the text for the picture study *Let Us Now Praise Famous Men* (1941); the narration for the documentary film *The Quiet One*; and the screenplays for *The Night of the Hunter* and *The African Queen*. He was awarded the Pulitzer Prize posthumously in 1958 for his novel *A Death in the Family* (1957).

Wilson is by no means the first film in which one might watch Hollywood hopping around on one foot, trying to put on long pants. Nor are the immense responsibilities and potentialties [sic] of moving pictures so nearly Mr. Darryl Zanuck's personal discovery, patent applied for, as he apparently feels them to be (*Intolerance*, after all, is nearly thirty years old). Yet Mr. Zanuck may be better than excused for regarding his new film as an important one, a test case. Very likely it is, not only for him but for Hollywood in general, for a long time to come. For as a hymn to international- [110/111] ism, performed with all the stops pulled out, at just this time, *Wilson* becomes an extremely powerful campaigner for the Fourth Term, whether or not Mr. Zanuck so intended it. It thus undertakes more crucial and specific responsibilities, more boldly, than any other American film to date. Still more important, from Hollywood's point of view, it represents the steepest investment, so far, in a would-be serious picture. When you count in a million dollars' exploitation costs, *Wilson* set Mr. Zanuck and the other little Foxes back about $5,200,000. No other film has ever cost so much.

If *Wilson* fails, Darryl Zanuck has promised never again to make a picture without Betty Grable. If *Wilson* fails, worse things than that may happen. It seems very possible that even any attempt at making "serious" or "idea" films of this sort might be postponed in this country for years to come. If *Wilson* succeeds, on the other hand, it is likely that we will get a lot of other pictures like it, not only because a new box-office formula will have been established but also because, I feel sure, Hollywood is as full as any other place of men of fairly good will who would gladly devote some of it to the public weal so long as no risk is involved.

If this conception of maturing and seriousness becomes generally accepted, I will be more sorry than glad. Pictures like *Wilson* have little if anything to do with mature serious cinema as such, and those who think of *Wilson* as a mature film are not in the least concerned with its liveliness or deadness as a work of art; they are excited because serious ideas are being used on the screen. Something well worth

* James Agee, "Films," *Nation*, CLIX (August 19, 1944), 221; reprinted in Agee, *Agee on Film* (New York: McDowell, Obolensky, 1958), I, 110-113. Copyright 1958 James Agee Trust. Review of *Wilson* from *Agee on Film I* by James Agee. Reprinted by permission of Ivan Obolensky, Inc., New York City.

excitement, I'll grant; but how much? None of the ideas used in *Wilson* is expressed in any better than primer fashion. Anyone who cares to can still get twice as much out of a newspaper and a dozen times as much out of even a mediocre book, so far as ideas are concerned. Perhaps this is a moment to be generous, as if toward a child who stumbles over unexpectedly big words; but that kind of contempt is peculiar to those who hate movies and think they like them, and is unavailable to those who love movies and are thought to loathe them. Furthermore, I believe that political ideas at their most mature and serious are still childish and frivolous as compared with those ideas or conceptions which attempt to work in, to perceive, and to illuminate, the bottoms of the souls of human beings. If political issues and a reverence for fact on the journalistic (or even the historical) level become a popular criterion for seriousness and maturity in films, the proper study of mankind is likely to be deferred even longer than by the present prospects. On the other hand, if great audiences, and those who fearfully try to give them what they want, get used to the idea [111/112] that thinking and entertainment are by no means autonymous, this postponement-period may serve both ends, valuably, as a period of transition and training.

The whole business makes me a little tired when I reflect that it is 99 per cent waste motion—that a dozen really good, really mature films, each made on a B-budget or less, would be more likely to do overnight what in this way won't happen with any firmness in twenty years. But the distinguishing faculty of the realist in [*sic*] his preference for the longest distance between two points—a preference which becomes virtually beatitude if the second point is never reached. As a realist, then, I hope that *Wilson* grosses ten million dollars and that no matter how disastrously misleading the whole process may be, the studios will spend the next few years tearing each other's throats out over political and social issues. Seriousness and courage on a political level are infinitely preferable, heaven knows, to no seriousness and courage at all.

I have left myself very little space in which to talk about *Wilson* in detail; but perhaps that is just as well. It is essentially a very sincere and even a brave picture, and I am bound to salute even an attempt to help prevent a third world war, and to wish it well. One might at great length talk about its virtues—for on its own level, and in so far as its tight intersection of anxious showmanship, conventional talent, and journalistic conscience allows it, it has a great many more virtues than faults, and is a big, splendid, competent, resourceful show. One might at even greater length, and still with no lack of basic sympathy, analyze its extremely characteristic fits and starts down to the least evidence of the effort to give it all that money can buy and that honest research can edge it with: for in every grand effect and little mannerism it is both fascinating and instructive. They copied the cracks in the paint in the original portraits of Presidents in the White House; but they were unable to learn anything whatever of primary value from their study of 160,000 feet of relevant newsreel.

But here again, I am just as glad to shirk my duty. No matter how friendly I feel toward *Wilson* and the people who made it, any such review would amount chiefly to a specification of occupational psychosis. With the best intentions in the world, Hollywood took a character and a theme of almost Shakespearian complexity and grandeur, and reduced the character to an astutely played liberal assistant professor of economics; the theme to a few generalizations which every schoolboy has half-forgotten; the millennial, piteous surge of hope and faith which bore Wilson to Paris, to nothing at all; the colossal struggles between Wilson and Clemenceau [112/113] and Senator Lodge, to one firmly written tizzy and one softly written one; Wilson's terrifying, possessed trip around the United States, to a set of pretty Thomas-Wolfean train-montages, culminating in the unprepared breakdown of a good insurance risk;

the American people, to a passive murmurous backdrop; and an extraordinarily grandiose prospect of powerful and original cinema, to a high-grade sort of magazine illustration. Every major problem, opportunity, and responsibility which the picture set its makers was, in other words, flunked—now through timidity, again through habitual half-blindness, and most of all perhaps through the desire to sell and ingratiate and essentially to render a two-and-a-half-hour apology for one sustained impulse of daring and disinterestedness.

If *Wilson* fails, I believe it will be because Mr. Zanuck and his associates were not up to their subject. For I am quite sure that the tremendous audiences which may or may not accept it as it stands would have been found more than ready for the same story, maturely told.

PART FOUR

CAN THE SCREEN INFLUENCE SOCIETY?

Propaganda and the Nazi War Film*

SIEGFRIED KRACAUER was on the editorial staff of the German newspaper *Frankfurter Zeitung* from 1920 to 1933. He analyzed Nazi film propaganda for the Rockefeller Foundation and the Museum of Modern Art in 1941-42 and incorporated a revised version of that report (part of which is reprinted here) in his book on the German theatrical film between the wars, *From Caligari to Hitler* (1947). His *Theory of Film* (1960) is an important contribution to motion-picture aesthetics.

. . . .
Totalitarian propaganda endeavored to supplant a reality based upon the acknowledgment of individual values. Since the Nazis aimed at totality, they could not be content with simply superseding this reality—the only reality deserving the name—by institutions of their own. If they had done so, the image of reality would not have been destroyed but merely banished; it might have continued to work in the subconscious mind, imperiling the principle of absolute leadership. To attain their aim, the Nazi rulers had to outdo those obsolete despots who suppressed freedom without annihilating its memory. These modern rulers knew that it is not sufficient to impose upon the people a "new order" and let the old ideas escape. Instead of tolerating such remnants, they persistently traced each independent opinion and dragged it out from the remotest hiding-place—with the obvious intention of blocking all individual impulses. They tried to sterilize the mind. And at the same time they pressed the mind into their service, mobilizing its abilities and [298/299] emotions to such an extent that there remained no place and no will for intellectual heresy. Proceeding ruthlessly, they not only managed to prevent reality from growing again, but seized upon components of this reality to stage the pseudo-reality of the totalitarian system. Old folksongs survived, but with Nazi verses; republican institutions were given a contrary significance, and the masses were compelled to expend their psychic reserve in activities devised for the express purpose of adjusting people's mentality, so that nothing would be left behind.

This is precisely the meaning of the following statement by Goebbels: "May the shining flame of our enthusiasm never be extinguished. This flame alone gives light and warmth to the creative art of modern political propaganda. Rising from the depths of the people, this art must always descend back to it and find its power there. Power based on guns may be a good thing; it is, however, better and more gratifying to win the heart of a people and to keep it." [299/300]

. . . .
Goebbels spoke these words at the Nuremberg Party Convention in 1934; and *Triumph of the Will,* the film about this Convention, illustrates them overwhelmingly. Through a very impressive composition of mere newsreel shots, this film represents the complete transformation of reality, its complete absorption into the artificial structure of the Party Convention. The Nazis had painstakingly prepared the

* Siegfried Kracauer, from "Propaganda and the Nazi War Film," *From Caligari to Hitler* (Princeton: Princeton University Press, 1947), pp. 298-303. *From Caligari to Hitler* is available also in a paperback edition (New York: Noonday Press, 1959). Reprinted by permission of the author.

ground for such a metamorphosis: grandiose architectural arrangements were made to encompass the mass movements, and, under the personal supervision of Hitler, precise plans of the marches and parades had been drawn up long before the event. Thus the Convention could evolve literally in a space and a time of its own; thanks to perfect manipulation, it became not so much a spontaneous demonstration as a gigantic extravaganza with nothing left to improvisation. This staged show, which channeled the psychic energies of hundreds of thousands of people, differed from the average monster spectacle only in that it pretended to be an expression of the people's real existence. . . .

. . . *Triumph of the Will* reveals that the Convention speeches played a minor role. Speeches tend to appeal to the emotions as well as the intellect of their listeners; but the Nazis preferred to re- **[300/301]** duce the intellect by working primarily upon the emotions. At Nuremberg, therefore, steps were taken to influence the physical and psychological condition of all participants. Throughout the whole Convention masses already open to suggestion were swept along by a continuous, well-organized movement that could not but dominate them. Significantly, Hitler reviewed the entire five-hour parade from his standing car instead of from a fixed dais. Symbols chosen for their stimulative power helped in the total mobilization: the city was a sea of waving swastika banners; the flames of bonfires and torches illuminated the nights; the streets and squares uninterruptedly echoed with the exciting rhythm of march music. Not satisfied with having created a state of ecstasy, the Convention leaders tried to stabilize it by means of proved techniques that utilize the magic of aesthetic forms to impart consistency to volatile crowds. The front ranks of the Labor Service men were trained to speak in chorus—an outright imitation of communist propaganda methods; the innumerable rows of the various Party formations composed *tableaux vivants* across the huge festival grounds. These living ornaments

not only perpetuated the metamorphosis of the moment, but symbolically presented masses as instrumental superunits.

It was Hitler himself who commissioned Leni Riefenstahl to produce an artistically shaped film of the Party Convention. In her book on this film,[2] she incidentally remarks: "The preparations for the Party Convention were made in concert with the preparations for the camera work." This illuminating statement reveals that the Convention was planned not only as a spectacular mass meeting, but also as spectacular film propaganda. Leni Riefenstahl praises the readiness with which the Nazi leaders facilitated her task. Aspects open here as confusing as the series of reflected images in a mirror maze: from the real life of the people was built up a faked reality that was passed off as the genuine one; but this bastard reality, instead of being an end in itself, merely served as the set dressing for a film that was then to assume the character of an authentic documentary. *Triumph of the Will* is undoubtedly the film of the Reich's Party Convention; however, the Convention itself had also been staged to produce *Triumph of the Will*, for the purpose of resurrecting the ecstasy of the people through it.

With the thirty cameras at her disposal and a staff of about 120 members, Leni Riefenstahl made a film that not only illustrates the Convention to the full, but succeeds in disclosing its whole significance. The cameras incessantly scan faces, uniforms, arms and again faces, and each of these close-ups offers evidence of the thoroughness with which the metamorphosis of reality was achieved. It is a metamorphosis so radical as to include even Nuremberg's ancient stone buildings. **[301/302]** Steeples, sculptures, gables and venerable façades are glimpsed between fluttering banners and presented in such a way that they too seem to be caught up in the excitement. Far from forming an unchangeable background, they themselves take wing. Like many faces and objects, isolated archi-

[2] *Hinter den Kulissen des Reichsparteitag Films*, Franz Eher, München, 1935.

tectural details are frequently shot against the sky. These particular close shots, typical not only of *Triumph of the Will,* seem to assume the function of removing things and events from their own environment into strange and unknown space. The dimensions of that space, however, remain entirely undefined. It is not without symbolic meaning that the features of Hitler often appear before clouds.

To substantiate this transfiguration of reality, *Triumph of the Will* indulges in emphasizing endless movement. The nervous life of the flames is played upon; the overwhelming effects of a multitude of advancing banners or standards are systematically explored. Movement produced by cinematic techniques sustains that of the objects. There is a constant panning, traveling, tilting up and down—so that spectators not only see passing a feverish world, but feel themselves uprooted in it. The ubiquitous camera forces them to go by way of the most fantastic routes, and editing helps drive them on. In the films of the Ukrainian director Dovzhenko, motion is sometimes arrested for a picture that, like a still, presents some fragment of motionless reality: it is as if, by bringing all life to a standstill, the core of reality, its very being, were disclosed. This would be impossible in *Triumph of the Will.* On the contrary, here total movement seems to have devoured the substance, and life exists only in a state of transition.

The film also includes pictures of the mass ornaments into which this transported life was pressed at the Convention. Mass ornaments they appeared to Hitler and his staff, who must have appreciated them as configurations symbolizing the readiness of the masses to be shaped and used at will by their leaders. The emphasis on these living ornaments can be traced to the intention of captivating the spectator with their aesthetic qualities and leading him to believe in the solidity of the swas-

tika world. Where content is lacking or cannot be revealed, the attempt is often made to substitute formal artistic structures for it: not for nothing did Goebbels call propaganda a creative art. *Triumph of the Will* not only explores the officially fabricated mass-ornaments, but draws on all those discovered by the wandering cameras: among them such impressive *tableaux vivants* as the two rows of raised arms that converge upon Hitler's car while it slowly passes between them; the bird's-eye view of the innumerable tents of the Hitler Youth; the ornamental pattern composed by torchlights sparkling through a huge cloth banner in the foreground. Vaguely reminiscent of abstract [302/303] paintings, these shots reveal the propagandistic functions pure forms may assume.

The deep feeling of uneasiness *Triumph of the Will* arouses in unbiased minds originates in the fact that before our eyes palpable life becomes an apparition—a fact the more disquieting as this transformation affected the vital existence of a people. . . . This film represents an inextricable mixture of a show simulating German reality and of German reality maneuvered into a show. Only a nihilistic-minded power that disregarded all traditional human values could so unhesitatingly manipulate the bodies and the souls of a whole people to conceal its own nihilism. The Nazi leaders pretended to act in the name of Germany. But the Reich's eagle, frequently detailed in the film, always appears against the sky like Hitler himself —a symbol of a superior power used as a means of manipulation. *Triumph of the Will* is the triumph of a nihilistic will. And it is a frightening spectacle to see many an honest, unsuspecting youngster enthusiastically submit to his corruption, and long columns of exalted men march towards the barren realm of this will as though they themselves wanted to pass away.

.   .   .   .

Searchlight on Democracy*

JOHN GRIERSON (1898-   ), after receiving a degree in philosophy at the University of Edinburgh, came to the United States to study the mass media on a Rockefeller Foundation grant. He became deeply interested in film; wrote film criticism (including a review of Robert Flaherty's *Moana*, which first used the term "documentary"); and went back to Britain to become film officer, first, of the Empire Marketing Board, and, later, of the General Post Office (1927-37). He supervised the making of hundreds of short films for governmental and private sponsors. Later he set up and headed the Canadian National Film Board (1939-45). Recently he has presided over a weekly program of short films on a Scottish television station.

Your dictator with a wave of the hand can clear a slum or rebuild a town—and this is always an attractive prospect to people who want slums cleared and towns rebuilt. But the communication of dictatorship is of orders given and of organization set in motion. Our democratic interest in communications is very different. It is integral to the democratic idea that constructive action shall bubble up all over the place. Initiative must be not only central but local. By the mere acceptance of democracy we have taken upon ourselves the privilege and the duty of individual creative citizenship and we must organize all communications which will serve to maintain it.

I know the waving hand of the dictator can more spectacularly clear the slums, if —and who can ensure it?—it is disposed to clear the slums. I know that efficiency is attractive and the beat of feet marching in unison is a remarkable source of persuasion. I know, too, that when, in the democratic way, we leave so much initiative to the individual and the locality, the result is sometimes only too local. Local taste may be terrible to the metropolitan aesthete. The perfectly sound scientist will be chal-

lenged by rustic pigheadedness. But what we lose perhaps in efficiency and taste— and it is just possible that the dictator may be a man of taste—what we lose with our shabby local methods, we gain in spirit. It may be poor but it is our own.

The moment we accept this decision a great obligation is laid upon education in a democracy. It must perfect its system of communication so that individuals and localities may draw from the deepest source of inspiration. It must create a flow of initiative and ideas which, while maintaining the vitality of democracy, will help it to challenge authoritarian standards in quality and efficiency. This is a tall order but I can see no way out of it. . . . **[192/194]**

. . . .

. . . I was discussing this with my friend, George Ferguson, the editor of the *Winnipeg Free Press* and one of Canada's most stalwart champions of the democratic idea. He said that the only thing you have to set against the spectacular appeal of the totalitarian State is the spectacle of liberty. I think the idea is worth examin- **[194/195]** ing. Looking back on our own documen-

* John Grierson, from "Searchlight on Democracy," *Grierson on Documentary*, ed. Forsyth Hardy (New York: Harcourt, Brace, 1947), pp. 192, 194-196, 198-201. From *Grierson on Documentary*, edited by Forsyth Hardy, copyright, 1946, 1947, by Harcourt, Brace & World, Inc. and reprinted with their permission and the permission of the editor.

tary films, I know I have tried to do something of this sort in every film with which I have been concerned. I have asked the directors to call down a cinematic blessing on the fact that people in our world are so natively out of step. I have asked them to express the beauty that goes with the tatterdemalion good humor of a London bank holiday. We have in our own fashion and in a hundred ways described those manifestations of the human spirit which are not mobilized, not regimented, not dictated from without. . . .

. . . When you think of it, the dictator States did a magnificent job in presenting their own brand of fraternity. They had their comrade-in-arms gambit. They had the spectacle of men joining together in the religious brotherhood of the blood. Their fraternity was expressed in exciting forms like parades, flags and mutual salutes. One does not wonder for a moment if it seems to fill a gap and meet a need for recognizable comradeship which our own system lacks. It seems to me, however, that the democratic idea must shrink a little from the outstretched hand, the hearty backslap, or any such form of mania. I like to think that in our presentation of the democratic idea we will know how to present fraternity and a common feeling for one's neighbor, with a degree of diffidence. But it puts a heavy burden on democratic statement when the very essence of it is that it should not be melodramatic and should not be spectacular.

We are faced indeed with a very difficult problem. It means that people must be taught to appreciate that being together, [195/196] talking together, living together and working together in common undemonstrative harmony is the whole fraternity. It means that we must praise and encourage every little grouping of common spirits who ride their bicycles out into the country, or hike across the downs, or meet in the local to organize a cricket team or hoist a pint. It means that we are concerned with a multitude of ordinary things and that the very secret of them is their ordinariness. We are led inevitably to the conclusion that if such simple human elements are to be made the basis of loyalty, then we must learn to make a drama and a poetry from the simple.

As in the case of liberty and fraternity, so with equality. One drives on inevitably to the conception that we cannot present a rich interpretation of dramatic virtues except we produce a poetry and a drama of ordinary things. The spectacular appeal, the organized uplifting emotion which the totalitarian system provided in its education could, I believe, be matched and could be matched tomorrow if the writers and the poets and the picture men among us would seize upon the more intimate and human terms of our society.

Our searchlight on democracy will in the end turn out to be a quiet soft light under which little things are rounded in velvet and look big. [196/198]

. . . .

. . . If you are to create interest in the community life, you are face to face with the Herculean task of articulating this monstrous new metropolitan world which we have built for ourselves. You must bring it alive, so that people will live intimately in it and will make an art of life from it. And you cannot do it by information alone or analysis alone, for the life escapes. You can only do it in those dramatic terms which present the life of the thing and the purpose of the thing and make intimacy possible. The radio, the picture, the poster and the story are the more obvious instruments in your hands and art has become inevitably half of your teaching.

Let me be specific. You will not succeed in bringing things alive in a general spate of new enthusiasm. Things do not happen that way either: vague enthusiasms are not the best of guides. As educationalists, you are concerned at every point with specific areas of interest. The child has to be prepared for citizenship in field or town. The world which has to be brought alive to him will, if you are wise, have a good deal to do with that field or that town, and only later with those wider perspectives of citizenship which reach out from it. The citizen, similarly, has his factory, his union, his family, his neighbors, his traditions, his news, his hobbies, his specialized world of discourse, his movies, his pub, his relationship with taxes and votes, and other aspects of local or national government. Perhaps he even has his church. These are the terms of his life and in each and every aspect of it, his understanding is not so great that it cannot be greater or his harmony so assured that it cannot be brighter. At a hundred points education can touch the quick of his life and light the way for him. It may excite him a bit more about his neighborhood. It may encourage him in his skill—as I kept asking the Kent County Council to encourage me in my strawberry-growing. It may, in general, make his world a more exciting place than at first it seems.

But again and again you will find yourself concerned with a dramatic or living process rather than a pedagogic or merely informational one. And I am thinking not only of the power of the movie and the newspaper. I am thinking of arts as separate as private discussion and child welfare: gardening and sport and music hall. These and a thousand more represent openings for [198/199] your imagination as educationists, for they are the opportunity and the substance of the work you must finally do. All are media of communication and a way to the art and spectacle of democracy.

In my own field of documentary filmmaking, this is the inspiration on which we operate and I am not sure we may not have done just enough (since 1929) to prove its truth. We have been concerned with those very problems of bringing specific fields of modern activity alive to the citizen. We have worked in a dozen very different areas, and made a first tentative shot at picturing the worlds of communication and science, public administration and social welfare. We have followed along the perspective of modern life and sought to find themes which gave a new significance to the terms of ordinary living. Sometimes we have approached the task

on a journalistic level or poetic level or analytical level or more dramatic level, but always we have been concerned to find a degree of beauty in the process and make our own contribution to the spectacle of democracy at work. It can be done and it can be done more widely. And all the thousand arts of human discussion and intercourse have their own special contribution to make. [199/200]

. . . .

We arrive inevitably at the thought that propaganda or education in a democracy must operate on a large number of specialized levels and should be deliberately organized on a large number of levels. There must, of course, be a general spate of information and uplift, affecting the minds of general audiences: and you have the film and radio organized for that purpose. But I like to think that those of us who are interested in special aspects of the community life will develop our own systems of communications and that film and radio and other media of vital communication will do much for us.

When you see this from the international viewpoint, you will realize how much these specialized services could mean to international understanding and to the expression of the democratic idea. Wandering about the world, one finds that while countries differ in their expression and in their local idioms, they are in one respect identical. We are all divided into groups of specialized interests and we are all, at bottom, interested in the same things. There are the same essential groups everywhere. Here is a group interested in town planning, or in agriculture, or in safety in mines or in stamp collecting. Whatever the different language they speak, they speak the common language of town planning, agriculture, safety in mines, and stamp collecting. In that sense, one never thinks of Geneva as representing the real internationalism. The real internationalism is in the manias we share with each other.

How great is the opportunity this provides for the creation of the democratic picture! Several years ago Basil Wright and I suggested a scheme to the International Labour Office. We said, in effect: "Why do you not create a great international overflow of living documents by which specialized groups will speak to their brethren in the fifty countries that operate within your system? You are anxious to raise the common standard of industrial welfare. Why do you not use the film to do it? If France [200/201] has the best system of safety in mines, let other countries have the benefit of this example. If New Zealand is a great pioneer of prenatal care, let other countries see the record of its achievement."

I hope the I.L.O. will do something about that, but I would not simply leave it to the I.L.O. Britain is now engaged in far-reaching efforts of education and propaganda. There has been a lot of talk about the projection of Britain. I say frankly that I do not think anyone in high quarters has seriously thought about how it should be performed in a truly democratic way, or has seen the enormous advantage in international communication which the democratic idea gives us. In Whitehall there is no philosophy of propaganda and certainly none that is recognizably democratic as distinct from authoritarian. There is the same exhausting effort to look spectacular. There is the same noise. I am sorry to say there is the same tendency toward the synthetic and unreal. Yet I believe that democratic education and democratic propaganda are an easy matter and indeed far easier than the authoritarian type, if these principles I have laid down are grasped. It will be done not by searchlight but in the quiet light of ordinary humanism. Speaking intimately and quietly about real things and real people will be more spectacular in the end than spectacle itself. And, in the process of creating our democratic system of communications, in bridging the gaps between citizen and community, citizen and specialist, specialist and specialist, we shall find that we have in the ordinary course of honest endeavor made the picture of democracy we are seeking. And we shall have made it not only national, but international too.

Movies and Propaganda*

LEO ROSTEN (1908-   ) combines the writing of fiction and nonfiction with a specialist's interest in the mass media. He taught both English and political science at the University of Chicago before completing his Ph.D. in 1937. Under Carnegie Corporation and Rockefeller Foundation grants, he wrote two analytical studies, *The Washington Correspondents* (1937) and *Hollywood: The Movie Colony, the Movie Makers* (1941). He is also the author of the short story collection *The Education of H*y*m*a*n K*a*p*l*a*n* (1937), the screenplay *Walk East on Beacon* (1952), and the novel *Captain Newman, M.D.* (1961).

. . . . No one accuses the press of conducting propaganda because newspapers report the speeches of foreign dictators or American demagogues; no one accuses the radio of insidious intentions when it presents programs which contain controversial material; but when a movie company produces one film which arouses public debate, the charge of "propaganda" cleaves the air.

There is behind this a hidden premise which is worth examining: people expect to encounter things with which they do not agree, or which they even violently oppose, when they purchase a newspaper or tune in on a radio program; but the public has been conditioned to expect movies to provide them with what is pleasant, undisturbing, and soporific. It has long been assumed that movies, unlike other agencies of public communication, *ought* to confine themselves to the noncontroversial.

This drum has, unfortunately, been beaten for many years by the movie producers themselves. One of the more banal clichés which issued from the motion picture industry for twenty years was that "movies are only concerned with entertainment." Whenever producers were criticized they promptly retreated, with pained and misunderstood gestures, behind the serene bulwark of "pure entertainment." However disarming this may have been as polemics, it fell into the disastrous error of creating an artificial antithesis between something called "entertainment" and something called "propaganda." This muddy distinction implied that what is entertaining cannot be significant, and that what is significant (dealing with group, rather than individual, problems) cannot be entertaining.

The movie producers have come to regret this fatal illogic; the inept dichotomy of "entertainment versus propa- [117/118] ganda" made it difficult for Hollywood to defend the continuing broadening of subject matter which the movies were compelled to undertake, under the pressures of both competition and conscience, and which, for reasons explored below, they cannot reject or avoid in the future.

WHAT IS PROPAGANDA?

What is the proper measure to use in determining what is "propaganda"? The

* Leo Rosten, from "Movies and Propaganda," in *The Motion Picture Industry*, ed. Gordon S. Watkins, *Annals of the American Academy of Political and Social Science*, CCLIV (November, 1947), 116-124. Reprinted by permission of the American Academy of Political and Social Science.

word itself comes from the Roman Catholic Church, which, in the seventeenth century, set up a College of Propaganda to educate its priests in the techniques of missionary work. The practice of propaganda is, of course, as old as that moment when the first cave man attempted to influence the conduct or attitudes of others by nonviolent methods.

Propaganda, according to the most cogent authority in the field, is the deliberate attempt to influence mass attitudes on controversial subjects by the use of symbols rather than force.[1] Three factors in this definition deserve special attention: "deliberate attempt," "mass attitudes," "controversial." It is crucial to recognize that it is *intention* that lies at the heart of propaganda. This must be stressed, since it is often crudely assumed that the *effect* of a publication (or a movie) upon those who see or read it determines whether or not propaganda is involved.

Laymen are often confused in the effort to identify propaganda because they find it difficult to distinguish propaganda from education or from patriotic reiterations or from entities of art, barren of ideas. A clear classification at this point will be helpful. Education represents the transmission of aptitudes or attitudes on subjects which are *not* controversial. Patriotic reiterations (pageants, poems, patriotic films) involve the dramatization of accepted political values. Entertainment is the communication of the pleasurable.[2]

A movie on physiology or golf or arithmetic is an educational film. A movie which dramatizes the prevailing civic emotions about our country, its institutions or national heroes, is a patriotic film. But a movie made for the *purpose* of changing attitudes about, say, American foreign policy or socialized medicine or monogamy would be a propaganda film.

It is imperative to keep these distinctions in mind, since it will be seen that the diagnosis of whether an entity is "propagandistic" depends not only upon the intention of those who create it, but also upon the intellectual commitments of the audience to which the work is exposed. In the United States, a movie about free elections is not propaganda: the same movie would be considered propaganda in Spain or the Soviet Union, since under each of these regimes, despite differences in formal ideology, positive affirmations about opposition parties or multiple choices violate the official political theology. Contrariwise, a film made in Moscow about the glories of Communism, the sanctity of Stalin, or the infallibility of the *Politburo* is a "patriotic" enterprise—for Russians; the same film would be considered a propaganda film in the United States. [118/119]

. . . .

During the First World War, some of the more conspicuous movie successes were flag-waving films, of the most crude and unsubtle nature, such as "The Kaiser, the Beast of Berlin" or "My Four Years in Germany." But it was not until the international crises of 1936-37 that there was any substantial concern in the United States about the propaganda potentialities of the screen. The shock effect of Nazism in Germany and the bloody and tragic civil war in Spain was reflected in the public controversy [119/120] which raged in the United States around the first tentative American movies which dared to mention the reality of fascism.

"Blockade," a melodramatic and rather naïve film about the Franco rebellion, and "Confessions of a Nazi Spy," a vigorous movie based on news accounts and Federal Bureau of Investigation materials which exposed the activities of German secret agents in the United States, created a national uproar of more than passing duration. That substantial proportion of the American public which favored an isolationist foreign policy recognized and feared the power of the screen to awaken Americans to a distant threat or to or-

[1] This definition follows Harold D. Lasswell, the first social scientist to study propaganda systematically. See Bruce Smith, Harold D. Lasswell, and Ralph D. Casey, *Propaganda, Communication, and Public Opinion*, 1947, pp. 1 ff.
[2] I have added this definition of entertainment to the three categories of Professor Lasswell.

ganize American attitudes toward something called fascism. The leaders of public opinion began to realize the political potential of movies—as a catalyst of political attitudes and as a lever on Congress and American foreign policy. The controversy about these first "political" films was significant not simply because of the position which those films took: what alarmed the politicos was the fact that movies dared to say anything about matters which were believed to be outside Hollywood's jurisdiction.

At the heart of the public debate lay the surprised recognition that the movies had violated a familiar pattern of escape and reassurance, and had shown the temerity to extend their province from the amorous to the political. The Senate, in the throes of profound conflict over American foreign policy, launched a formal investigation of "war propaganda in motion pictures." The movie producers engaged Mr. Wendell Willkie, the defeated but immensely popular Republican candidate for President, as special counsel.

DECLARATION OF PRINCIPLES

Even before the hearings opened in Washington, it became clear that a philosophical point would confound the pragmatic opponents of Hollywood: it was the *intent* of the movie producers, no less than the effect of the films they had made, that would form the critical focus of the investigation. Mr. Willkie seized the initiative by making an opening statement to the Senators which became a new (and long overdue) Magna Charta for Hollywood:

The motion-picture screen is an instrument of entertainment, education and information. Having been pioneered and developed in our country, it is peculiarly American. . . . The motion picture industry has always been permitted freedom of expression. The impression has now arisen, and very naturally, that one of the hoped-for results of the pressure of your investigation will be to influence the industry to alter its policies so that they may accord more directly with the views of

its critics. The industry is prepared to resist such pressure with all of the strength at its command.[6]

This declaration of principles was supported by those movie producers who were called before the public tribunal. They maintained that the allegedly "propagandistic" films which they had produced were based on indisputable facts; that their movies faithfully brought to the screen the contents of books or plays which had already won widespread public approval; and that movies are made under free competitive conditions—with the primary intention of earning a profit by providing a salable commodity for consumers on a market in which consumers are free to make choices. More important, the motion picture industry resolutely embraced the principle that movies were not to be denied that freedom of expression which the Constitution unequivocally grants to the press. This [120/121] defense, which was an attack on the investigation itself, proved singularly successful: the failure of the Senate committee to demonstrate an avowed intention to produce "un-American" or war propaganda on the part of Hollywood represented a historic liberation of the movies as an instrument of mass communication.[7] [121/123]

.   .   .   .

If propaganda requires the intention to change mass attitudes on controversial subjects, few movies are or will be propagandistic, since even such movies as do invade the area of social problems are ordinarily made in order to make money or win prestige or allay the inner dissatisfactions of those who make them. But the problem for Hollywood is whether any film can be made about an important controversial subject without suffering instant denunciation as "propaganda" and

[6] Quoted by Bosley Crowther, Sunday *New York Times*, July 6, 1947, p. 1, dramatic section.
[7] For data on the Senate investigation, see U. S. Senate, Interstate Commerce Committee, *Propaganda in Motion Pictures: Hearings, 77th Cong., 1st sess., on S. Res. 152, Authorizing Investigation of War Propaganda Disseminated by Motion-Picture Industry*, Washington, D. C.: Government Printing Office, 1942.

penalization at the box office. It is one thing to publish a news story or book about the position of the Negro in the South; it is another thing to risk the sums involved in a film which is certain to be barred from the Southern states of the Republic. (This happened to the movie called "The Southerner.")

But a powerful demand is growing, in the critical and intellectual ranks of our society, for movie-makers to fulfill the *responsibility* (even at the cost of profit sacrifices) which movies, no less than the press or the radio, owe to the democracy in which they are produced and from which they derive that freedom of expression which is unfettered by government control, censorship, or persuasion. Even the province of entertainment, long permitted the luxury of eschewing reality, must recognize its obligations to public information and enlightenment, and to a national interest which, if not altruistically served, cannot be blindly evaded. An admission of this newly recognized responsibility, on one level at least, was recently voiced by Louis B. Mayer, production head of the largest and most profitable motion picture company in the world, Metro-Goldwyn-Mayer: [123/124]

The message of the screen reaches approximately 235,000,000 persons throughout the world. . . . There is a heavy responsibility upon the producers of motion pictures. Therefore a motion picture should not only afford entertainment, but be of educational value. In this crisis it can portray fairly and honestly the American way of life, and can be a powerful influence in the lives of the millions in other countries who are either denied access to our way of life, or who have never had the opportunity of experiencing it. This is not propaganda . . . unless one would say that presenting to the world our way of life, our freedom, our opportunities, our defense of liberty, our emphasis on the dignity of the human being [is] . . .[13]

FREEDOM INVOLVES RESPONSIBILITY

Freedom in the arena of public opinion involves obligations no less than license. The public can properly make claims upon those who control the avenues of communication and to whom the people have granted the inviolable protection of the Bill of Rights. And this brings the modern democratic state face to face with the dilemma of a freedom which is often enjoyed and exploited without a corresponding sense of responsibility. Justice Felix Frankfurter (in *Pennekamp* v. *State of Florida*) has stated, "Freedom of the press is not freedom from responsibility for its exercise." [14]

The distinguished scholars who functioned for three years as the Commission on Freedom of the Press ("the press" was defined as embracing all agencies of communication, including movies) have concluded that freedom no longer sanctions the right to suppress truths, present lies, practice injustice, corrupt the public mind, or be irresponsible in the fulfillment of that public obligation for which the guarantees of free communication were established.[15]

This position has been brilliantly explored by Professor William Ernest Hocking of Harvard in what is surely the most trenchant analysis of freedom and responsibility since John Stuart Mill's *On Liberty*. The final recommendation of the Commission on Freedom of the Press offers a standard by which the movie-makers should be judged, and by which they might well, in the confused days of the future, judge themselves:

The press must know that its faults and errors have ceased to be private vagaries and have become public dangers. Its inadequacies menace the balance of public opinion. It has lost the common and ancient human liberty to be deficient in its function or to offer half-truth for the whole. The press must remain private and free, *ergo* human and fallible; but the press dare no longer indulge in fallibility—it must supply the public need.[16]

[13] Quoted in the *Hollywood Reporter*, July 8, 1947, p. 4. Let it be noted that movies made in Hollywood for the purpose of influencing attitudes about democracy in countries which do not enjoy it *would* be classified as propaganda.

[14] Quoted by William Ernest Hocking, *Freedom of the Press*, 1947, p. 10.

[15] The Commission on Freedom of the Press consisted of Robert M. Hutchins, chairman, Zechariah Chafee, Jr., John M. Clark, John Dickinson, William E. Hocking, Harold D. Lasswell, Archibald MacLeish, Charles E. Merriam, Reinhold Niebuhr, Robert Redfield, Beardsley Ruml, Arthur M. Schlesinger, and George N. Shuster.

[16] Hocking, *op. cit.*, Appendix, p. 30.

The Movies and Political Propaganda*

UPTON SINCLAIR (1878-   ), novelist and crusader, graduated from
the College of the City of New York in 1897. He is the author of a great many
books, including *The Jungle* (1906), a novel of social protest that called attention to unsanitary practices and poor working conditions in the stockyards;
Upton Sinclair Presents William Fox (1933), the story of one of Hollywood's
giants; and the Lanny Budd series of international adventure novels. An ardent
Socialist, he ran unsuccessfully for Congress in New Jersey and California; in
1934 the California Democratic party accepted him as its candidate for governor, with a program called EPIC (End Poverty in California). The heated
battle that followed his nomination is described in the following selection.

I have had dealings with the movies since
their infancy. Twenty years ago the late
Augustus Thomas made a really honest
version of "The Jungle." That caused me
to have hopes, but they were quickly
dashed. I sold to a movie concern a story
telling about a self-confident young rich
man who made a wager that he could go
out as a hobo and get a quick start in life.
When I next heard of that story, it had to
do with a lost will. Soon after the War,
my old friend, Ben Hampton, historian of
the industry, undertook to make a picture
of "The Moneychangers," which tells how
the elder J. P. Morgan caused the panic
of 1907. When I went to see it, it was a
story of the drug traffic in Chinatown!

I don't think I am egotistical in saying
that I have offered to the motion picture
studios some good opportunities. "King
Coal," "Jimmie Higgins," "100%," "They
Call Me Carpenter," "Boston"—all these
are motion picture scenarios ready made.
There is only one thing wrong with them,
they indict the profit system. "Oil" has
been read by every concern in the business
—I suppose a dozen agents have set out

full of confidence to handle it, and never
have they reported but one thing: "Magnificent, but dangerous." [189/190]

That I know what I am talking about
was proved when I happened to write on
a subject that did not involve the profit
system. Several concerns were bidding for
"The Wet Parade" before the book was
out. Metro-Goldwyn-Mayer paid twenty
thousand dollars for it, and they spent half
a million and made an excellent picture,
following my story closely.

Now I loomed on the horizon, no longer
a mere writer, but proposing to apply my
rejected scenarios! While I was in New
York some reporter asked: "What are you
going to do with all the unemployed motion picture actors?" I answered: "Why
should not the State of California rent one
of the idle studios and let the unemployed
actors make a few pictures of their own?"
That word was flashed to Hollywood, and
the war was on.

Louis B. Mayer, president of Metro-
Goldwyn-Mayer, was vacationing in Europe when he got this dreadful news, and
he dropped everything and came home to

* Upton Sinclair, from "The Movies and Political Propaganda," in *The Movies on Trial*, ed. William J. Perlman
(New York: The Macmillan Company, 1936), pp. 189-195. Reprinted with permission of The Macmillan Company from
The Movies on Trial by William J. Perlman. Copyright 1936 by William J. Perlman.

take charge of the campaign to "stop Sinclair." You see, he is chairman of the State Committee of the Republican party, so he had a double responsibility. I have met "Louie Bee," as he is called, now and then. I once took Bertrand Russell to lunch with him by invitation and learned that a great film magnate doesn't have time to talk with a mere philosopher, but politely appoints a substitute to see that he is properly fed and escorted round the lot.

Also Mr. Hearst was summoned from his vacation. Mr. Hearst belongs to the movie section. Hearst had been staying at Bad Nauheim. He was hobnobbing with Hanfstaengel, Nazi agent to the United States. You see, Hearst [190/191] wants to know how the Reds are to be put down in America; so "Huffy," as they call him, flew with Hearst to interview Hitler.

As soon as Hearst learned of my nomination, he gave out an interview comparing me with the Pied Piper of Hamlin; and then he came back to New York and gave another interview, and from there to California, where he called me "an unbalanced and unscrupulous political speculator." His newspapers began a campaign of editorials and cartoons denouncing me as a Communist. I didn't see any denouncing me as a free-lover, and a menace to the purity and sanctity of the American home.

The first threat of the movie magnates was to move to Florida. Warner Brothers said they would go—and proceeded to start the construction of two or three new sound stages in Hollywood. Joseph Schenck of United Artists travelled to Florida to inspect locations, and the Florida legislature announced its intention to exempt motion picture studios from all taxes, and a mob of new "come-ons" rushed to buy lots.

Of course, this talk of moving was the veriest bunk. It would cost a billion dollars to move, and the British would grab the business meanwhile. Where would they get their mountains, and their eucalyptus trees, which represent the foliage of North and South America, Europe, Asia, Africa, and Australia? Above all, what would they do about the mosquitoes? I

have lived in Florida, and I said to my audiences: "Right in the middle of a scene, one would bite the lady star on the nose and cost them fifty thousand dollars."

But that didn't keep them from building up the terror. [191/192] Orders for an assessment came; and in Hollywood an assessment means that the check is written for you, and you sign it. In this case it was for one day's pay of everybody in all the studios—except the big "execs." The total amount raised was close to half a million. There was a little rebellion, but I didn't hear about it in any paper in California. I had to go to the London *News-Chronicle* to learn that Jean Harlow and James Cagney were among the Protestants. From the same paper I learn that Katharine Hepburn was threatened with dismissal if she supported Upton Sinclair.

I am happy to say that a few Hollywood writers showed political independence. Frank Scully got up a committee in my support, and it was joined by Dorothy Parker, Morris Ryskind, Gene Fowler, Lewis Browne and Jim Tully.

Also they started in making newsreels. Will Hays sent a representative to attend to this. They invented a character called the "Inquiring Reporter." He was supposed to be travelling around California, interviewing people on the campaign. They were supposed to be real people, but of course they were actors. On November 4, the New York *Times* published a two-column story from their Hollywood press correspondent, from which I quote:

FILMS AND POLITICS

HOLLYWOOD MASSES THE FULL POWER OF HER RESOURCES TO FIGHT SINCLAIR

The City of Los Angeles has turned into a huge movie set where many newsreel pictures are made every day, depicting the feelings of the people against Mr. Sinclair. Equipment from [192/193] one of the major studios, as well as some of its second-rate players, may be seen at various street intersections or out in the residential neighborhood, "shooting" the melodrama and unconscious comedy of the campaign. Their product can be seen in leading motion-picture houses in practically every city of the State.

In one of the "melodramas" recently filmed and shown here in Los Angeles, an interviewer approaches a demure old lady, sitting on her front porch and rocking away in her rocking chair.

"For whom are you voting, Mother?" asks the interviewer.

"I am voting for Governor Merriam," the old lady answers in a faltering voice.

"Why, Mother?"

"Because I want to have my little home. It is all I have left in the world."

In another recent newsreel there is shown a shaggy man with bristling Russian whiskers and a menacing look in his eye.

"For whom are you voting?" asked the interviewer.

"Vy, I am foting for Seenclair."

"Why are you voting for Mr. Sinclair?"

"Vell, his system vorked vell in Russia, vy can't it vork here?"

All these releases are presented as "newsreels." Another "newsreel" has been made of Oscar Rankin, a colored prizefighter and preacher who is quite a favorite with his race in Los Angeles county. Asked why he was voting for Governor Merriam, he answered that he liked to preach and play the piano and he wants to keep a church to preach in and a piano to play.

Merriam supporters always are depicted as the more worthwhile element of the community, as popular favorites or as substantial business men. Sinclair supporters are invariably pictured as the riff-raff. Low paid "bit" players are said to take the leading roles in most of these "newsreels," particularly where dialogue is required. People conversant with movie personnel claim to have recognized in them certain aspirants to stardom.

At another studio an official called in his scenario writers to give them a bit of advice on how to vote. "After all," he is reputed to have told his writers, "what does Sinclair know about anything? He's just a writer." [193/194]

Hitherto the movies have maintained that they could not do any kind of "educational" work; their audiences demanded entertainment, and they could have nothing to do with "propaganda." But now, you see, that pretense has been cast aside. They have made propaganda, and they have won a great victory with it, and are tremendously swelled up about it. You may be sure that never again will there be an election in California in which the great "Louie Bee" will not make his power felt; and just as you saw the story of

"Thunder Over California" being imported from Minnesota, so will you see the "Inquiring Reporter" arriving in Minnesota, Mississippi, Washington, or wherever big business desires to ridicule the efforts of the disinherited to help themselves at the ballot-box.

Listen to the lords of the screen world vaunting themselves: The front page of the *Hollywood Reporter* eleven days prior to the election.

This campaign against Upton Sinclair has been and is dynamite.

When the picture business gets aroused, it becomes AROUSED, and, boy, how they can go to it. It is the most effective piece of political humdingery that has ever been effected, and this is said in full recognition of the antics of that master-machine that used to be Tammany. Politicians in every part of this land (and they are all vitally interested in the California election) are standing by in amazement as a result of the bombast that has been set off under the rocking chair of Mr. Sinclair.

Never before in the history of the picture business has the screen been used in direct support of a candidate. Maybe an isolated exhibitor here and there has run a slide or two, favoring a friend, but never has there been a concerted action on the part of all theatres in a community to defeat a nominee. [194/195]

And this activity may reach much farther than the ultimate defeat of Mr. Sinclair. It will undoubtedly give the big wigs in Washington and politicians all over the country an idea of the real POWER that is in the hands of the picture industry. Maybe our business will be pampered a bit, instead of being pushed around as it has been since it became a big business.

Before Louis Mayer, Irving Thalberg, Charlie Pettijohn (a good old democrat under ordinary conditions) and Carey Wilson stepped into this political battle here, the whole Republican party seemed to have been sunk by the insane promises of Mr. Sinclair. With that group in the war, and it has been a WAR, things took a different turn. Governor Merriam's party here in the South had a HEAD, something that was missing before. It received the finances it so direly needed AND the whole picture business got behind the shove.

Sinclair is not defeated yet, but indications point to it, and California should stand up and sing hosannas for their greatest State industry, MOTION PICTURES, and that same industry should, for itself, point to its work whenever some of the screwy legislation comes up in the various State Legislatures during the next few months.

Research: The Immature*

MORTIMER ADLER (1902-   ) received his Ph.D. at Columbia University in 1928 and was professor of the philosophy of law at the University of Chicago from 1930 to 1952. He was one of the editors of the Great Books of the Western World, one of many intellectual enterprises in which he has been associated with Dr. Robert Hutchins. In *Art and Prudence* (1937), a wide-ranging study of public restraints on the arts, in particular the film, he included a long, analytical criticism of the Payne Fund studies. This series of volumes explored the relationship between motion pictures and youth, with emphasis on the possible influence of motion pictures on crime. The Payne Fund study discussed in the following selection is one concerned with the influence of motion pictures on political and social ideas.

. . . .

... There is no question that in its scientific technique the work of Professor L. L. Thurstone and Miss R. C. Peterson of the Department of Psychology of the University of Chicago is clearly the best of the Payne Fund researches.[283] The experimental procedure involved the use of attitude scales and paired-comparison schedules to detect a shift in the attitude of children on some issue having affective value, as a result of their witnessing a motion picture bearing on that issue. The attitudes of the subjects were recorded about two weeks before their exposure to the movie, and then on the day after exposure, the amount and [411/412] direction of change was measured with fair precision by means of the scales. The pictures used were selected for their suitability from between six and eight hundred films. Many of the test instruments, though not all, were especially constructed for the purposes of the experiment. The experimental groups included children of the fourth to the eighth grade, high-school students and, in one experiment, college students, either in the city of Chicago or in smaller towns in Illinois. The statistical treatment of the data and the statistical processes involved in the construction of the scales are impeccable. These techniques are among the best available in the field of psychometrics to which Professor Thurstone is a leading contributor. In only a few instances can one criticize the verbal statements, which the scales involve, for ambiguity or unclarity; thus, such statements as "Some Chinese traits are admirable but on the whole I don't like them" or "The Negro should have freedom but should never be treated as the equal of the white man" or "In a thousand years the Negro *might* become the white man's equal; then his social position *should* be equal to the white man's" (italics mine), complicate the interpretation of the responses. The student is asked to put an x next to the statement if he disagrees with it. In cases of this sort, does the x negate both parts of the statement, or only the first? But the number of such statements is few, and hardly invalidates the results obtained from the scale.

The first series of experiments was concerned with the effect of single pictures. In the first of these, the testing of 133 children in Genoa, Illinois, a town of about 1200, discovered that the motion picture "Four Sons" resulted in a change of atti-

[283] *Motion Pictures and the Social Attitudes of Children*, The Macmillan Company, Publishers, New York, 1933.

* Mortimer Adler, from "Research: The Immature," *Art and Prudence* (New York: Longmans, Green, 1937), pp. 411-415. Reprinted courtesy of David McKay Company, Inc.

tude favorable to the German people, and slightly less favorable to war. In another, conducted with 240 children in Mendota, a town of about 4000, the motion picture "Street of Chance" made the children less favorable to gambling "even though the gambler was an interesting, likeable character in the film."[284] In another, conducted with 254 children in Princeton, Illinois, a town of about 4700, the motion picture "Hide Out" had no measurable effect on the children's attitudes toward prohibition or bootlegging, although some effect had been expected in the light of the criticism of the movie as a portrayal of a college bootlegger. In similar experiments, using "Son of the Gods" [412/413] and "Welcome Danger"—the first a movie that had been considered friendly toward Chinese culture, and the second one which the Chinese had criticized as unfriendly—it was found that the first made the children more favorable to the Chinese, whereas the second made the children less favorable, but to a much slighter degree. The motion picture "The Valiant," which was used to test a change of attitude toward capital punishment, did not give a statistically significant result, although the change was in the expected direction toward greater disfavor. "Journey's End" similarly gave an extremely small change, of questionable statistical significance, in the direction of an unfavorable attitude toward war; whereas "All Quiet on the Western Front" gave an extremely large change in the same direction. The investigator's comment is that probably "Journey's End" is too sophisticated in its propaganda for high-school children.[285] To test change of attitude toward the punishment of criminals, "The Criminal Code" was used. This experiment was performed with both a high-school and a college group. The latter were more in favor of leniency toward criminals before seeing the picture, although their change in the direction of leniency was slightly less than the change in that direction of the high-school group. In still another experiment with the same film, no statistically significant result was obtained. Finally, "The Birth of a Nation" was used to measure shifting attitudes toward Negroes. Here the largest effect was found, the children becoming much less favorable toward Negroes. The power of Thomas Dixon as a propagandist is again confirmed.

In another series of experiments, Professor Thurstone and Miss Peterson attempted to measure the cumulative effect of a number of motion pictures. Thus, for example, using both "Journey's End" and "All Quiet on the Western Front," they found a cumulative effect on the children's attitude, the pictures tending to reinforce each other. But it should be noted that the group who saw "Journey's End" after they had seen "All Quiet on the Western Front" showed no greater absolute change in attitude than the group who saw only the latter; whereas the group who saw both in the order indicated showed the largest absolute change in attitude. And, in an experiment on attitude [413/414] toward the punishment of criminals, it was found that two pictures, "The Big House" and "Numbered Men," neither of which by itself had a measurable effect, did however cause a significant change when combined. [414/415]

. . . .

. . . We simply know, as a result of Professor Thurstone's efforts, that movies do have an effect upon the formation of children's attitudes with respect to certain social questions. We have a limited scientific measurement of the propaganda power of the movies, the first that has probably been made of any type of art. Science here confirms what is an ancient and generally accepted opinion among men of experience that works of art, particularly literature, and the stage, are potent media of propaganda. Whether for good or ill is a question that can be answered only in the particular case in terms of the merits of each side of the issue toward which the propaganda is being directed. . . .

. . . .

[284] *Op. cit.*, p. 15.
[285] *Op. cit.*, p. 26.

PART FIVE

SHOULD THE SCREEN BE CONTROLLED?

The Problem in Practical Philosophy*

MORTIMER ADLER. For biographical data, see "Research: The Immature," p. 85. Having dealt with the history of social control of the arts and having judged largely inadequate the "scientific" attempts of the Payne Fund studies to gauge the effects of films on young people, Dr. Adler in this selection attempts to lay out a philosophical base for censorship.

. . . .
. . . Though the prudent man is obligated to take account of the arts because they produce goods and evils which fall within his view of the means and circumstances of human life to be ordered and controlled, he is not by virtue of prudence competent to direct the work of the arts. In the sphere of his own activity, the artist must be relatively independent. He alone has the special competence for making or doing well whatever is subject to his technique. Furthermore, the work of art which is good technically may be morally pernicious in its effects, or the reverse may be the case. Such discrepancies may occur even though the artist is a man of moral integrity and works with the best intentions, because the effect of the work depends upon the moral fibre of its recipients as well as upon its intrinsic morality, whereby it reflects the soul of its maker.

The position of prudence is, therefore, anomalous. It has a task of ruling which exceeds its competence. It is a limited sovereign charged with responsibilities disproportionate to its limited powers. The prudent man cannot ignore the artist and his work, as the artist is able to ignore the prudent man. Considering the positive values of the arts in human life, he must [448/449] seek to increase their production, he must strive to preserve and enhance these values. Considering the negative values, he would be unwise if he tried to interfere with the operations of art, but he must nevertheless try to prevent them from interfering with his own efforts for the sake of human happiness.

4. In the light of this analysis, a few principles of practical wisdom can be formulated. They do not solve the antinomy of art and prudence. On the contrary, they acknowledge its insolubility except in ideal terms—the ideal of a supernatural perfection, healing the wound of intellect divided against will. They do not seek to *reconcile* art and prudence, but only to effect a *compromise* between them [141].

. . . .
. . . to grant an art freedom in its proper domain—the process of production [449/450] itself, in which the artist's technique is the instrument of the artist's soul—does not mean that it should be allowed to run wild in the community. It is proper for the prudent man to supervise the ways in which works of art reach their audience, to say, not what shall be made, but what shall be received and by whom and under what conditions.[71] Here the difficulties of the prudent man are of another order. He does not go out of his proper sphere in imposing a censorship which rejects a work of art as unfit to be received. But he must be guided in such action by knowledge or opinion concerning the effects of the par-

[71] Cf. the practical proposals of the encyclical, *Vigilanti Cura*, July 2, 1936.

* Mortimer Adler, from "The Problem in Practical Philosophy," *Art and Prudence* (New York: Longmans, Green, 1937), pp. 448-452, 652-655. Reprinted courtesy of David McKay Company, Inc.

ticular work upon moral character and conduct [142]. Knowledge, in the proper sense of this word, he cannot have. If opinion is uncertain and conflicting, and if scientific evidence is either not available or no more certain and unambiguous than opinion, the casuistical problem may be genuinely insoluble. This, of course, does not abrogate the principle that the prudent man should seek to do what he can to increase the benefits of a particular art and to minimize its undesirable consequences: *to do what he can,* within the limitations imposed upon him by the inviolable autonomy of art, on the one hand, and by his honest doubts and uncertainties concerning the relevant facts, on the other.

One other principle is clear. The proper end of the artist is to do good work according to the standards of his art. Moral instruction is not his task [143]. The artist *qua* artist seeks neither to help nor hinder the moralist and statesman. As an artist his virtue is that of making *things* as they should be made, and not of making *men* as they should be, by aiding them toward their proper end. The latter task belongs to the moralist or statesman, as well as to the parent, the priest and the teacher, through their possession of prudence. . . . [**450/451**]

. . . .

. . . The fact that works of art can be used by parent, priest and teacher to serve their ends, does not make the artist a moralist or teacher any more than it makes him a parent or a priest.

This division of responsibilities indicates another course of action for the prudent man. Granting the arts their freedom, he can safeguard human welfare by concerning himself with what is most properly subject to his power: moral training [144] . . . .

. . . The prudent man, seeking to cultivate moral character, is justified in using works of art in the process, or in excluding them if they threaten to interfere with his work. We must not overlook, as Maritain points out, "the necessity for prohibitive measures. Human frailty makes them indispen-

sable: it must be protected. It is none the less clear that prohibitive measures, however necessary they may be, remain by nature less effective and less important than a robust intellectual and religious training, enabling mind and heart to resist *vitally* any morbid principle."[72]

The compromise between art and prudence is accomplished by recognizing their limitations, unless they are aided by superior wisdom. Eric Gill has said: "Look after goodness and truth, and beauty will take care of herself."[73] The formula is [**451/452**] true, and also convertible: look after truth and beauty, and goodness will take care of herself. It is the human task to look after all three, but by means of different powers or virtues. Only confusion and misfortune can result from the transgression of a natural division of labor in the realization of these basic values. If the artist and the prudent man are not one —if the conflicting virtues are not perfectly reconciled by a unity of intellect and will—then each must do what is within his limited power as well as possible. On the one hand, the prudent man can best meet the opposition of the arts to his work by reinforcing his own efforts in the moral sphere. On the other, the artist can best meet the opposition of the moralist and the statesman to his work by producing what is good as art. This is by no means a solution of the conflict. But to ask for a real solution is to ask for too much. We must be satisfied with what we can achieve according to the circumstances of our time and the universal limitations of human nature. . . .

. . . .

[72] Maritain, p. 224, by permission of Messrs. Sheed and Ward, Publishers. See Note 145 *infra.*
[73] *Beauty Looks After Herself,* New York, 1933: p. 245. See the remainder of this essay, pp. 208-245, and the essay entitled *Art and Prudence* in the same volume, pp. 11-29.

141. A compromise is effected when conflicting parties are kept *apart* by courtesies reciprocally extended. It is a practical expedient and superficial with respect to the basis of the issue. Art and prudence are reconciled only when they are *united* by a harmony of intellect and will. This can be accomplished, as Maritain points out, only by Wisdom "endowed with the outlook of God" (*Art and Scholasticism,* p. 86, Sheed and Ward). Human

wisdom is not enough. The gifts of a supernatural religion are needed. "Truth to tell, I believe it to be impossible outside Catholicism to reconcile in man, without diminishing or forcing [652/653] them, the rights of morality and the claims of intellectuality, art or science. Morality as such aims only at the good of the human being, the supreme interests of the acting Subject; intellectuality as such aims only at the Object, its nature, if it is to be known, what it ought to be, if it is to be made. . . A super-human virtue is necessary to secure the free play of art and science among men under the supremacy of the divine law and the primacy of Charity, and so to realize the higher reconciliation of the *moral* and the *intellectual*" (*op. cit.,* pp. 138-139).

In an essay devoted to this subject and acknowledging its discipleship to Maritain, Eric Gill describes the opposition of art and prudence as a lover's quarrel. Each is devoted in part to the interests of the other, yet each claims a precedence and a dominion over the other, each is jealous of its rights in human life. He concludes that, although the prudent man should have no quarrel with good art, the conflict goes on and will "never be settled until most men of prudence are also artists and most artists have become men of prudence. This pleasing state of affairs will not come about until the present civilization has passed away" (*Beauty Looks After Herself,* Sheed and Ward, New York, 1933: p. 29).

The makers of motion pictures are not the only artists in our day about whom it can be asked whether they are also prudent men. If the unity of Christian wisdom, the existence of a truly Christian civilization, is needed to prevent "the ungodly divorce between Art and Prudence," the deficiency of it will exhibit itself in all fields of human endeavor, in science and philosophy as well as in the fine arts, in music and painting as well as in the novel, the play and the motion picture. For this, as for other modern evils, the only remedy may be the re-establishment of Christendom. Those who do not share this faith and hope must move to a solution on a lower level.

142. In his recent encyclical *Vigilanti Cura* (July 2, 1936), Pope Pius XI said: "Everyone knows what damage is done to the soul by bad motion pictures. They are occasions of sin; they seduce young people along the ways of evil by glorifying the passions; they show life under a false light; they cloud ideals; they destroy pure love, respect for marriage and affection for the family. They are capable also of creating prejudices among individuals, misunderstanding among nations, among social classes and among entire races. On the other hand, good motion pictures are capable of exercising a profound and moral influence upon those who see them. In addition to affording recreation, they are able to arouse noble ideals of life, to communicate valuable conceptions," etc. [653/654] The question must be asked whether the judgment of motion pictures here made is in terms of their content or in terms of their effects. If the former, the judgment is an aesthetic one; and indirectly it involves moral condemnation of the makers of motion pictures in so far as "bad" motion pictures betray the souls of their makers. But if the latter, the judgment must rely upon knowledge or become tautological. If a "bad" motion picture is one which has certain deleterious effects, then the difficult question is which motion pictures are bad, i.e. which have these effects? By definition every one *knows* that a motion picture is bad if it has these effects; but everyone does not *know* the answer to the question of fact indicated. Nor can it be answered by a judgment of the morality or immorality of the content of motion pictures, because the intrinsic and extrinsic values of works of fine art are independently variable.

143. It is interesting to note that the encyclical *Vigilanti Cura* takes the Platonic position with respect to the function of art: "We call to mind that it is necessary to apply to the cinema a supreme rule which must direct and regulate the greatest of arts in order that it may not find itself in continual conflict with Christian morality or even simply with human morality based upon natural law. The essential purpose of art, its *raison d'être,* is to assist in the perfection of moral personality, which is man, and for this reason must itself be moral." . . . We therefore recommend "the necessity of making the motion picture 'moral, an influence for good morals, an educator.' " In another place, Pope Pius asks: "Why, indeed, should there be a question of merely avoiding evil? Why should the motion picture simply be a means of diversion and light relaxation to occupy an idle hour? With its magnificent power it can and must be a light and a positive guide to what is good." This conception of art as essentially didactic confirms the Platonism of the encyclical, elsewhere revealed in the identification of intrinsic and extrinsic criticism. See Note 142 *supra.*

144. If the home, the church and the school, or the State, succeeded in the task of training youth, there would be little to fear from the arts. If human character, formed as well as possible, is still corruptible by works of art, then nothing can be done to safeguard men from corruption because it is the weakness of their souls that no human effort can remedy. This was Milton's insight when he praised Plato for his positive programme of good institutions. The arts can interfere in moral affairs only to the extent that men [654/655] are susceptible to such interference. The wise course for the prudent man is, therefore, to make them less susceptible by the efficiency of his positive efforts. In following this programme it may be necessary, of course, for the Church or the State or the individual parent to prevent the arts from interfering with these efforts. Preventive measures should seek, not to regulate the arts directly, but only to regulate the conditions of their reception: what shall be seen and what rejected. This is the policy recommended in the recent papal encyclical. It is the policy ever pursued by vigilant parents.

There is no question that protection from misleading influences is justified during the course of moral training and even for adults to the extent that they must be treated as children. But fears about the effects of external factors is often more a confession of the weakness of home, church and school as positive moral forces than an indication of the existence of the menace feared. That school teachers should be so concerned about what children learn from the movies is a terrifying admission of doubt about the influence of their own teaching. A good teacher so instructs the mind that it is incapable of being hurt by the multifarious errors received from all other sources. In fact, assured of his power and of the strength of his discipline, he is happy to assume the role of antagonist to all other teachers, in school or out, who seem to oppose him. The same is true of the home and the church in the matter of moral training. The agitation about the movies, resulting in extensive scientific research, has not resulted in any findings that are nearly as much cause for alarm as the terrible confession of inadequacy which the agitation itself so plainly bespeaks.

145. "Prudence is right in being apprehensive of the effect on the masses of many works of art. And Catholicism, knowing that evil is to be encountered *ut in pluribus* in the human race, and yet obliged to concern itself with the good of the multitude, must in certain cases deny to art, in the name of the essential interests of the human being, liberties which art would jealously assert. The 'essential interests of the human being' here in

question must be understood not only in relation to the passions of the flesh, but also in relation to the subject-matter of all the virtues, the integrity of the mind first of all—not to mention the interests of art itself, and the need it has of being protected by the disciplines of religion against the dissolution of everything there is in man. It is difficult no doubt in such a case to preserve the balance. At all events to be frightened of art, to flee from it or to put it to flight, is [655/656] certainly no solution. There is a superior wisdom in trusting as much as possible to the powers of the mind" (Maritain, *Art and Scholasticism*, Note 154, Sheed and Ward).

The Cinema and Society

ROGER MANVELL (1909-   ), who received his Ph.D. from London University, became the first director of the British Film Academy when it was established in 1947. He has written many articles and books about motion pictures, including *Film* (1944), *The Animated Film* (1954), *A Seat at the Cinema* (1951), and *Film and the Public* (1955), from which this selection is taken. He has broadcast and lectured on motion-picture subjects and reviewed films for more than twenty years. He edited the *Penguin Film Review* (1946-49) and an annual called *The Cinema* (1950-52).

. . . .

THE PUBLIC AND FILM CENSORSHIP

Are you the sort of person who wants to decide absolutely for himself whether he should attend a play or see a film or [241/242] read a book or visit an exhibition *whatever it may be about?* This question is the first test of your own attitude to censorship. If you answer 'yes' to the whole of it without any reservation whatsoever, then I would say that you are against any form of censorship in the arts, that is as far as you yourself are concerned.

Only a minority of people would have the courage to answer 'yes' if they were really pressed. When you consider that without some form of censorship, whether administered by an official or a policeman is for the moment beside the point, it would be possible for the arts to portray to the public, quite indiscriminately, lewdness and blasphemy, unrestrained vice and perversion, sadism and the cruelties of the jungle, you will begin to see where censorship quite naturally begins. The real problem lies in deciding at what point it should end.

Now this bold minority of people who are prepared to face anything rather than seek the protection of the police or hide behind a censor, may well draw the line when the same freedom is permitted to other people who they think are weaker-minded than themselves! What is all right for you may not, in your opinion, be all right for your maiden aunt or your four-teen-year-old daughter or your brother-in-law who is a country parson. So you guide them away, or perhaps tell them bluntly they are not to look. And so you will have become a censor yourself.

All this goes to show that there is no easy answer to the censorship problem. Abolish it altogether, and you will soon get an exploitation of public curiosity which will invite some kind of police intervention. Public behaviour over street accidents and murder trials shows there are always plenty of people about who are keen to get a low sort of thrill at any price. It was because of this that censorship began here, and, for that matter, in America.

It is a curious story. Most people think the film censor is a Government official like the Lord Chamberlain, who has been the official Censor of Plays since an Act of 1737 and is a member of the Royal Household. The plays are actually [242/

* Roger Manvell, from "The Cinema and Society," *The Film and the Public* (Harmondsworth: Penguin Books, 1955), pp. 241-252. Reprinted by permission of Penguin Books Ltd.

93

243] read by one or other of a number of official Readers of Plays appointed by the Lord Chamberlain. But the film Censor is not a Government official: he is an official of the film industry itself. The films of forty or fifty years ago, especially the comedies and farces, were gradually getting so low in tone that the British film producers felt it was time to put their own house in order before someone else from outside came and did it for them; there are always plenty of people only too ready to clean up the activities of others in the name of virtue.

So the Kinematograph Manufacturers' Association, as the main film producers' organization was then called, set up the British Board of Film Censors in 1912. G. A. Redford, who had been the Lord Chamberlain's official Reader of Plays for nearly twenty years, was appointed the first President, and he was succeeded by T. P. O'Connor in 1916. O'Connor's name became famous on the smudgy censorship certificate which preceded the tens of thousands of films shown to the public during his Presidency. F. Brook Wilkinson, who died in 1948, was the Secretary of the Board from its commencement. The President now is Sir Sydney Harris, and the Secretary is A. T. L. Watkins, who was Brook Wilkinson's chief assistant. It is perhaps typically British that the Kinematograph Manufacturers' Association, which has long been superseded as a representative organization of the British film producers, still survives as the body which appoints the President of the British Board of Film Censors. The President is then left free to choose his own small staff of censors, who are responsible for viewing every film, long or short, shown on our public screens, except the newsreels which are not required to be censored.

Yet if you were to ask the Censor what is really the protective or prohibitive power in the cinema, he would tell you it is the Local Authority. Although the certificate which precedes the film looks as official as a dog licence, it is really only an advisory certificate warning all comers that in the view of the Censor the film is in a special class (X) entirely unsuitable for showing to children under sixteen years of **[243/244]** age, or Adult (A) and therefore only to be seen by children if the adult with them will take on the responsibility of introducing them, or Universal (U) which means that anyone of any age can go into the cinema if he has got the money. But the individual certificates given are advisory only. Any Local Authority can alter them for its own locality; for example, a good many authorities changed the certificate A given to Walt Disney's *Snow White and the Seven Dwarfs* to a U.

The main distinction between the British and American systems of self-censorship, built up in each case by the film industries themselves in order to avoid intervention by the state, is that the American Hays Office committed itself to a written code while the British Censor has so far left matters to direct argument with the film-maker. In Britain, therefore, the general rules concerning what is forbidden remain open to discussion. This, at any rate, allows for a certain elasticity, and British film censorship since A. T. L. Watkins became Secretary has achieved a reputation for liberality which is not entirely shared by the American Censors.

All censorship is a dead weight on the more progressive artist. The idealist in these matters has always said that the artist alone should take responsibility for what he says, and that the public itself is the best judge of whether its baser instincts are being exploited. The greatest freedom of expression undoubtedly belongs to the writer, provided he can find a publisher for his work.

The dramatist has to be more circumspect, for his work is performed in public. But the least freedom of all belongs to the film-maker; because his audience is so extensive his work has come to be hedged in by restraints unknown to any other art in Britain. The more accessible a work of art becomes to an assembled audience representing all ages, child and adult, the more it has to observe the restrictions of codes or unwritten rules.

Nevertheless, if the Censor suddenly decided to abolish himself, it would almost certainly be necessary to re-create him again in one form or another. The conditions of film- [244/245] going in this country make it a very mixed affair; audiences are dominated by the permanent presence of young adolescents and family parties, whereas in some Continental countries children under sixteen years are excluded from the cinemas altogether.

But the Censor claims he does not exist to administer or reform the industry, but to deal with it as it is. He must take into account the youthful element in virtually all the cinema audiences in Britain. Therefore he gives *Snow White and the Seven Dwarfs* an A and not a U certificate on account of the frightening scenes of witchcraft, and *Oliver Twist* and *Great Expectations* similarly became A pictures on account of certain scenes which appear in them. The only certificate which excludes children is that for the X category. This was introduced in January 1951, partly to enable the censor to pass with as little interference as possible foreign language films made in countries where censorship restrictions do not operate in so narrow a way as in Hollywood, and partly to enable him to deal more strictly with films containing horrific, violent, or 'difficult' themes totally unsuitable for children. The X certificate is unpopular with exhibitors when it is applied to American or British films intended for wide distribution, because it keeps the family audience away from the cinema, and the family audience is an important part of the regular patronage. Typical of the better films gaining an X Certificate have been the American productions *A Streetcar named Desire, The Well, Death of a Salesman, War of the Worlds,* and *Sound of Fury,* and the foreign-language films, *Rashomon, Los Olvidados, Casque d'or, Les Jeux interdits,* and *La Ronde.*

The attitude of the British censorship is expressed in an article written by A. T. L. Watkins, Secretary to the Board of Film Censors, for *Penguin Film Review* (9):

The Board has no written Code, no neatly docketed list of things which are allowed and things which are not. It has been suggested that such a Code would help producers. The Board thinks it would have the reverse effect. The absence of a Code enables it to treat each picture, each incident, each line of dialogue [245/246] on its merits. No two pictures are alike, everything depends on the treatment and the context. If the Board worked to a Code, it would have to stick to the Code. Films would be dealt with on the basis of hard-and-fast rules, no discretion would be exercised—and producers and public alike would be the losers.

But if the Board has no Code, there are certain broad principles on which it works. In judging a film there are three main questions to be considered: Is it likely to impair the moral standards of the audience by extenuating vice or crime or by depreciating social value? . . . Secondly, is the story, incident, or dialogue likely to give offence to any reasonably minded section of the public? Repeat 'reasonably minded'. . . . Thirdly, what will be the effect of the story, incident, or dialogue on children—that is to say, children of all ages under sixteen?

In America the chief form of censorship is once again that of the industry itself, administered by the Motion Picture Association of America. The famous Code, the full and fascinating text of which can be found in the annual publication *The Motion Picture Almanac,* was first drafted in 1929 by Father Daniel A. Lord, S.J., in association with Martin Quigley and Father F. J. Dineen, S.J. This Code was finally accepted by the M.P.A.A. (the Hays Office) in March 1930, and after a trial period the M.P.A.A. set up the Production Code Administration under Joseph J. Breen, a Roman Catholic, who has administered it ever since. The Code occupies eight closely printed pages, and lists every kind of offence conceivable which could be committed in a film against the moral susceptibilities of society.

An introduction to the Production Code (published in 1944) explains that, though it is not obligatory for producers to conform to the Code, producers in fact do observe it; this is meant to underline the producers' own sense of responsibility which self-regulation implies. It ends by claiming that the freedom of the artist is not curbed by the Code, and that it reflects responsible public opinion as to what is 'clean and artistic' in film entertainment.

Few writers would agree with this claim that the Code leaves them free.

The main implications to be derived from the regulations which follow in the Code are examined very fully by Ruth [246/247] Inglis in her book *Freedom of the Movies* (1947). Here only a brief reference can be made to the main clauses. Crime comes first; the details of technique of murder and methods of theft must never be shown in detail, the illegal drug traffic and the use of drugs must be kept in the background so that curiosity may not be stimulated, and 'the use of liquor in American life, when not required by the plot or for proper characterization, will not be shown'. Sex follows: 'The sanctity of the institution of marriage and the home shall be upheld.' 'Adultery and illicit sex, sometimes necessary plot material, must not be explicitly treated, or justified, or presented attractively.' Scenes of lust and passion must be restrained; seduction and rape should never 'be more than suggested'. Among the direct prohibitions are references to or representations of sex perversion, white slavery, and miscegenation. Obscenity and profanity are forbidden, and a list of indecent words is appended which must not be used; these include 'damn' and 'hell' used as expletives. Nudity (except where it is natural in natives), indecent exposure, and indecent dances are prohibited, and 'undressing scenes should be avoided, and never used save where essential to the plot'; 'the treatment of bedrooms must be governed by good taste and decency'. Religious ceremonies, ministers of religion, the national feelings of other countries and the appearance of the American flag must all be treated with respect. Finally certain 'repellent subjects' must be 'treated within the limits of good taste'; these are actual hangings, electrocutions, third degree methods, brutality, branding of people and animals, apparent cruelty to children or animals, the sale of women, women selling their virtue, and surgical operations.

Further special regulations modify the representation of crime; they affect the slaughter of police and law-enforcement officers by criminals, the use of murder and suicide in films, the use of illegal firearms, or the flaunting of weapons by gangsters, the use of kidnapping, the inclusion of minors as criminals, or scenes using animals which may have been made to suffer in the process of film-making. [247/248]

STATE CONTROL OF THE FILM

Another form of censorship, this time political rather than moral, is that imposed by the Government of the U.S.S.R. on Soviet film-making. The film industry was nationalized in August 1919, and, after supervision by a series of different authorities reflecting the changes of policy of the regime, came under the Ministry of Cinematography in 1946, replacing the former Committee on Cinematography founded in 1938. Each constituent Republic of the U.S.S.R. has a corresponding though subsidiary Ministry of its own.

It has always proved difficult to supervise the work of the Soviet film-makers effectively. At its worst the controls may be so irksome that the repressed artist loses his creative energy or declines into a conformist technician providing what is needed and no more. Soviet film production has never been adequate to the needs of the vast potential audiences which still remain relatively cut off from the cinema.* The Communist Party watches most carefully every stage in a film's scripting, production, and exhibition. The Ministry of Cinematography must obtain the approval of the Council of Ministers, one of the hierarchies of Government, for its annual programme of film production, and the Council usually makes annual pronouncements on the industry and its shortcomings. Directives for individual film subjects may be given from the highest level. An Art Coun-

* The population of the Soviet Union was about 200 million in 1950. The annual audience for films in 1939 was only 1,200 million, and in 1945 573 million. In 1950 it had not reached the 1939 figure, in spite of the efforts made to replace equipment damaged during the war. In 1951 the audience figure for Great Britain was 1,350 million.

cil was established in 1944 by order of the Party within the Committee of Cinematography and later within the Ministry, to supervise the progress of each film during production and to ensure its ideological correctness. Many films have been withdrawn after production on ideological grounds—famous examples were the second part of Eisenstein's trilogy *Ivan the Terrible,* and the film of the post-war reconstruction [248/249] of the mines and industries of the Donets Basin, *A Great Life.* This latter was condemned because it concentrated on the so-called 'primitive' description of the private lives of certain miners and narrowed its scope to only one example of reconstruction in an area where so much had been done. The very title was considered to be ironic, and therefore anti-social!

Socialist realism is the basis of the policy behind Soviet film production. The words of Lenin and Stalin about the powers of the film are famous. Lenin declared as early as 1907: 'When the masses take possession of the film and it comes into the hands of the true supporters of socialist culture, it will become one of the most powerful means of educating the masses.' Stalin said that 'the film is a great means of mass agitation', and that it is 'a great and invaluable force . . . aiding the working class and its Party to educate the toilers in the spirit of socialism, to organize the masses . . . and to raise their cultural and political battle-fitness'.

Socialist realism did away with what was regarded as the bourgeois and reactionary stylization of such film-makers as Eisenstein and Pudovkin during the famous period of the Russian silent film. These self-conscious techniques did not speak directly to the mass audience; they were the product of the intellectual. They were supposedly swept away twenty years ago when, in 1934, the slogan for all workers in the arts became 'socialist realism'.

The basis of socialist realism in the arts was very clearly summarized in an article by G. Nedoshivin called *On the Relation of Art to Reality,* published by Voks in 1951. The following quotations give the essence of his arguments, and they are of great importance, for they explain the philosophy of all Communist film-making since the War.

The basic problem of aesthetics as a science may be defined as the relation of art to reality. . . . Thus art is one of the forms through which all human mind reflects social being.

Art loses all meaning as soon as it divorces itself from reality. Modern formalism clearly bears this out. Abstract cubistic or [249/250] suprematistic combinations of forms do not contain a grain of the real content of objective reality; this makes them absolutely empty, meaningless, devoid of the least objective value.

In other words, reality existing outside of us is primary and its artistic reflection is secondary. 'The existence of matter does not depend on sensation. Matter is primary. Sensation, thought, consciousness are the supreme product of matter organized in a particular way.' (Lenin.)

. . . .

Art generalizes about these matters through carefully selected characters in action. The essence of this generalization in art derives from the ideas these characters and their actions represent.

The great Lenin was the author of the principle that art must be partisan; this was one of the elements of his theory of the partisanship of ideology generally in antagonistic class societies. Mercilessly exposing reactionaries of all hues and shades, Lenin showed that their assertion that art is independent of life screened their defence of the interests of the exploiting classes. Lenin developed this brilliant principle of the partisanship of art in struggle against the theory of 'art for art's sake', against all spokesmen of reaction. Counterposing the false 'freedom' of bourgeois art to the tasks of the art which links its destinies with the emancipation movement of the working class, he said in this article:

'In contrast to bourgeois customs, in contrast to the bourgeois privately-owned and commercialized press, in contrast to bourgeois literary careerism and individualism, "aristocratic anarchism" and rapacity—the Socialist proletariat must advance the principle of *Party literature,* must develop this principle and put it into effect as fully and completely as possible.' . . .

Social consciousness has always served human society as a weapon of struggle with nature, as a weapon of social struggle, forming the basis of practice and acting as its conscious expression. And art has been just such a weapon from the very first days of its existence, remaining such to the present. In the hands of the progressive classes it has been a powerful means of revolutionizing consciousness; reactionary classes have exploited and are still exploiting it as a brake on the development of society. In the latter case, art loses its true content and significance, and generally ceases to be art, as we see with modern reactionary imperialistic 'artistic creation'. Art has reached its true heights only when it has [250/251] performed its function as a force revolutionizing society. . . . Stalin's brilliant definition of the artist as an engineer of the human soul reveals the innermost kernel of this aspect of the problem. . . . The life-giving power of the idea is the basis of the florescence of the art of socialist realism, which is advancing on the foundation of growing ties between art and the struggle the Soviet people are waging under the guidance of the Bolshevik Party, led in its creative work by the genius of Lenin and the genius of Stalin, to build Communism.

The sharp contrast between the communist and democratic attitude to the artist is fully explained by these quotations. In democratic society the burden of social judgement rests with the artist himself; short of offending society utterly he may seek his own values and speak his mind about society as he finds it. In this way the rich, complex evolution of human consciousness is developed like a great river with a hundred twists and turns, or a thousand exploratory rivulets. Experiments and mistakes are part of the larger process of learning; art can learn just as much by being wild, absurd, extravagant as by being wise and far-seeing. In communist society the artist must conform to the Party view in all the facets of its policy, expressing in literature, drama, film, poetry, sculp-

ture, and even music the current ideology, changing his viewpoint only when policy dictates that this change is necessary.

Soviet culture does not recognize the right of the artist to comment *as an individual* on the life of the society in which he lives. The responsibility of criticism rests with the Party and with those placed in authority by it; the artist's responsibility is a technical one, to translate the directions he receives about Soviet society into the most effective form of propaganda through the medium in which he specializes. When the artist is a man of the calibre of the late Sergei Eisenstein the result is a tragic frustration even when he is a sincere Communist. For there are in any generation a few men and women endowed with a superlative understanding of their fellow-beings and with an overwhelming desire to express what they observe and know through the arts. Their [251/252] work is often regarded as antisocial because of the universal unpopularity of the truth when it is expressed with an undisguised vitality. As a result they are persecuted as Eisenstein was persecuted both by the Soviets and by the West when he visited the United States, where he was felt to be a troublesome and difficult man. The artist is almost always difficult and troublesome; he is meant to be so both by nature and temperament, otherwise he would conform and become as other men are. But there is no place for this kind of individualism in Soviet society; . . .

.   .   .   .

Reasons Underlying the General Principles
[of *The Motion Picture Production Code*]*

THE MOTION PICTURE ASSOCIATION OF AMERICA is the organization of the major American film-distribution companies, with headquarters in Washington, D.C. Its principal purpose has been to represent the industry in relations with government—state, national, and foreign, including boards of censors. *The Motion Picture Production Code* of the MPAA is summarized in other selections in this anthology (see "The Cinema and Society," p. 93, and "Movies and Censorship," p. 108). It was actually written in 1929 by Martin Quigley (for biographical data see "Importance of the Entertainment Film," p. 101) and Father Daniel A. Lord, a Jesuit priest from St. Louis who had a special interest in theater and films. This authorship was not generally known until some years later. Specific provisions and applications were in large part developed from earlier lists; but Mr. Quigley and Father Lord added the broader philosophical base of "Reasons Supporting the Code," "Reasons Underlying Particular Applications," and the following statement, which expands upon the three principles given at the beginning of the code proper.

. . . .

I. No picture shall be produced which will lower the moral standards of those who see it. Hence the sympathy of the audience should never be thrown to the side of crime, wrong doing, evil or sin.

This is done:

1. When evil is made to appear attractive or alluring, and good is made to appear unattractive.

2. When the sympathy of the audience is thrown on the side of crime, wrong-doing, evil, sin. The same thing is true of a film that would throw sympathy against goodness, honor, innocence, purity or honesty.

Note: Sympathy with a person who sins is not the same as sympathy with the sin or crime of which he is guilty. We may feel sorry for the plight of the murderer or even understand the circumstances which led him to his crime. We may not feel sympathy with the wrong which he has done.

The presentation of evil is often essential for art or fiction or drama.

This in itself is not wrong provided:

a. That evil is not presented alluringly. Even if later in the film the evil is condemned or punished, it must not be allowed to appear so attractive that the audience's emotions are drawn to desire or approve so strongly that later the condemnation is forgotten and only the apparent joy of the sin remembered.

* [Martin Quigley and Daniel A. Lord], "Reasons Underlying the General Principles," *The Motion Picture Production Code*, rev. ed. (Washington: Motion Picture Association of America, 1956), pp. 9-10. Reprinted by permission of the Motion Picture Association of America, Inc.

b. That throughout, the audience feels sure that evil is wrong and good is right.

II. Correct standards of life shall, as far as possible, be presented.

A wide knowledge of life and of living is made possible through the film. When right standards are consistently presented, the motion picture exercises the most powerful influences. It builds character, develops right ideals, inculcates correct principles, and all this in attractive story form. If motion pictures consistently hold up for admiration high types of char- [**9/10**] acters and present stories that will affect lives for the better, they can become the most powerful natural force for the improvement of mankind.

III. Law—divine, natural or human— shall not be ridiculed, nor shall sympathy be created for its violation.

By natural law is understood the law which is written in the hearts of all mankind, the great underlying principles of right and justice dictated by conscience.

By human law is understood the law written by civilized nations.

1. The presentation of crimes against the law is often necessary for the carrying out of the plot. But the presentation must not throw sympathy with the crime as against the law nor with the criminal as against those who punish him.

2. The courts of the land should not be presented as unjust. This does not mean that a single court may not be represented as unjust, much less that a single court official must not be presented this way. But the court system of the country must not suffer as a result of this presentation.

.   .   .   .

Importance of the Entertainment Film*

MARTIN QUIGLEY (1890-1964) was for many years publisher of the weekly trade magazine *Motion Picture Herald*. He established the *Exhibitors' Herald* in Chicago in 1915 (having been deeply impressed by D. W. Griffith's film *The Birth of a Nation*) and acquired *Moving Picture World* (established 1907) in 1928. In 1931 he moved his publishing activities to New York with the purchase of the daily *Motion Picture News,* later called *Motion Picture Daily.* He was the coauthor of *The Motion Picture Production Code* (see "Reasons Underlying the General Principles," p. 99) and was the author of *Decency in Motion Pictures* (1937).

. . . .
The subject matter of the typical motion picture comprises the circumstances of life and living. It presents human beings in action and reaction upon one another. It shows people confronted with problems of conduct and behavior, and the manner and the ways they meet and solve, or attempt to solve, these problems. Of the essence of morality are the manner and the ways in which these problems are approached and solved.

Screen conduct, in the forcefulness of its presentation, in the public's aptitude for imitation of screen personalities whom they admire, influences, or tends to influence, the concepts and the conduct of an audience. Motion picture history reveals countless examples of the power of the screen to influence customs of dress and habits of public behavior. The result of such influence is readily discernible to all observers. Not so readily discernible, but certainly as wide and as thorough, are those other influences which result in concepts that determine attitudes toward those essential moralities which distinguish man from beast, moralities which either make or mar a civilization. [65/66]

. . . .

As an entertainment medium the motion picture is not a natural inheritor of academic responsibility. To assume that it is burdened with such responsibilities is both illogical and dangerous. It is illogical because the origin, the development, and the operation of the entertainment film place it clearly apart from the commonly accepted area of academic responsibility. The millionfold public to whose support it owes its existence does not hold it accountable for service in the field of education. Such assumption is dangerous because argument as to a function which the entertainment film might conceivably serve accomplishes nothing and tends only to hinder and confuse correct understanding of the responsibility inherent in the function which it actually does serve.

While the entertainment film should not be held accountable for a service which it is not consistent for it to render and which it does not purpose to render, there remains charged against it an enormous burden of responsibility in relation to the influence and effects arising out of its function of supplying to America and the world that form of public amusement which in interest, attractiveness, and audience effect transcends all others.

* Martin Quigley, from "Importance of the Entertainment Film," in *The Motion Picture Industry,* ed. Gordon S. Watkins, *Annals of the American Academy of Political and Social Science,* CCLIV (November, 1947), 65-69. Reprinted by permission of the American Academy of Political and Social Science.

The entertainment motion picture should serve those purposes traditionally associated with the ideal of the theater. It must, as a matter of primary responsibility, avoid any word or act which may reasonably be expected to lead to an invasion of public or private morality.

It should deal faithfully and honestly with whatever type and kind of subject matter it touches, whether in the current scene or in the field of history.

It should seek, in good faith, to promote cultural progress.

It should seek, in good faith, to widen the acceptance of right and useful standards of thought and conduct for the individual and for society. Controversial pleading and the pursuit of theoretical and experimental causes should have no place in the theatrical film. As a dramatic medium it is entitled to a reasonable measure of dramatic license—but not to a measure so loose and vague as to create and perpetuate serious misrepresentation relating to events and personalities, either of history or of our own day. [66/67]

. . . .

The motion picture industry makes the kind of motion pictures which it wishes to make—the wish being fathered by the individual producer's judgment of what the public wants. The eventual controlling influence over the kind of pictures the industry makes is exerted by the public's ballot as registered at the box office. It is not to be expected that the industry will be found responsive in any major degree to causes other than these, namely, its own wishes and the box-office declaration of public taste.

SAFEGUARDING THE MORAL CONTENT

The primary responsibility of the entertainment industry—the governing of the moral content of the entertainment film—involves a thoroughly practical problem. The producer, in order to sur-

vive in a highly competitive business in which mistakes may run into losses of millions of dollars, must, however great may be his good faith, have before him a rule of guidance. He must know with reasonable certainty, before his investment is made, whether the resultant film—if made in accordance with the rule—will be acceptable on moral grounds to the general public and will hold him free from responsible criticism and attack.

The entertainment industry in the United States has adopted such a rule in the Motion Picture Production Code. The code is based on the objective principles of morality in their relation to public entertainment. It involves no doctrinal distinctions. Its address is simply and solely to the fundamental criteria of human obligation and responsibility as set forth in the Ten Commandments.

While the code has accomplished no miracle of betterment, its effectiveness has been of enormous proportions. Day after day, for more than a decade and a half, it has blocked or lessened the flood of unfit material seeking access to the screen; it has guided the producer in the treatment of stories and characterizations; it has completely eliminated many objectionable types of dramatic incident and language. In the light of experience, it remains today the best conceivable instrument for the support and encouragement of those who, mindful of the potent moral and social influence of the entertainment film, are anxious to lend their efforts in a direction that will produce desirable and effective results.

But the existence of this code or any code, this system of regulation or any system of regulation, offers in itself no continuing assurance of the maintenance of right moral standards in motion picture entertainment. An enlightened and articulate public opinion is essential if this great influence over the thought and behavior of a vast public is to be a force for good and not evil.

. . . .

[The *Miracle* Case]*

Joseph Burstyn, Inc., motion-picture distributor, was the appellant in the so-called *Miracle* case, which was appealed to the United States Supreme Court in 1952. In question was the right of the appellant to exhibit the Italian motion picture *The Miracle* in the state of New York.

Lewis A. Wilson, commissioner of education of the state of New York (1950-55), was the appellee in the case. Associate Justice Tom C. Clark in this selection delivers the opinion of the Court. Although the decision of the Court was unanimous, two concurring opinions were written that added further considerations to the case.

JOSEPH BURSTYN, INC. *v.* WILSON, COMMISSIONER OF EDUCATION OF NEW YORK, *et al.*

APPEAL FROM THE COURT OF APPEALS OF NEW YORK.

No. 522. Argued April 24, 1952.—Decided May 26, 1952. [495/497]

. . . .

Mr. Justice Clark delivered the opinion of the Court.

The issue here is the constitutionality, under the First and Fourteenth Amendments, of a New York statute which permits the banning of motion picture films on the ground that they are "sacrilegious." That statute makes it unlawful "to exhibit, or to sell, lease or lend for exhibition at any place of amusement for pay or in connection with any business in the state of New York, any motion picture film or reel [with specified exceptions not relevant here], unless there is at the time in full force and effect a valid license or permit therefor of the education department. . . ."[1] The statute further provides:

"The director of the [motion picture] division [of the education department] or, when author-ized by the regents, the officers of a local office or bureau shall cause to be promptly examined every motion picture film submitted to them as herein required, and unless such film or a part thereof is obscene, indecent, immoral, inhuman, sacrilegious, or is of such a character that its exhibition would tend to corrupt morals or incite to crime, shall issue a license therefor. If such director or, when so authorized, such officer shall not license any film submitted, he shall furnish to the applicant therefor a written report of the reasons for his refusal and a description of each rejected part of a film not rejected in toto."[2]

Appellant is a corporation engaged in the business of distributing motion pictures. It owns the exclusive rights to distribute throughout the United States a film produced in Italy entitled "The Miracle." On November 30, 1950, after having examined the picture, the motion picture division of the New York education depart- [497/498] ment, acting under the statute quoted above, issued to appellant a license authorizing exhibition of "The Miracle," with English subtitles, as one part of a trilogy called "Ways of Love."[3]

[1] McKinney's N. Y. Laws, 1947, Education Law, § 129.

[2] *Id.*, § 122.

[3] The motion picture division had previously issued a license for exhibition of "The Miracle" without English subtitles, but the film was never shown under that license.

* *Joseph Burstyn, Inc. v. Wilson, Commissioner of Education of the State of New York, et al.,* 343 U.S. 495, 497-506 (1952).

Thereafter, for a period of approximately eight weeks, "Ways of Love" was exhibited publicly in a motion picture theater in New York City under an agreement between appellant and the owner of the theater whereby appellant received a stated percentage of the admission price.

During this period, the New York State Board of Regents, which by statute is made the head of the education department,[4] received "hundreds of letters, telegrams, post cards, affidavits and other communications" both protesting against and defending the public exhibition of "The Miracle."[5] The Chancellor of the Board of Regents requested three members of the Board to view the picture and to make a report to the entire Board. After viewing the film, this committee reported to the Board that in its opinion there was basis for the claim that the picture was "sacrilegious." Thereafter, on January 19, 1951, the Regents directed appellant to show cause, at a hearing to be held on January 30, why its license to show "The Miracle" should not be rescinded on that ground. Appellant appeared at this hearing, which was conducted by the same three-member committee of the Regents which had previously viewed the picture, and challenged the jurisdiction of the committee and of the Regents to proceed with the case. With the consent of the committee, various interested persons and [498/499] organizations submitted to it briefs and exhibits bearing upon the merits of the picture and upon the constitutional and statutory questions involved. On February 16, 1951, the Regents, after viewing "The Miracle," determined that it was "sacrilegious" and for that reason ordered the Commissioner of Education to rescind appellant's license to exhibit the picture. The Commissioner did so.

Appellant brought the present action in the New York courts to review the determination of the Regents.[6] Among the claims advanced by appellant were (1) that the statute violates the Fourteenth Amendment as a prior restraint upon freedom of speech and of the press; (2) that it is in-valid under the same Amendment as a violation of the guaranty of separate church and state and as a prohibition of the free exercise of religion; and, (3) that the term "sacrilegious" is so vague and indefinite as to offend due process. The Appellate Division rejected all of appellant's contentions and upheld the Regents' determination. 278 App. Div. 253, 104 N. Y. S. 2d 740. On appeal the New York Court of Appeals, two judges dissenting, affirmed the order of the Appellate Division. 303 N. Y. 242, 101 N. E. 2d 665. The case is here on appeal. 28 U. S. C. § 1257 (2).

As we view the case, we need consider only appellant's contention that the New York statute is an unconstitutional abridgment of free speech and a free press. In *Mutual Film Corp.* v. *Industrial Comm'n,* 236 U. S. 230 (1915), a distributor of motion pictures sought to enjoin the enforcement of an Ohio statute which required the prior approval of a board of censors before any motion [499/500] picture could be publicly exhibited in the state, and which directed the board to approve only such films as it adjudged to be "of a moral, educational or amusing and harmless character." The statute was assailed in part as an unconstitutional abridgment of the freedom of the press guaranteed by the First and Fourteenth Amendments. The District Court rejected this contention, stating that the first eight Amendments were not a restriction on state action. 215 F. 138, 141 (D. C. N. D. Ohio 1914). On appeal to this Court, plaintiff in its brief abandoned this claim and contended merely that the statute in question violated the freedom of speech and publication guaranteed by the Constitution of Ohio. In affirming the decree of the District Court denying injunctive relief, this Court stated:

[4] McKinney's N. Y. Laws, 1947, Education Law, § 101; see also N. Y. Const., Art. V, § 4.
[5] Stipulation between appellant and appellee, R. 86.
[6] The action was brought under Article 78 of the New York Civil Practice Act, Gilbert-Bliss N. Y. Civ. Prac., Vol. 6B, 1944, 1949 Supp., § 1283 *et seq.* See also McKinney's N. Y. Laws, 1947, Education Law, § 124.

"It cannot be put out of view that the exhibition of moving pictures is a business pure and simple, originated and conducted for profit, like other spectacles, not to be regarded, nor intended to be regarded by the Ohio constitution, we think, as part of the press of the country or as organs of public opinion."[7]

In a series of decisions beginning with *Gitlow* v. *New York*, 268 U. S. 652 (1925), this Court held that the liberty of speech and of the press which the First Amendment guarantees against abridgment by the federal government is within the liberty safeguarded by the Due Process Clause of the Fourteenth Amendment from invasion by state action.[8] That principle has been [500/501] followed and reaffirmed to the present day. Since this series of decisions came after the *Mutual* decision, the present case is the first to present squarely to us the question whether motion pictures are within the ambit of protection which the First Amendment, through the Fourteenth, secures to any form of "speech" or "the press."[9]

It cannot be doubted that motion pictures are a significant medium for the communication of ideas. They may affect public attitudes and behavior in a variety of ways, ranging from direct espousal of a political or social doctrine to the subtle shaping of thought which characterizes all artistic expression.[10] The importance of motion pictures as an organ of public opinion is not lessened by the fact that they are designed to entertain as well as to inform. As was said in *Winters* v. *New York*, 333 U. S. 507, 510 (1948):

"The line between the informing and the entertaining is too elusive for the protection of that basic right [a free press]. Everyone is familiar with instances of propaganda through fiction. What is one man's amusement, teaches another's doctrine."

It is urged that motion pictures do not fall within the First Amendment's aegis because their production, distribution, and exhibition is a large-scale business conducted for private profit. We cannot agree. That books, newspapers, and magazines are published and sold for profit does not prevent them from being a form of expression whose liberty is safeguarded by the First Amend- [501/502] ment.[11] We fail to see why operation for profit should have any different effect in the case of motion pictures.

It is further urged that motion pictures possess a greater capacity for evil, particularly among the youth of a community, than other modes of expression. Even if one were to accept this hypothesis, it does not follow that motion pictures should be disqualified from First Amendment protection. If there be capacity for evil it may be relevant in determining the permissible scope of community control, but it does not authorize substantially unbridled censorship such as we have here.

For the foregoing reasons, we conclude that expression by means of motion pictures is included within the free speech and free press guaranty of the First and Fourteenth Amendments. To the extent that language in the opinion in *Mutual Film Corp.* v. *Industrial Comm'n, supra,* is out of harmony with the views here set forth, we no longer adhere to it.[12]

To hold that liberty of expression by means of motion pictures is guaranteed by the First and Fourteenth Amendments, however, is not the end of our problem. It does not follow that the Constitution requires absolute freedom to exhibit every

---

[7] 236 U. S., at 244.

[8] *Gitlow* v. *New York*, 268 U. S. 652, 666 (1925); *Stromberg* v. *California*, 283 U. S. 359, 368 (1931); *Near* v. *Minnesota ex rel. Olson*, 283 U. S. 697, 707 (1931); *Grosjean* v. *American Press Co.*, 297 U. S. 233, 244 (1936); *De Jonge* v. *Oregon*, 299 U. S. 353, 364 (1937); *Lovell* v. *Griffin*, 303 U. S. 444, 450 (1938); *Schneider* v. *State*, 308 U. S. 147, 160 (1939).

[9] See *Lovell* v. *Griffin*, 303 U. S. 444, 452 (1938).

[10] See Inglis, Freedom of the Movies (1947), 20-24; Klapper, The Effects of Mass Media (1950), *passim;* Note, Motion Pictures and the First Amendment, 60 Yale L. J. 696, 704-708 (1951), and sources cited therein.

[11] See *Grosjean* v. *American Press Co.*, 297 U. S. 233 (1936); *Thomas* v. *Collins*, 323 U. S. 516, 531 (1945).

[12] See *United States* v. *Paramount Pictures, Inc.*, 334 U. S. 131, 166 (1948): "We have no doubt that moving pictures, like newspapers and radio, are included in the press whose freedom is guaranteed by the First Amendment." It is not without significance that talking pictures were first produced in 1926, eleven years after the *Mutual* decision. Hampton, A History of the Movies (1931), 382-383.

motion picture of every kind at all times and all places. That much is evident from the series of decisions of this Court with respect to other [502/503] media of communication of ideas.[13] Nor does it follow that motion pictures are necessarily subject to the precise rules governing any other particular method of expression. Each method tends to present its own peculiar problems. But the basic principles of freedom of speech and the press, like the First Amendment's command, do not vary. Those principles, as they have frequently been enunciated by this Court, make freedom of expression the rule. There is no justification in this case for making an exception to that rule.

The statute involved here does not seek to punish, as a past offense, speech or writing falling within the permissible scope of subsequent punishment. On the contrary, New York requires that permission to communicate ideas be obtained in advance from state officials who judge the content of the words and pictures sought to be communicated. This Court recognized many years ago that such a previous restraint is a form of infringement upon freedom of expression to be especially condemned. *Near* v. *Minnesota ex rel. Olson,* 283 U. S. 697 (1931). The Court there recounted the history which indicates that a major purpose of the First Amendment guaranty of a free press was to prevent prior restraints upon publication, although it was carefully pointed out that the liberty of the press is not limited to that protection.[14] It was further stated that "the protection even as to previous restraint is not absolutely unlimited. But the limitation has been recognized only [503/504] in exceptional cases." *Id.,* at 716. In the light of the First Amendment's history and of the *Near* decision, the State has a heavy burden to demonstrate that the limitation challenged here presents such an exceptional case.

New York's highest court says there is "nothing mysterious" about the statutory provision applied in this case: "It is sim-

ply this: that no religion, as that word is understood by the ordinary, reasonable person, shall be treated with contempt, mockery, scorn and ridicule. . . ."[15] This is far from the kind of narrow exception to freedom of expression which a state may carve out to satisfy the adverse demands of other interests of society.[16] In seeking to apply the broad and all-inclusive definition of "sacrilegious" given by the New York courts, the censor is set adrift upon a boundless sea amid a myriad of conflicting currents of religious views, with no [504/505] charts but those provided by the most vocal and powerful orthodoxies. New York cannot vest such unlimited restraining control over motion pictures in a censor. Cf. *Kunz* v. *New York,* 340 U. S. 290 (1951).[17] Under such a standard the most careful and tolerant censor would find it virtually impossible to avoid favor-

[13] *E. g., Feiner* v. *New York,* 340 U. S. 315 (1951) ; *Kovacs* v. *Cooper,* 336 U. S. 77 (1949) ; *Chaplinsky* v. *New Hampshire,* 315 U. S. 568 (1942) ; *Cox* v. *New Hampshire,* 312 U. S. 569 (1941).

[14] *Near* v. *Minnesota ex rel. Olson,* 283 U. S. 697, 713-719 (1931) ; see also *Lovell* v. *Griffin,* 303 U. S. 444, 451-452 (1938) ; *Grosjean* v. *American Press Co.,* 297 U. S. 233, 245-250 (1936) ; *Patterson* v. *Colorado,* 205 U. S. 454, 462 (1907).

[15] 303 N. Y. 242, 258, 101 N. E. 2d 665, 672. At another point the Court of Appeals gave "sacrilegious" the following definition: "the act of violating or profaning anything sacred." *Id.,* at 255, 101 N. E. 2d at 670. The Court of Appeals also approved the Appellate Division's interpretation : "As the court below said of the statute in question, 'All it purports to do is to bar a visual caricature of religious beliefs held sacred by one sect or another . . . .' " *Id.,* at 258, 101 N. E. 2d at 672. Judge Fuld, dissenting, concluded from all the statements in the majority opinion that "the basic criterion appears to be whether the film treats a religious theme in such a manner as to offend the religious beliefs of any group of persons. If the film does have that effect, and it is 'offered as a form of entertainment,' it apparently falls within the statutory ban regardless of the sincerity and good faith of the producer of the film, no matter how temperate the treatment of the theme, and no matter how unlikely a public disturbance or breach of the peace. The drastic nature of such a ban is highlighted by the fact that the film in question makes no direct attack on, or criticism of, any religious dogma or principle, and it is not claimed to be obscene, scurrilous, intemperate or abusive." *Id.,* at 271-272, 101 N. E. 2d at 680.

[16] Cf. *Thornhill* v. *Alabama,* 310 U. S. 88, 97 (1940) ; *Stromberg* v. *California,* 283 U. S. 359, 369-370 (1931).

[17] Cf. *Niemotko* v. *Maryland,* 340 U. S. 268 (1951) ; *Saia* v. *New York,* 334 U. S. 558 (1948) ; *Largent* v. *Texas,* 318 U. S. 418 (1943) ; *Lovell* v. *Griffin,* 303 U. S. 444 (1938).

ing one religion over another, and he would be subject to an inevitable tendency to ban the expression of unpopular sentiments sacred to a religious minority. Application of the "sacrilegious" test, in these or other respects, might raise substantial questions under the First Amendment's guaranty of separate church and state with freedom of worship for all.[18] However, from the standpoint of freedom of speech and the press, it is enough to point out that the state has no legitimate interest in protecting any or all religions from views distasteful to them which is sufficient to justify prior restraints upon the expression of those views. It is not the business of government in our nation to suppress real or imagined attacks upon a particular religious doctrine, whether they appear in publications, speeches, or motion pictures.[19]

Since the term "sacrilegious" is the sole standard under attack here, it is not necessary for us to decide, for ex- [505/506] ample, whether a state may censor motion pictures under a clearly drawn statute designed and applied to prevent the showing of obscene films. That is a very different question from the one now before us.[20] We hold only that under the First and Fourteenth Amendments a state may not ban a film on the basis of a censor's conclusion that it is "sacrilegious."

Reversed.

[18] See *Cantwell* v. *Connecticut*, 310 U. S. 296 (1940).

[19] See the following statement by Mr. Justice Roberts, speaking for a unanimous Court in *Cantwell* v. *Connecticut*, 310 U. S. 296, 310 (1940):

"In the realm of religious faith, and in that of political belief, sharp differences arise. In both fields the tenets of one man may seem the rankest error to his neighbor. To persuade others to his own point of view, the pleader, as we know, at times, resorts to exaggeration, to vilification of men who have been, or are, prominent in church or state, and even to false statement. But the people of this nation have ordained in the light of history, that, in spite of the probability of excesses and abuses, these liberties are, in the long view, essential to enlightened opinion and right conduct on the part of the citizens of a democracy.

"The essential characteristic of these liberties is, that under their shield many types of life, character, opinion and belief can develop unmolested and unobstructed. Nowhere is this shield more necessary than in our own country for a people composed of many races and of many creeds."

[20] In the *Near* case, this Court stated that "the primary requirements of decency may be enforced against obscene publications." 283 U. S. 697, 716. In *Chaplinsky* v. *New Hampshire*, 315 U. S. 568, 571-572 (1942), Mr. Justice Murphy stated for a unanimous Court: "There are certain well-defined and narrowly limited classes of speech, the prevention and punishment of which have never been thought to raise any Constitutional problem. These include the lewd and obscene, the profane, the libelous, and the insulting or 'fighting' words— those which by their very utterance inflict injury or tend to incite an immediate breach of the peace." But see *Kovacs* v. *Cooper*, 336 U. S. 77, 82 (1949): "When ordinances undertake censorship of speech or religious practices before permitting their exercise, the Constitution forbids their enforcement."

Movies and Censorship*

BOSLEY CROWTHER (1905-   ), a graduate of Princeton University, joined the staff of the New York *Times* in 1928 as a reporter. In 1932 he became assistant drama editor and since 1940 has been motion-picture reviewer. He is the author of a history of Metro-Goldwyn-Mayer, *The Lion's Share* (1957), and a biography of Louis B. Mayer, *Hollywood Rajah* (1960).

"What in heaven's name is happening to the movies?" an anxious mother said to me recently at a private dinner party in a New York suburban home. "The other day I took my 15-year-old daughter to see one she particularly asked to see—an Italian movie about a mother and her daughter— and I was absolutely appalled. You probably know the picture. At the climax, the mother and daughter both were raped! No doubt about it! And by a gang of soldiers! I was never so shocked and embarrassed at anything!"

Of course, I knew the picture. It was a fine and successful Italian film, "Two Women," starring Sophia Loren, which had been one of the outstanding dramas of the year. To be sure, it was intensely realistic, with no punches pulled, no curtains drawn, but it carried a powerful message of love and compassion. I asked my friend what she and her daughter thought of it. [1/2]

"Well," she replied, with some caution, "it was a very moving, a very disturbing film. We were both rather deeply shaken. But, really, it's not the sort of thing I think a child should see. Where are the censors? Where is the Hays office? I'm surprised they permit such a thing. We never saw stuff like that in the movies of Ginger Rogers and Loretta Young when I was a girl!"

Here, in one sudden burst of feeling, was concentrated and conveyed a fair sample of sentiment towards the movies that many parents are expressing these days, disturbed as they are by the candor and rawness of some pictures and by the public objections of certain religious and civic elements. Here, too, was a typical example of the lack of understanding of the majority of people today about what is happening in the realm of motion pictures.

THE CHANGING MOTION PICTURES

For the fact is that large and significant changes in the culture of motion pictures have been occurring in the past decade— and these are but a part of and in line with a whole complex of developments and shifts in our ways of living, our facilities for pleasure, our educational expansion, and our intellectual growth.

The characteristics of the motion picture audience have changed considerably in the past fifteen years, due largely to the effect that television has had upon the American people and upon the use of our leisure time. The number of movies available each year for the theatre-going public to see has been steadily declining, as has the number of conventional theatres in which

* Bosley Crowther, from *Movies and Censorship*, Public Affairs Pamphlet No. 332 (New York: Public Affairs Committee, 1962), pp. 1-2, 8-28.

these films may be seen. The nature and quality of theatrical motion pictures have been changing perceptibly, and the level of sophistication of movies in general has shown an appreciable rise. **[2/8]**

. . . .

FOREIGN FILMS

Withal, there has been a marked expansion in one area of motion picture culture that was of comparatively little importance before the emergence of TV. That is the area of foreign pictures, those French, Italian, Swedish, and other films imported to this country. These films, which were generally imported in limited numbers and for only a limited audience until after World War II, are now a considerable element in movie culture and trade.

What happened was that, with the falloff in attendance and the decrease in the number of American films, certain theatres in the larger cities turned to the exhibition of imported films. These pictures, distinguished by generally more realistic and sophisticated content than American films, attracted a more perceptive and demanding audience. Shown in what were at first called "art houses," they began pulling, indeed, a marginal element of the population that seldom went to films.

Now the Italian films of Roberto Rossellini, Vittorio de Sica, Federico Fellini, and Michaelangelo Antonioni; the films of the so-called French "new wave" directors such as Francois Truffaut, Roger Vadim, Alain Resnais; the films of the Swedish Ingmar Bergman and even Akira Kurosawa's Japanese films have opened new territories of thought and emotional stimulation for the American audience and have reached an opposite pole of cultivation from that of the cheap American "B" pictures, which they have in a sense replaced. . . . **[8/9]**

. . . .

HISTORY OF CENSORSHIP

The first ordinance empowering a censor to look at motion pictures in advance of their exhibition in theatres and determine whether they were morally fit for the public to see was adopted by the city of Chicago in 1907. The responsibility for making the determination was assigned to the police. (Censorship is still **[9/10]** practiced in Chicago under a special Mayor's committee.)

New York City set up reviewing arrangements in 1909, and other cities followed. The first state censorship board was adopted in Pennsylvania in 1911; Ohio and Kansas came next in 1913.

At first, the theatre men were agreeable to the arrangements which they felt would provide them with a flow of pictures that had been officially approved and thus free them from the frequent harassment of censorious elements in their communities. But soon it was discovered by film producers and distributors that the practice was jeopardizing many of their films—and was also adding the heavy expense of the inevitable reviewing and licensing fees charged by the censor boards.

. . . .

FIRST CHALLENGE TO CENSORSHIP

The first all-out formidable challenge to the system of censorship as a denial to motion pictures of the right of free press and free speech was taken to the United States Supreme Court in 1915 by a distributor in Ohio. Lawyers argue that pre-release policing of motion pictures constitutes illegal prior restraint. Such prior restraint cannot legally be imposed on newspapers, books, or magazines. This is the classic and continuing argument against censorship.

However, the United States Supreme Court did not take this view in 1915. In a historic ruling, it said: "The exhibition of motion pictures is a business pure and simple, originated and conducted for profit, like other spectacles, not to be regarded, nor intended to be regarded . . . as a part of the press of the country or as organs of public opinion."

This judgment put the stamp of legitimacy on film censorship and became the accepted doctrine during the next four decades. It left the motion picture, then growing by leaps and bounds, without legal safeguards or defenses against those that would impose restraints on it. Within a few years after that ruling, a succession of states passed censorship laws—Maryland, Virginia, New York, Florida, and Massachusetts. [10/11]

Typical of their mandate was that of the New York law, which provided that a film be licensed "unless such film or a part thereof is obscene, indecent, immoral, inhuman, sacrilegious or is of such character that its exhibition would tend to corrupt morals or incite to crime." The determination of whether it contained these elements was left to a dubiously qualified panel of state-employed reviewers.

By 1922 there were censorship bills before the legislature of thirty-two states and a surge of moral indignation against the movies was once more billowing across the land. [11/12]

. . . .

THE MOTION PICTURE INDUSTRY'S CODE

It was at this point that industry leaders, well aware that there had been an excess of bolder pictures made after World War I—and also that the public had been excited and aroused with elaborate reports of a few private scandals that had occurred among the people of Hollywood—pulled themselves together and formed their own organization for the advancement of their public relations and the political protection of the industry. Will H. Hays, then Postmaster General of the United States, was prevailed upon to accept the position of chairman of the organization which was

called the Motion Picture Producers and Distributors of America (MPPDA). Within a year, Mr. Hays, who was a remarkable combination of shrewdness and piety, succeeded in having all the pending censorship bills killed or pigeonholed.

With a great deal of skill and persuasion, Mr. Hays continued to stave off the objections of the screen's moral critics and the further spread of censorship all through the 1920's, but with the arrival of sound and talking films, which brought a new element of realism and theatrical sophistication to the screen, there were fresh assaults upon the medium for its exposures of "sex and violence."

To pacify these critics, Mr. Hays recommended to the MPPDA that it adopt a "code of morals" drawn up by a trade paper publisher and a Roman Catholic priest as a guide to what should and should not be in pictures. This was the origin of the so-called "Hays code," adopted in 1930. Significantly, the code was but an arbitrary restraint upon the operation of the member producers. They could abide by its regulations or leave them alone.

However, three years later, when the Roman Catholic Church, concerned about the content of motion pictures, established its Legion of Decency to play an active role in watchdogging the medium, the MPPDA found it expedient to "put teeth into the code." It set up a Production Code Administration which was [12/13] organized to read all film scripts of its member producers, advise as to the undesirable elements in them, and then pass upon the acceptability of the finished films. Those acceptable were given what was known as the "seal," and were free to be released and shown in the theatres of the member companies that had agreed to show only Code-approved films.

Thus, under definite pressure, mainly from the Catholic Church, the motion picture industry established its own device of self-restraint, which was apart and different entirely from the various agencies of state and municipal censorship.

So, through the 1930's and 1940's, the American motion picture was under two moral controls of a generally rigid nature —the initial control of the Production Code, and then the second line of control in the state and municipal censor boards.

LEGION OF DECENCY

Beyond these stood yet another considerable barrier to be passed by the film seeking wide circulation. That was the "rating" of the National Legion of Decency. Shortly after its formation, the Legion began a practice of reviewing and classifying films according to their moral content and their suitability for showing to audiences. These classifications now are: "A-1," films deemed morally unobjectionable for general patronage; "A-2," morally unobjectionable for adults and adolescents; "A-3," morally unobjectionable for adults; "B," morally objectionable in part for all persons; and "C," totally condemned.

These ratings, arrived at by a panel of voluntary lay persons (mostly women, members of the Motion Picture Department of the International Federation of Catholic Alumnae), receive wide circulation in the Catholic press, and annually members of the faith are asked in their churches to take a pledge to be guided by the recommendations in their and their families' film going.

Thus, while the Legion's ratings do not impose enforced restraints and are, of course, a legitimate service of the church to [13/14] its parishioners, the effect of a "B" or "C" rating in many Catholic-populated communities has been found a liability to a film. Some theatres in such communities have refrained from showing "B" or "C" films, especially when priests in such communities have brought overt or subtle pressures to bear, such as threats of Catholic boycott of the theatres.

WEAKENING RESTRAINTS

Such was the general picture until after World War II. Then began the great change in the patterns of motion picture attendance described earlier, and the inevitable challenge to the whole structure of restraints was begun by new elements moving into the field of films.

One reason for the weakening of the structure of restraints was the long-threatened dissolution of the monopoly structure of the motion picture industry. When the major motion picture companies (which were the chief factors of intra-industry control) were forced in 1948 to divest themselves of their theatre holdings and stick solely to the production and distribution of films, the tight grip which had enforced the rulings of the Production Code was loosed. With the control of theatres by producers eliminated, theatres that chose to show films without the seal of approval could do so. And since many of the films imported from Italy and France did not have seals, there was an increasing temptation for the theatres to disregard that lack.

THE ISSUE OF FREEDOM OF THE PRESS

It was in connection with a ruling of the United States Supreme Court on "divorcement" of theatres that the first hint came that the court might now be ready to look upon motion pictures differently from the way it had looked upon them in 1915. In conveying the court's opinion, Justice William O. Douglas wrote: "We have no doubt that moving pictures, like newspapers and radio, are included in the press whose freedom is guaranteed by the First Amendment." [14/15]

This was an open invitation to challenge statutory censorship, and the motion picture people moved to do so in several instances. But it was not until four years later that two cases ultimately came before the U.S. Supreme Court almost simultaneously. It is interesting that the first to be ruled on—and now the historic one of these—served to protect the right to show one of the new imported foreign films.

THE CASE OF "THE MIRACLE"

The film was a short dramatic fiction called "The Miracle," made in Italy by Roberto Rossellini and having Anna Magnani as its star. It told a story of an unmarried peasant woman, a bit of a simpleton, who became pregnant by a passing vagrant and then thought, in her simple faith, that Saint Joseph had caused her to conceive. The manner in which she was taunted in her village and her later ordeal of the birth were the solemn and poignant substance of it.

This film, presented by Joseph Burstyn, an independent importer, was initially passed by the New York censor and opened at the Paris Theatre, a so-called "art house," in December, 1950. Twelve days later, the New York City Commissioner of Licenses informed the theatre that he found the film "officially and personally blasphemous" and threatened to suspend the theatre's license if the film were not stopped. In the course of the next few weeks, there were several new developments.

The film was temporarily removed, then reinstated, the action of the Commissioner was taken to court and, on January 5, it was ruled that the License Commissioner had no authority to stop the showing of a film he did not like.

Meanwhile, the Legion of Decency had condemned the film and formidable individuals and groups of organized Roman Catholics, including Francis Cardinal Spellman of New York, had expressed their contempt for it.

Now the film was re-reviewed by a three-man committee of the Board of Regents, under which the New York censor is main-[15/16] tained. This committee ruled it "sacrilegious." Hearings were then held on the authority of the Regents to revoke a license. They ruled they had the power. Burstyn now sued the Regents for denial of a license on constitutional grounds. The "Miracle" case dragged through the state courts and finally reached the top court in the land.

In the meantime, another case arose out of the censoring of an American film. "Pinky" (a film about a Negro girl who had "passed" for white in the North returning to her home in the South and being subject to strong racial discrimination) had been banned by municipal action in Marshall, Texas, as it had also been banned in other cities of the South. The manager of a theatre in Marshall was induced to make a test. He showed the film, was fined $300, and took an appeal. This case reached the Supreme Court simultaneously with the "Miracle" case. **[16/17]** . . . "The Miracle" was the first to be passed on. On May 26, 1952, the court handed down a unanimous decision which removed the New York ban, holding "sacrilege" not a cause for which a state could censor a film.

More important, however, the decision boldly proclaimed that motion pictures are a medium of communication and are entitled to the constitutional guarantees of free speech and free press under the First and Fourteenth Amendments. This finding, of course, reversed the previous ruling of the court in the Ohio case that had stood for forty years. However, it did not automatically render null and void all censorship statutes then in force. It simply stood as a judicial guide to state legislatures or courts. All that the "Miracle" decision specifically nullified was the validity of "sacrilege."

Indeed, the court stated clearly, "Since the term 'sacrilegious' is the sole standard under attack here, it is not necessary for us to decide, for example, whether a state may censor motion pictures under a clearly drawn statute designed and applied to prevent the showing of obscene films. That is a very different question from the one now before us." And this has remained the considerable and critical question ever since the revolutionary ruling in the "Miracle" case.

One week after that ruling, the decision in the "Pinky" case came through. It repeated the court's determination that motion pictures are a part of the free press and, in effect, held that a film could not be banned from showing because it might offend the prejudices of a community.

EFFECT ON CENSOR BOARDS

Thus the demand that all censor boards justify their rulings and themselves has been a persistent feature for the past ten years.

But censor boards and the censor-minded die hard, and the running battle to reduce the scope and authority of the censors has been tough. In a series of cases ruled upon by the Supreme [17/18] Court since the "Miracle" ruling, the authority of the state censor boards has been whittled away to the point where it is limited now to the determination of obscenity. And the court has ruled that the test of obscenity must be "whether, to the average person applying contemporary community standards, the dominant theme of the material taken as a whole appeals to prurient interests."

The first state to give up censorship after the "Miracle" case was Ohio. In January 1955, the court of appeals in Franklin County of that state declared its censorship statute illegal and unconstitutional, and efforts to pass new censorship bills in the Ohio legislature have been unsuccessful. The Pennsylvania Supreme Court, in a six-to-one decision, declared the censorship act of that state unconstitutional on March 13, 1956. The state adopted a new statute in 1959, which provided for classification of motion pictures as to those unsuitable for persons under seventeen as well as those unsuitable for all audiences, and it was made a criminal offense to show a film that had been classified unsuitable. This statute, too, was killed by the State Su-

preme Court, which held that it violated the free speech and free press guarantees of the Pennsylvania constitution.

Massachusetts and Florida have also abandoned state censorship. New York, Maryland, Kansas, and Virginia are the only states that persist.

However, the practice of censorship on the municipal level remains and is a sporadic problem for film distributors. Chicago, for instance, still has its local censor. Although his power is limited to rulings on obscenity, he sometimes takes in a wide range with this power, compelling the film distributors to seek redress in the courts.

THE CURRENT SITUATION

An effort to get the United States Supreme Court to take the final step and rule all censorship—or prior restraint of movies—unconstitutional was made in 1960-61 by a foreign film distribu- [18/19] tor who applied for a license to distribute a film in Chicago but refused to submit the film for the censor to view. In a 5-4 decision, the court upheld the city's right of inspection on the ground that "it is not for this court to limit the state in its selection of the remedy it deems most effective" to cope with the problem of determining whether a piece of material contains matter against which the community should be on guard.

In a dissenting opinion, Chief Justice Earl Warren said of this reasoning, "It comes perilously close to holding that not only may motion pictures be censored but that a licensing scheme may also be applied to newspapers, books, periodicals, radio, television, public speeches, and every other medium of expression. The court in no way explains why moving pictures should be treated differently than any other form of expression."

Here the situation now stands, with censorship still being practiced, with the censor—particularly the one in New York State—often making rather broad interpretations of the prevalence of obscenity, but with lawyers generally expecting that, within the next few years, there may well be a Supreme Court ruling that will render unconstitutional the whole practice of prior restraint.

Of course, this would not mean that the showing of movies of a grossly obscene or pornographic nature—movies that are clearly designed to appeal solely to prurient interests—might not be challenged by the police and their exhibitors arrested and made to stand trial *after* they have shown the film. This would be consistent with the practice of safeguarding the community against the circulation of offensive materials in other media, including television and radio.

INDUSTRY CODE REVISED

In line with the steady erosion of the extent and effectiveness of censorship, there has been a parallel moderation of the restraints of the film industry's Production Code. Aware that the ideas and customs of society are undergoing change and that the spread of [19/20] education and sophistication has been rapid since World War II, the Production Code administrators made an extensive revision of the code in 1956.

The previous absolute taboos against depicting narcotic traffic, prostitution, abortion, and kidnapping were removed. Miscegenation was no longer a forbidden topic. Ordinary profanity (such as "hell," "damn," etc.) was cleared when dramatically valid and used with discretion, and the code's administrators were allowed to be more "liberal" in interpreting the other guiding rules. In [20/21] 1961, the code was further interpreted to permit reference to homosexuality, so long as it is treated "within the careful limits of good taste."

IS "CLASSIFICATION" THE ANSWER?

While the informed and comprehending public has generally accepted as the right and democratic thing the steady elimination of pre-release film censorship and has conceded the cultural desirability of liberalizing the code, there continues an intelligent and responsible segment which feels that some method should be found to differentiate between films that are suitable for everybody and those which only adults should see. This feeling is based upon the notion which seems ingrained in our thinking that children may be harmed by seeing films of a particularly candid or violent nature, just as the mother described previously assumed that something "bad" had happened to her daughter from seeing a drama which included a double rape.

In recent years there has been a growing sentiment on the part of parent organizations and church groups that "classification" is the answer—that in this procedure lies the best way of keeping children from seeing pictures the adults think they shouldn't see.

What is classification? It is the practice of estimating films on the basis of their moral and emotional content (not their artistic qualities) and grading them according to whether they are suitable for everybody or just persons over a certain age to see.

COMPULSORY CLASSIFICATION

Classification may be of two sorts—and in the difference between them lies a wide range of philosophical disagreement and likely impracticality. The first is compulsory classification. This would be a function of a state (or municipal) authority which would classify all films according to their suitability. Then its classifications would be enforced by law. A theatre manager who permitted a person under the legally established age to see a film [21/22] classed as not fit for such a person would be subject to prosecution and penalty. This sort of classification would be perilously close to censorship.

ADVISORY CLASSIFICATION

The other sort of classification—the sort that is most widely advocated by the various organizations now leaning heavily towards this new protective means—is termed advisory classification. Under it, the classifying would be done by either a statutory agency or one acceptable to the populace, such as the Code administrators of the motion picture industry, and its advices on the suitability of individual pictures would be publicized with each one as it was released. Thus parents would presumably be guided by this advice as to what films were suitable (or unsuitable) for their children to see. No penalty would be imposed upon a theatre that admitted a child to a disapproved film.

The arguments *pro* and *con* classification are many and variable, and the individual's readiness to accept them seems to depend largely upon the slant of his sentiments. Here again the extent of comprehension is generally limited. Much more thought should be given to the matter before any big decisions are made.

For instance, a basic assumption by the advocates of classification, both compulsory and advisory, is that it is reasonable and practicable to pass a judgment as to the suitability (or unsuitability) of a picture for *all* persons under a certain age. Corollary to it is their assumption that it would be reasonable and practicable for *all* parents to accept this more or less official judgment as fitting for their children. The flaws in these assumptions are vigorously cited by those who oppose classification.

In the first place, they note that the establishment of a cut-off age would be completely arbitrary and unrealistic because chronological age is a hopelessly unreliable index to the intellectual, emotional, and social maturity of a person. There are as many youngsters at 16 who have the sophistication and stability of the [22/23] average person at 21 as there are youngsters at 16 who have the emotional stability of the average person at 10. There is

no scientific way of measuring the impact of dramatic and entertainment material upon the mind of a child.

The advocates hold that, regardless of the logic of this argument, the state nonetheless establishes age levels below which individuals cannot legally do certain things such as buy alcoholic beverages, obtain a license to drive an automobile, or be employed in a steady job. Therefore, there is no reason why an arbitrary age level should not be set for the suitability of viewing films.

The answer to this by the opposition is that the effect of film content cannot be measured and thus can in no way be compared with the measurable effect of alcohol on a teen-ager or the statistical incidence of automobile accidents involving young drivers. There is dependable medical and police evidence for the latter; there is no substantial evidence—only conjecture—as to the "harmfulness" of films.

WHOSE STANDARDS?

Then there is the question of the standards of suitability that would prevail. Whose experience—or taste—would determine the official judgment of a film? At present, the greatest anxiety of the advocates of classification is the moral content of pictures, the prevalence of "sensationalism" and "sex." These are the elements that are supposedly most insidious and harmful to young people.

But a frequent concern of parents and child psychologists is the occurrence of horror, violence, and other emotionally disturbing elements in films. These, say the child psychologists, are invariably more upsetting to a tot who is emotionally disturbed or highly sensitive than are adult presentments of sex. The latter are usually either meaningless or annoying to the younger child, they say.

The advocates of classification who have given the matter serious thought contend that this consideration of film content [23/24] should be as much in the minds of the classifiers as are considerations of sexual excess and immorality. The younger child needs to be guarded from possible abrasion as much as the teen-ager.

The opponents of classification say that this theory would logically require the subdivision of classification into ratings of films suitable for children in different age groups, and they observe that such stratification would only make the judgments of the classifiers more delicate, esoteric, and confusing to the average parent and child. (Incidentally, it has been wondered whether any official classification board would have the nerve to rate such a "fright"-laden picture as Walt Disney's "101 Dalmatians" as unsuitable for children under ten?)

It is strongly questioned by its opponents whether classification would be of much use on the advisory basis and as a purely voluntary thing. The point is made that most of the conscientious parents who might avail themselves of it are already sufficiently sophisticated and generally well-informed by critics and existing film-rating services to know something about the current pictures and which ones are generally suitable for their children. Such parents usually prefer to make up their own minds and not have someone else make up their minds for them.

On the other hand, it is reasoned that labeling and finger-pointing to films that are suitable "for adults only," without any restriction on who can attend, only arouses the curiosity and attracts the attendance of those teen-agers who are looking for sensations and are not under parental control. Thus advisory classification might serve as much to guide the undisciplined to the "unsuitable" pictures as to keep the disciplined away.

THE BRITISH SYSTEM

In discussions of classification, the advocates usually point to what they understand is the "success" of a system of classification in England. The operation of the English system is generally misunderstood by people in this country. [24/25]

Actually, the British Board of Film Censors, which classifies films in that country, is a non-governmental body financed by the motion picture industry. This board now rates films in three categories: "U" which is suitable for all (Universal); "A" suitable for adults, with under-16's admitted if accompanied by an adult; and "X" for adults only (no under-16's allowed).

These ratings are then passed along to local authorities who must decide whether they are to be made mandatory in the theatres in their areas. Most of the counties and municipalities impose them, but some do not. Oftentimes local authorities make further demands and classifications of their own, creating confusion and anomalies that are as absurd as some consequences of municipal censorship in the United States.

For instance, the film "Saturday Night and Sunday Morning" [25/26] was given an "X" certificate, but the Warwickshire County Council refused to let it be shown within its jurisdiction even with that classification unless two scenes were cut. The distributor refused to make them and as a consequence the film was banned in Warwickshire.

However, within the boundaries of the county are the cities of Birmingham and Coventry, which, under their municipal authority, allowed the film to be shown with an "X" rating. Thus anyone in the county over 16 could see the film by taking a trip to one of those nearby cities. And, ironically, the scenes that were banned by the county council were shown on a Midlands television program that went into all the county homes.

It is a recognized fact that "X" ratings are often boastfully advertised. One film was recently blazoned as "the X-iest film on the screen."

INDEPENDENT RATINGS

Instead of some official form of classification, administered either by the state or by the motion picture industry, opponents feel that the public is already provided with adequate guides to movie content in the existing independent rating services.

Best known of the existing agencies is the Legion of Decency, whose ratings and operation have been described. It is calculated that its recommendations are brought to the attention of most of the 43,000,000 Catholics in the United States.

It is true that the Legion is sometimes forward and has been known to suggest that, if certain cuts be made in certain pictures, a "C" (condemned) rating might be avoided. This has been remarked by some observers as having the effect of a tacit form of private censorship. But, of course, the Legion's answer is that no one is compelled to make the cuts it suggests; it is simply trying to be constructive—to help make films recommendable to persons of the Roman Catholic faith.

Perhaps the most objective of the film information services is that provided by *The Green Sheet*, a monthly publication of [26/27] brief reports and classifications of current pictures, prepared by a large panel of voluntary women reviewers representing ten recognized educational and religious organizations. Suggested classification for all audience levels are provided in *The Green Sheet* reviews, which are published by the Motion Picture Association of America (522 Fifth Avenue, New York City) primarily for mass media dissemination and the use of educators, librarians, clergymen, theatre managers, and others who are able to circulate its information widely.

Ratings of films as to their suitability for different age groups and interests are also run in *Parents' Magazine*, the *PTA* (Parent-Teachers Association) Magazine, *Consumer Reports, Consumer Bulletin,* the *Protestant Motion Picture Bulletin* and the *DAR* (Daughters of the American Revolution) Magazine.

And, of course, many newspapers and magazines throughout the country carry, in addition to critical reviews, assorted thumbnail reports and recommendations on current movie fare.

Indeed, the amount of information about movies that is available—the news stories, critical appraisals, and rating services—should be enough to provide anybody who is genuinely interested in determining what films are suitable for children with all the information they need. And the notion of setting up another master agency for putting tags on pictures as a quick and easy guide for those comparatively few nervous parents who might use it seems patently superfluous.

In the new-blown sentiment for classification appears a curious carryover, indeed, of the old custom of putting the responsibility for "protecting" the public against "harmful" movies upon some remote higher authority such as the state. Just as it used to be argued that censorship was as much justified as a protective device against "poison" as the pure food and drug laws (an argument, incidentally, which is easily demolished by the point that it is impossible to make a chemical analysis of the dramatic contents of a film), so people are now devoutly arguing that classification is required to save our youth from corruption. [27/28]

ROLE OF PARENT AND TEACHERS

What will best guard the youth of this country from those occasional perverse and seamy films that present a distorted, inartistic, and often untrue picture of life is intelligent guidance by parents and teachers who draw upon a wide range of information for their own guidance and not on some agency's arbitrary tag. The latter dependence smacks too strongly of the Big Brotherism of George Orwell's *1984*.

Now, with the motion picture medium advancing into broader and deeper explorations of the complexities and meanings of life, it should behoove the public to greet its advancement gratefully, to encourage its explorations with excitement and eagerness, to be well informed about it, and to give it its full cultural due— not to be squeamish and suspicious about what it may do to youth.

The significance of this potent medium is that it is available to and embraces everyone. Only by personal investigation and discovery will the individual learn to appreciate and appraise it, to sense what he and his children should take and what he and they should leave alone.

What Should We Do About the Crisis in Movie Morals?: The Answer: "Graded" Films*

JOE HYAMS (1923-   ) received an M.S. in education from New York University in 1948 and has taught journalism at U.C.L.A. He has been Hollywood columnist for the New York *Herald Tribune* and for *This Week,* the Sunday magazine section distributed with newspapers in many cities in the United States. The author of many magazine articles about Hollywood, he collaborated with Walter Wanger on the recent book *My Life with Cleopatra* (1963).

The American movie industry . . . is against classification. It supports this position with several arguments which don't impress me greatly.

One of them is economic. A 1957 survey showed that half of all movie-goers are under 20 and to turn them away from a number of films would be to turn away millions of dollars. In England, a picture with an "X" (adults only) certificate does 20 per cent less business than a "U" (for everyone) picture.

The answer: Well, what's more important, children or profits? Also, it seems to me that there's a good chance that classification would increase the total audience, as parents found they could rely on movies not to shock them or their children.

Another argument against grading movies was given by a spokesman for the Motion Picture Association of America. He claimed movies have become more "adult" along with plays and books.

The answer: If plays and books and movies had the same audience, limited largely to adults, this argument might have some force. But the movie audience contains many adolescents and children.

Eric Johnston, President of the MPAA, rejects the "adults only" label for certain pictures, contending it would be impossible to agree on which pictures to include and also what minimum age to set. "It is not and never has been the function of the Code to say that every film it grants a seal is suitable for children," Mr. Johnston said. "A Code seal merely indicates that a picture is generally acceptable for the general American public, leaving it wholly up to [9/10] the parents to decide whether or not their children should see a picture."

The answer: It's true that the responsibility for what children should see devolves on parents. The film producers themselves, the U.S. Army, and church groups agree that the parent is the best qualified judge of his family's entertainment. But how can they make an intelligent, well-informed decision unless they have the facts readily available? After many hours of discussion with parents, movie producers and distributors, with foreign censors and legal experts, I suggest a plan which is, I believe, both effective and practical:

Classify all pictures shown in the U.S. as "recommended for adults" or "recommended for family."

Such a system will serve the purposes of protection without infringing on Con-

* Joe Hyams, from "What Should We Do About the Crisis in Movie Morals?: The Answer: 'Graded' Films," *This Week*, February 26, 1961, pp. 8-10.

stitutional freedom. We will be able to avoid shocking unprepared spectators without lowering the content of all movies to a level suitable for children.

The next problem is to decide who is going to administer the plan. In my opinion the MPAA, which now decides whether a movie gets the Code seal, could at the same time classify it as "adult" or "family." The exhibitor would put the seal in his ads and on his marquee.

You might wonder if the industry can be trusted to police itself, but I think the answer is "yes." Once public demand has created a classification system, the MPAA can be trusted to apply it sensibly and firmly, as it has enforced the Code for the past 30 years.

It will be up to the parent to decide whether to follow or ignore the recommendation—but he will have readily available the information needed to decide which of the hundreds of pictures available each year are suitable for his child.

Will this system of classification work in America despite the opposition of the movie industry? Most concerned adults think it is the only system. Many creative men in Hollywood like the idea.

"I'm all in favor of voluntary classification," producer-director Otto Preminger says. "It would show we don't want freedom of the screen just for the sake of sensationalism. In fact, I'd be proud if all my pictures were recommended for adults."

. . . .

Champions of graded movies say it is bound to come. They feel that there is no other way to let Hollywood make the "adult" films it feels the times demand and still protect the morals of minors. With pressure from parents it may come, and soon.

Motion Pictures and Juvenile Delinquency*

THE SUBCOMMITTEE TO INVESTIGATE JUVENILE DE-LINQUENCY was formed according to Senate Resolution 62 (84th Congress, 1st Session), on the investigation of juvenile delinquency in the United States. Chairman of this subcommittee was Senator Estes Kefauver of Tennessee, whose skills as an investigator were often exercised during his membership on the Committee on the Judiciary, especially in inquiring into the effectiveness of federal laws against crime. This selection presents excerpts from a special report on theatrical motion pictures, a report based primarily on hearings held in Los Angeles on June 16 and 17, 1955.

. . . .

Mr. Goeffrey [*sic*] Shurlock, director, Production Code Administration of the Motion Picture Association of America, testified before the subcommittee. Mr. Shurlock has worked for the Motion Picture Association since 1932, and has been on the staff of the Production Code Administration since its formation in June 1934 under its first director, Joseph I. Breen. Upon Mr. Breen's retirement in October 1954 Mr. Shurlock became the director.

Mr. Shurlock stated that it is his duty, and the duty of the seven members of his staff, to review and pass on all pictures produced by the members of the Motion Picture Association who are signatory to the code, and also on any and all other scripts or pictures which independent producers may wish to submit voluntarily to the staff for review. Mr. Shurlock estimated that approximately 99 percent of the pictures produced in the United States for theatrical entertainment went through the Motion Picture Production Code. Funds for the operation of the Motion Picture Production Code are secured from the producers who submit a picture and pay a fee based on the negative costs of the picture.

Mr. Shurlock stated that during the last year or so, he has been aware of criticism, both in this country and from abroad, of motion- [30/31] picture content which contained excessive brutality and violence. This information was brought to the attention of the producers of these motion pictures by the Production Code Administration. In November of 1954 Mr. Shurlock went to New York and discussed the matter with the president of the Motion Picture Association, Eric Johnston. He then returned to Los Angeles and started a definite campaign to warn producers that there seemed to be an increasing resistance on the part of the public to being entertained or amused by seeing violence or brutality in pictures, or pictures that seemed to be of a violent nature. Mr. Shurlock stated that, as in former cases, the producers agreed that if there is a public reaction against any element in motion pictures to the point where pictures are not being enjoyed, they will change the type of production and their approach. He feels that motion pictures which contain crime, violence, and brutality are definitely beginning to change. With the complaints against violence and the campaign to urge producers to tone down these scenes, there should be noticeable improvements in the

* Staff of the Subcommittee to Investigate Juvenile Delinquency, Senate Committee on the Judiciary, 84th Congress, 2d Session, *Motion Pictures and Juvenile Delinquency* 30-35, 39-40, 42, 47-48, 61-62, 64-65, 67-70 (Committee Print 1956).

pictures released by fall or winter of 1955. Because of production schedules, it will take at least 6 months before the effect of this campaign will be noticed. [31/32]

. . . .

. . . Many of the complaints against certain motion pictures, although justifiable, are submitted by complainants who have no idea of how violent many motion pictures would have been had not many scenes already been cut from the film by the code administrators. One film in particular, Fort Yuma, might be used as an example. The files of the Code Administration yielded the information that the film contained 24 personalized killings in the script. The code administrators advised the producer that the film would not be given a seal of approval unless the number of killings was reduced from 24 to approximately 10. This course of action was followed and the film was given a seal of approval.

The following excerpts are taken from letters in the files of the Production Code. They constitute a small sampling of the types of suggestions and recommendations sent to several producers who were making pictures that contained scenes of violence:

This office has been receiving many and formidable complaints about scenes of men striking women in pictures. We have been endeavoring to tone down this problem. Consequently the acceptability of this action in scene _____ will depend on the discretion and taste with which it is actually photographed in the finished picture. This kind of action should be gotten over by suggestion rather than photographed in detail.

In the fight between _____ and _____, and in other fights throughout the script, please be advised that it would be unacceptable to indulge in any kneeing, kicking, gouging, or other forms of excessive brutality.

We have been receiving many and angry complaints on the score of excessive brutality in our motion pictures. Conesquently, it is necessary for us to insist that scenes involving fights and beatings of any sort be handled with a good deal more care than usual, and be done within the careful limits of good taste and discretion. * * * [32/33]

. . . .

If the Production Code Administration feels that in a certain film there is an ex-

cessive amount of violence and brutality or an excessive amount of sex suggestiveness, it is possible for them to withhold their seal if the producer is a signatory member of the association. If a signatory member of the association proceeds to release a film that has not been approved by the Production Code Administration, he is liable to a fine of $25,000.

In the last 15 years, there have been only 2 films produced by major companies that did not receive the seal of approval from the Motion Picture Production Code. There have also been a number of foreign films submitted to the Code Administration which have been refused a seal. One of these pictures was an independently produced film called The Moon Is Blue and one was the picture produced by one of the major studios, RKO, called The French Line. Both of these films were released without the seal of approval. In the case of The Moon Is Blue, neither the producer nor the distributing company was then a member of the association. Consequently, they were not subject to the $25,000 fine. In the case of The French Line, the fine was never assessed against the producer. However, when the film was subsequently brought into line with the code, the violation was overlooked.

Mr. Shurlock indicated that the following reasons should be underlined as causative factors in the apparent increase in violence, brutality, and sadism in motion-picture films.

(1) The reason that some of this violence is being objected to is that it no longer appears in the old-type western picture, but has been brought up to date into a type of picture in which the characters are more readily recognizable and identifiable. In the standard westerns there is an aura of the fairytale about the portrayal that does not bring an audience into direct identification. However, when this type of story is told in a modern setting, the violence and brutality seem to affect the public more strongly.

(2) There seems to be on the part of the public a greater resentment against violence because, unfortunately, there have been recently fewer of the old-style family type of picture. That is, pictures of a violent nature are not increasing in number; however, fewer of the domestic comedies

and pictures completely divorced from violence have been produced, so that when the family goes to the movies they see during the course of the year a greater proportion of violent pictures than they may have done previously.[32] [33/34]

. . . .

In discussing the connection of the Motion Picture Production Code with foreign countries and films produced by them, Mr. Shurlock stated that occasionally a foreign producer would like to get his picture released in the United States and that there is nothing to prevent him from releasing the picture without the seal of approval. Many times, however, the foreign producer would like to obtain the services of one of the major releasing companies which require the seal of approval before they will handle the picture. In that case, the producer sends, or brings, the film to the Code Administration and asks that it be reviewed to determine whether or not it conforms with the code; and if he is granted the seal, this enables him to ask a major releasing company to handle the picture. Many foreign films of the objectionable type, however, play in the so-called art houses, i. e., a limited number of theaters. Therefore, the producers of these films do not need the seal of approval because of their limited play and their limited audiences. This, in part, may account for the relative freedom in sexually suggestive scenes which have come under much criticism from the public. The producers of these films know that the content centers on sex exploitation and they know they cannot conceivably get the Production Code seal of approval.

There actually is no relationship between the Production Code Administration and the exhibiting houses or the theater owners themselves. The theater owners, through their organizations, Theater Owners of America and the Allied States Association of Motion Picture Exhibitors, do not require the seal of approval as a prerequisite for the showing of pictures in their particular movie houses. Because of a monopoly suit, the Government ordered divorcement of the producing and distrib-

uting companies from the theaters which they owned. Thus, the Motion Picture Association of America, which is a combination of both producing and releasing companies, no longer owns its own theaters. The result is that there is no working agreement in regard to requiring a seal of approval on the part of the theater owners at the present time. [34/35]

. . . .

In the course of reviewing a film script and film for the seal of approval, two members of the code staff always review the finished film, although sections of the sound track may not have been "dubbed" in as in the final production. It is mandatory upon the producer to submit the finished picture to the code staff before the seal is given and when the final letter is written granting the seal of approval on the script, a paragraph is added which reads:

You understand, of course, our final opinion will be based upon the finished picture.

. . . .

ALLEGED VIOLATIONS OF THE MOTION PICTURE PRODUCTION CODE [35/39]

. . . .

In the January 29, 1955, issue of the Motion Picture Herald, an industry journal, a review of the motion picture Ten Wanted Men, released through Columbia Pictures, Inc., reads:

There appears to this observer to have been growing up in recent months among the producers of westerns, a propensity for over-much bloodshed, even to the point of a sort of cinematic sadism. It apparently has become almost axiomatic that it must be gory to be good.

That does not mean that Ten Wanted Men is not a good, or a satisfactory western, or that it will not be successful of its type in almost any situation, for it is good. It is merely that this film is a case in point and could have been just as

[32] Shurlock, Geoffrey, statement in hearings before the Subcommittee To Investigate Juvenile Delinquency, Motion Pictures, U. S. Senate, held on June 17, 1955, pp. 190-191.

good, just as successful, and just as active and lively a western without carrying the killings as far as it does.

In discussing the film further the reviewer finishes by saying:

There is, however, en route to that conclusion (of the film) much killing which seems unnecessary for story purposes, beating and lashing which is not all vital to the narrative.[34]

Upon viewing the motion picture, it is found that this is not at all an unfair description. There can be counted a total of 17 personalized killings throughout the running of the film. Mr. Harry Joe Brown, one of the coproducers of Ten Wanted Men, stated at the hearings that there are only 5 or 6 killings in this picture, and each one contained a moral and gave a good example to American children. He did admit that the scene wherein a character in the film was shot first in the hand, then in the upper arm, and then apparently in the chest as he sat in a horse-drawn buggy was subject to some criticism. He did feel, however, that this scene provided a good example to children; i. e., the love of a father for his son. (This scene was an attempt by outlaws to derive information as to the whereabouts of the man's son. He preferred, however, to be systematically shot to death rather than reveal the information.)

Mr. Shurlock was also questioned about this picture. If 24 personalized killings, as originally existed in the script of the film Fort Yuma, had to be reduced to 10 in order to receive a code seal of approval, and Ten Wanted Men was released with a total of 17 personalized killings, what criteria are used to determine the number of [**39/40**] killings that can be portrayed in any one film. [*sic*] Mr. Shurlock felt that this was a good indication of the change in motion-picture content, as Ten Wanted Men had been produced 6 months earlier and the decisions on Fort Yuma were relatively recent. [**40/42**]

. . . .

On viewing the film, Big House, USA,

there can be no doubt that the film contains scenes of excessive brutality in violation of the Production Code. One scene depicts the kidnaper throwing the child into a ravine in a heartless, cold-blooded manner. Another scene shows the closeup of the face of a convict caught in a steam-pipe screaming wildly as he is about to be scalded to death. In what is probably one of the most morbid scenes that has ever been shown in motion pictures, the following sequence of scenes appeared: After having successfully escaped from prison by swimming underwater aided by breathing devices that had been smuggled into prison, five convicts reach a boat in the middle of the bay. The "kidnaper" has been forced to escape with the prisoners in order to get the $200,000 he received in ransom money. In an attempt to throw the police off the track, the leader of the gang, played by Broderick Crawford, orders one of the members of the gang murdered, his hands and face mutilated, and the clothes and other identifying articles of the "kidnaper" put on the body. This is done in hopes that the police will think the "kidnaper" is dead and will no longer wait for him in the area where the ransom money is hidden. Despite the fact that he has just been saved from drowning by one of the convicts, the leader of the gang orders him killed. The executioner is shown as he raises the hammer to bring it down on the head of the convict who has fallen asleep on the floor of the boat, exhausted from his exertions. The executioner is then ordered to take a blow-torch and mutilate the face and hands of the dead convict. The next few seconds are devoted to the awakening of the other convicts to the odor of burning flesh. The men operating the boat in the forward cabin also look out of the window, sniffing the air to see where the odor is coming from. The last to awaken is Lon Chaney, Jr., another member of the gang and friend of the criminal who is being mutilated. He goes berserk and attempts to attack the leader

[34] Review of Ten Wanted Men, in Motion Picture Herald, vol. 198, No. 5, January 29, 1955, p. 305.

of the gang and, as the camera pulls back slightly, we see the dead man lying on the floor of the boat, his head and his hands the color of charcoal. The leader of the gang then proceeds to shoot Lon Chaney, Jr., several times in the chest. He staggers back against the side of the boat, with fluid oozing from his chest. He is then shoved into the sea. The next scene shows the remaining gangsters calmly fishing off the side of the boat. The final scene is an extensive gun battle between the remaining convicts and the forces of the law. One of the convicts is apparently blasted to death with the entire magazine from a carbine. [42/47]

. . . .

. . . the subcommittee viewed another film produced in 1948 entitled "City Across the River," which at that time was supposed to expose the problem of delinquency and in some way alleviate the problem. The film was based on the book, the Amboy Dukes, which was the story of a teen-age group of delinquents. This book was subject to much discussion during a congressional investigation of 25-cent pocket magazines.[42] There was concern at that time of the possible harmful effects that the book may have had on predisposed delinquent youth. Many gangs apprehended by the police at that time had taken on both the gang name and the individual names of members of the gang as depicted in the book. While purporting to be a film to reduce delinquency, we have seen the delinquency rates rising since 1948, and, while we cannot say what effect this film had, if any, we may assume that it was hardly one of reducing delinquency. [47/48]

. . . .

The following is a discussion of the motion picture They Were So Young, taken from the February 5, 1955, issue of the Motion Picture Herald. It reads as follows:

The title of the picture pertains to a shipment of girls from Paris, where they've been trained as fashion models, to Rio de Janeiro, where their employers deprive them of their passports and work permits and make it clear to them that their basic obligation is to entertain, in whatever way may be required of them, the wealthy men who are the nonbuying nocturnal customers of the pretended women's-wear wholesaler.

Most of the unfortunate girls meet disastrous fates, including death and that which is classically alluded to as worse, before a Brazilian security-police investigator catches up with the white slavers and puts an end to their operations.

The picture, like others which dramatize materials not often presented on the American screen, has impact and contains a liberal allotment of incidents calculated to set up active, and probably profitable, word-of-mouth.

The following is further discussion of the above-mentioned motion picture:

* * * She flees to the jungle, Brady rescues her again, and when they stop for the night she is again taken captive and dispatched to the "river pleasure boats" which, the dialogue and action make plain, are the final destination of all enslaved girls who have outlived their attractiveness in the swankier salons of sin. * * *

It's a drab and distressing story, and while it does not glamorize vice it is a white-slave picture and as such is questionable subject matter for theatrical exhibition. The picture has not received approval of the production code.[46]

Subsequently the subcommittee found that the picture has now received a Motion Picture Production Code seal of approval. The technique used to get the film the seal of approval was similar to that used in Big House, USA, i. e., a slight change in terminology describing the story content and a prologue given by a police official which indicates that the entire theme of the film is something other than what it actually is. [48/61]

. . . .

X. CONCLUSIONS AND RECOMMENDATIONS

The investigation of the effect of crime and violence in motion pictures has been a three-part study wherein crime and hor-

---

[42] See, Report of the Select Committee on Current Pornographic Materials, House of Representatives, 82d Cong., 2d Sess., H. Rept. No. 2510, pp. 107-110.

[46] Review of They Were So Young, in Motion Picture Herald, vol. 198, No. 6, February 5, 1955, p. 315.

ror comic books, crime and violence in television and motion pictures were considered in terms of their relationships between delinquent behavior and the reading or viewing of these media. While once again, as with the comic books and television, no wealth of scientific data can be given as to a causal relationship between delinquent behavior and the mass media, it is quite clear that professional people generally view the presentation of brutality and violence in these media as definitely deleterious to the personality development of normal, predelinquent, and delinquent children. . . .

. . . the following generalizations can be made:

1. The mass media, including the movies, reflect many of the abnormal or deleterious attitudes, desires, wishes, etc., of adult society and, to that extent, they are reflecting the prevailing "atmosphere."

2. These media have a tremendous influence on the young child in his early development and, while reflecting the major attitudes of the society, they are in turn influencing to a great degree the attitudinal development of children. Given an emotionally stable child who has had what may be termed the proper emotional relationship with his parents, this type of presentation may have little or no effect in terms of influencing well established attitudes. However, given (a) a child with a more or less undeveloped attitudinal framework, the mass media may go a long way toward providing ideas both in the development of attitudes and predisposing the child for certain types of behavior; and (b) given a child who has had what may be interpreted as poor emotional relationships between the mother, the father, and the child, and who may be in the throes of a frustration-aggression complex, this child may gain support and ideas from viewing aggressively brutal and violent scenes as presented in motion pictures and as presented both in pictorial form and in the terminology present in motion-picture advertising. The motion picture, it was pointed out, could provide the many so-called "trigger mechanisms" that may

initiate and provide the content for antisocial behavior on the part of emotionally disturbed children. [61/62]

Much of the present concern over motion pictures is derived from ideas similar to the foregoing as to the effects of certain productions on children and adolescents. If this is the basic foundation on which regulation must rest, then it follows that the solution to the problem must be accommodated to the evil to be prevented.

Exactly what the influence of the motion picture, or any mass media, might be is a very complex problem about which specialists do not specifically agree. Other factors that must be taken into consideration are, firstly, that the impact of the movie depends greatly on what the personality makeup of the child already is; and secondly, that the impact must be seen in the perspective of the total environment, an environment which includes the school, the neighborhood, the gang, the church, the newspaper, the comic booklets, the radio programs, other movies, and, above all, the family.

COMPARISONS OF MOTION PICTURES WITH OTHER MASS MEDIA

When the motion picture is viewed in relation to the other media of mass communication, certain conclusions may be drawn. On the one hand, movies are less easily attainable than "comic" books or television. The presentations are less numerous and relatively more expensive. However, branching off from the original thesis of saturation which was considered to be of paramount importance in the television investigation, further discussions with professional people indicate that it may not be the saturation point that is the most important factor, but the degree of sadism, brutality, and violence that is portrayed in any one motion-picture presentation. However, again, the more presentations of this type available, the greater chance they have of being seen.

It has been definitely established at the hearings that, while there has not been a substantial increase in quantity of the type of film under consideration, that is, the western or modern crime variety, there has been a change in the ratio of crime and western movies to noncrime movies. That is, while the production of crime and western movies has remained constant or increased slightly, the production of noncrime movies has decreased greatly, making a greater proportion of the crime and western variety available on the market in the long run. The fact that producers and directors have increasingly emphasized sadism, brutality, and violence in their pictures was also established. **[62/64]**

. . . .

The type of film content under consideration has been outlawed since the beginning under the prevailing provisions of the Motion Picture Production Code. The subcommittee feels that the laxness on the part of the code and the loose interpretations placed on many obvious violations were a result of a genuine feeling of appreciation for the stiff competition faced by motion-picture producers from television and the feeling on the part of the code administrators that these were not indeed violations, but a more or less facing of reality in keeping with television productions. The subcommittee further feels that the Motion Picture Production Code staff has relinquished the necessity for strict adherence to the code by producers in the name of artistic liberalism, because they no longer feel a responsibility toward children.

. . . .

Increased objections on the part of concerned individuals throughout the United States and abroad are apparently going to put a stop to the trend toward more violence and, indeed, a reversal seems to be forthcoming. The real motivation underlying this reversal of form, however, cannot be placed at the level of a sudden social awareness of public resentment on the part of the motion-picture producers, but at the level of monetary remuneration. That is, there is fear on the part of the motion-picture producers that their box office will be hurt as a result of the recent trends in motion picture producing and the resulting criticism. The desire for a return to the code restrictions seems to be inspired by fear rather than by any growth of professional consciousness or sense of responsibility for the public interest on the part of a few who control the industry.

The subcommittee feels that Mr. Shurlock is a man of integrity and intelligence who is making every effort to bring the minority of producers making objectionable films toward the goal of more strict adherence to not only the provisions, but the spirit of the Motion Picture Production Code. The subcommittee also feels that Mr. Shurlock has been honest and forthright in performing his job. He has, however, himself stated that the Production Code Administration's responsibility toward children has lessened, and there the subcommit- **[64/65]** tee disagrees.[60] Aside from this, the subcommittee appreciates some of the difficulties faced by Mr. Shurlock. He is, after all, employed by the people whose product he passes on and is under continual pressure. . . . **[65/67]**

. . . .

Traditionally, three solutions have been developed for the problem of keeping motion pictures within their proper function: Censorship, penal sanctions, and self-regulation. Censorship, though its status is still unsettled, appears to have spent its force. Complete freedom for motion pictures within the limits of the penal laws is impossible to achieve, for organized interest groups are unlikely to give up their review boards, and they will see that the Production Code is perpetuated. Self-regulation through the Production Code has the advantage of being a method of control integrated with the production process, and the cost is borne by the industry. However, there are important defects. The interests of motion-picture producers do not always coincide with those of the public, and the public can exercise no direct control over the procedure established to administer

[60] Shurlock, Geoffrey, see statements in article, "How Hollywood Has Dropped Its Taboos," People Today, vol. 10, No. 7, April 6, 1955, pp. 2-6; and, People Today, vol. 10, No. 8, April 20, 1955, pp. 2, 64.

the code. There is also the possibility that producers with unacceptable productions will increasingly simply issue those films without the Production Code seal. It must be concluded that none of these methods will produce any universal solution.

The primary argument for censorship is usually the necessity for protecting young minds from contact with sights or ideas unsuited to their tender years. But many feel it is unthinkable that a medium designed for entertainment should be permanently hobbled by the mental and moral requirements of the immature. A realistic approach is taken by the British and Canadians who meet the situation by classifying some pictures as unfit for juvenile patronage.

Conceivably States could forbid the exhibition of unacceptable films to minors, in accord with the practice now followed with respect to liquor, tobacco, and firearms. In this connection, it might be profitable for State legislatures to examine the British system of film regulation. In Great Britain, there is no statutory provision for censorship of films. There is a board of film censors, but they are without statutory powers. They classify films into four categories: A (adult and children under 16 if accompanied by adults); H (horror films); U (universal exhibition); and X (unsuitable for children under 16 even if accompanied by adults). Obviously the only purpose of this classification is to indicate films which are suitable for children. Exhibition of films not passed by the board is not an offense as such, but such classifications are given legal effect under the Cinematograph Act [**67/68**] which allows revocation of exhibitor's licenses for failure to enforce the classifications. [**68/ 69**]

. . . .

The motion-picture industry, by its own action, should place increasing stress on its role as a civic and informational agency conscious of the changing character of many social problems. The industry as a responsible member of society cannot shirk its obligation to promote, so far as possi-

ble, an intelligent understanding of domestic and international affairs. While the subcommittee has criticized in this report many films that motion-picture producers may feel were in this category, the criticism raised was not whether the social prob- [**69/70**] lem should or should not be presented, e. g., Blackboard Jungle, but the manner of presentation, especially the emphasis on violence run rampant.

The public itself should insist upon the highest attainable accomplishment by the movies. Too often the customers fail to exert their influence. Newspapers and magazines could help by adopting the practice already followed by some of devoting regular space to serious criticism. In addition, every community should maintain one or more citizen's committees, not to further narrow purposes, but to encourage worthy achievement. These committees should be broadly representative, including persons jealous for the artistic integrity of the screen. The public has an important role to play also in encouraging the movie outside the commercial theater. Educational institutions, public libraries, churches, business clubs, trade unions, women's groups, and the like should cooperate in making available suitable films for nontheatrical audiences and in drawing on nationwide sources for information and comment to indicate to producers the principal needs.

All such efforts would be greatly strengthened if universities and foundations should pay appropriate attention to this potential in American life. In particular, they should set up centers of advanced study and research, whose investigations and reports would incite both producers and public to higher standards. The subcommittee has, since the outset of its investigation into the mass media, advocated the granting of funds by foundations and the utilization of university facilities to determine the effect of the various media on behavior and the developing of criteria for programs of a positive nature.

. . . .

PART SIX

SHOULD FILM DISTRIBUTION OVERSEAS BE RESTRICTED?

The Free Ride*

NORMAN COUSINS (1912-   ), editor of the *Saturday Review* since 1942, graduated from Columbia University Teachers College in 1933 and was managing editor of *Current History* from 1935 to 1940, when he joined what was then called the *Saturday Review of Literature* as executive editor. Under his direction, the weekly magazine has added to its book reviews a wide coverage of public affairs, education, science, and the arts, including film and television. Among his books are *Modern Man is Obsolete* (1945) and *Who Speaks for Man?* (1953).

In Osaka last summer I observed several thousand people in a line three-deep that ran completely around a large city block. The line was not unfamiliar; I had seen lines like it everywhere in Japan, and, indeed, in many other cities throughout the world. If you haven't guessed it already, it was a line of people waiting to buy tickets to American movies with translated subtitles.

What impressed me most of all about this particular line, however, was that it was formed despite difficult conditions, to say the least. All morning long the radio had sounded warnings of a possible typhoon sweeping in from the sea. By noon, when I happened to pass this particular theatre, the rain had already begun. I took shelter in an office building and observed the line across the street. The people pressed against the sides of the buildings and many of them looked up apprehensively from time to time at the darkening sky, but the line held. A half-hour later the rain developed into a heavy downpour swept along by high winds. This was a little more convincing and about one-third of the people decided to run for cover. But the others closed ranks and huddled together resolutely as the wind and the thunder struck up a Wagnerian finale. Such umbrellas as I could observe were of little use against the gusts that ripped through the streets.

An hour later the weather had eased off to a drizzle and the sky began to brighten. The expected typhoon had only skimmed the edge of Osaka. By this time the people on line looked as though they had been swimming with their clothes on, but their war against the elements was won, and they grinned at each other triumphantly.

It was a striking demonstration of the pulling power of the American movies, which far outdraw films produced anywhere else. Only Hollywood's assembly line can turn out pictures fast enough and slick enough to meet the craving for inexpensive film entertainment throughout the world. There is no such thing as a selective audience. People, starved for amusement and diversion, are being given and are taking anything they can get.

The first time an American abroad is confronted by direct evidence of the popularity of American films—the long lines outside theatres, pictures of American movie stars posted in conspicuous places, prominent newspaper notices—the first

* Norman Cousins, "The Free Ride" (editorial), *Saturday Review of Literature*, XXXIII (January 21, 1950), 24-25. Reprinted by permission of the *Saturday Review* and the author.

time he sees all this, he is pleasantly surprised and impressed, even awed. But let him talk, as I have done, to American officials abroad, particularly in the embassies and the information sources. Let him listen to the growing concern of the men and women abroad whose job it is to create good will for the American people. Out of these discussions will come serious doubts and apprehensions about the effects of our films on world public opinion.

"Don't take my word for it," I was told in Paris by a friend who was attached to the Embassy. "There is a simple and direct test. All you have to do is see an American movie in a foreign theatre. It's one thing to sit back in a theatre in the United States and dismiss what you see on the screen as a harmless Hollywood distortion of American life. But see how you feel about it when you see the same distortions soaked up by Frenchmen or Englishmen or Italians or any other people who know little about America outside of what they see on the screen."

It was good advice. Since then I have taken pains to see American movies whenever I have happened to be in a foreign country. It is a painful experience, difficult to describe. You find yourself even more interested in the people around you than you are in the motion picture. You are surprised to find them laughing heartily in places where you are certain the movie producers had intended no laughs, and you are even more surprised at the lack of even a ripple during scenes which would have delighted audiences back in America.

Most of all, however, you experience the unhappy sensation of observing yourself on the screen, for whether we like it or not, American films abroad speak for Americans. You shudder when you realize that these movies, for better or worse, are about *you*. They describe you intimately—so intimately, in fact, that at times you feel like the character in Shaw's "Heartbreak House" who suddenly began to tear off all his clothes because he felt he had nothing left to conceal. In a foreign setting American movies have a meaning and an effect

which are difficult to imagine back home. Every word, every gesture becomes almost part of a score card for or against Americans. You realize that what you are seeing is more than mere entertainment: it is a projection of America, and, as such, of vital importance to the American people at a time when they are spending millions of dollars to create good will abroad and a real understanding of themselves.

This is not a mere matter of pride or a matter of being hyper-sensitive to an unfavorable interpretation of America by other peoples as the result of American films. Nor is this minor issue to be debated leisurely under some such abstract heading as, "responsibility and the arts." What is involved here is a major matter hitting squarely upon America's stake in world public opinion. Whether Hollywood cares to recognize the fact or not, it happens that a full-fledged propaganda war is being waged at the [24/25] moment, and the stakes are large and real. It should be no secret that a vast attempt is being made by the Soviet, as it was made by Germany in the years leading up to and during World War II, to split off world public opinion from America, to create a deep distrust of Americans as individuals and as a nation, to picture us as selfish, degenerate, depraved, ruthless, acquisitive, anti-humanitarian, and anti-cultural. It is doubtful, however, whether anything under way or contemplated by Soviet propaganda is as widespread or effective in creating these impressions as our own films.

In the final analysis, of course, the question comes down to this: Do our movies accurately reflect America and Americans? For if they do, then there is no argument. If they do, then we deserve to be held up to scorn and ridicule. In that case we ought to save the millions of dollars we have been spending through the Voice of America and our information services abroad, for the attempt to deodorize ourselves would be beyond possibility of achievement.

But the fact is that the movies do not

accurately reflect America and Americans. We have more than our share of humanity's faults, but we by no means monopolize them. Nor are we predominantly a nation of murderers, gangsters, idlers, deadbeats, dipsomaniacs, touts, tarts, and swindlers, as Hollywood would have us appear. We don't all work in swanky buildings with private offices large enough to house a small army. We don't all live in plush duplex apartments with elaborate cocktail bars and retinues of servants. We don't all sleep in kingsize beds with silk topsheets, nor do we all arise languidly at noon for breakfast in bed. Some of us find something to do with our hands other than to drape them around long cocktail glasses, expensive cigarette holders, or smoking revolvers. Some of us even read a book occasionally and find something to talk about other than a scheme to murder our wives or our business partners. And, while we like to hold our own in discussion or debate it isn't true that the only rebuttal is a sock on the jaw.

The next pertinent question to ask is this: Is there any reason to suppose that people in foreign countries don't make the necessary allowances, realizing that the movies are dealing largely with fictional material and concepts? The easiest way to answer this question is to talk to the people themselves. It becomes immediately clear that too many of them see us as we look to them under the klieg lights. All the old stereotypes and misconceptions about the United States as a vastly wealthy but yet culturally undeveloped country come gushing forth.

Frequently in the past two years, while attending American movies in such cities as London, Brussels, Paris, Berlin, Milan, and Hiroshima, I have had to fight down the impulse to rise up in my seat and shout out that what was being shown was a lie, and to try to refute the dangerous impressions about America that were being hammered home—sometimes in Technicolor. For it makes little sense to set up elaborate agencies in our State Department at great cost for building good will abroad when a large part of the problem was being mass-produced right here on the West Coast.

There is no way of knowing how much Russia spends for her propaganda against the United States, but it would seem she is foolish to spend anything at all so long as Hollywood continues to give her a free ride.

Hollywood: America's Travelling Salesman*

ERIC JOHNSTON (1896-1963) graduated from the law school of the University of Washington in 1917. Active in the manufacturing and retail aspects of the electrical business in Spokane, Washington, and in Chamber of Commerce affairs, he was elected president of the U.S. Chamber of Commerce for four terms. He was president of the Motion Picture Association of America from 1945 until his death in 1963. The following selection is from a speech delivered to the New York Sales Executives Club on May 28, 1957.

This afternoon I'd like to talk to you about Hollywood—the Hollywood I've known for the past dozen years—the Hollywood that is America's travelling salesman to all the world, a salesman of goods and services, of language and culture, of ideas and hopes. With or without our industry's own adjectives, there has been no place like this particular Hollywood before or since.

For the Hollywood film has provided massive global communication which no other man-made device has ever equalled —from Gutenberg's movable type to—and including—Dr. Zworykin's television tube. Hollywood never had any such grand intention in mind. It didn't mean to Communicate with a capital C—it merely wished to entertain. It didn't set out as America's or anybody else's travelling salesman, or to spread culture, or enlightenment, or even the democratic way of life to our fellow residents of the earth.

Hollywood rendered these and other services on the side, as by-products incidental to its mission of entertainment. It rendered these by-products successfully because it was extraordinarily successful in entertaining, and it is so today.

As the magic screen spread across our continent and then across other continents, Hollywood created demand for sewing machines, refrigerators, rumble seats, the pop-up toaster—the [572/573] list is endless. It created demand for sleek porcelain bathtubs instead of the lion-clawed monstrosities of B.C.B.D.—before Cecil B. de-Mille—because people wanted sleek bathtubs and the bathtub industry was eager to accommodate them.

Hollywood, as I noted, wasn't trying to sell anything but motion pictures, which it did. But it also sold America into mass production, which wasn't on its mind at all. It created demands of the most powerful sort. It provoked the handcraft homebuilders of a generation ago into mass-producing the Cape Cod love nest and the builders of today into mass-producing the Western-style rambler. It stimulated the mass manufacture of men's wear and it influenced women to a degree that no ordinary man would dare attempt.

A generation ago, Hollywood sent women to beauty parlors to emulate Greta Garbo's long bob; a half generation ago, it sent them in pursuit of the hair-in-the-face outlook of Veronica Lake; today it sends them after Audrey Hepburn's short-cropped gamin coiffure. And during these years Hollywood and Marlene Dietrich sent women into slacks—whether built for them or not.

* Eric Johnston, from "Hollywood: America's Travelling Salesman," *Vital Speeches of the Day*, XXIII (July 1, 1957), 572-574. Reprinted by permission of the author.

. . . .

Sometimes the films have been accused of stirring too many demands in too many places, of fostering, if not inventing, materialism. To my mind, there is nothing wrong with stirring up demands in the world—and showing that productivity can meet them. If Hollywood does that, aren't we surely on the side of the angels?

I think so and so does that salty, articulate angel from Britain, Professor Dennis Brogan of Cambridge. To his own countrymen, he said:

"If the movies make the British housewife demand revolutionary changes in kitchen and house-planning, I'm all for it. The American film shows a society full of energy, faith, industry and hope.

"Well," the professor demanded, "what's wrong with that?"

Before I turn to my next point, I'd like to summarize what I've said in these words:

American mass production . . . the American assembly line . . . received its momentum and reached full speed in very large degree from the selling power of the Hollywood film.

That seems to me a prodigious accomplishment. And now for my second point —Hollywood's even greater role . . . its intangible role . . . as an agent for democracy, for the worth and dignity of man throughout the world.

During the past dozen years, I've been privileged to travel to every continent on motion picture business. I've seen our movies in Damascus and Hongkong and Bombay. I've watched with tribesmen in the Belgian Congo who'd never seen a movie before. I've seen them with Bushmen sitting cross-legged on the floor in a thatched hut in Australia. I've seen them in Japan and the Philippines and, a while back, in Soviet Russia and the satellites.

The films I saw in all these places were the same varied fare as our own audiences find in their neighborhood theatres—from musicals to social dramas, from epics to animated cartoons. Seen through the eyes of Asia, Africa, Latin America, these Hollywood films were somehow different—in glamor, in excitement, but also in another quality beyond entertainment.

I'd like to tell you a few incidents. Shortly after the war I went to a screening in Warsaw given by the communist minister of labor for Stakhanovite workers, the elite of the communist labor force. An American film was shown, a rather innocuous romance, and it went over big. What most moved the audience was a scene in which the heroine met her fiance at a factory where he worked. Outside the factory were thousands of American workers' cars.

The minister of labor was deeply disturbed. "Why do you try to fool us?" he asked me. "What do you mean, fool you?" I said. "Oh, now, you know your exploited workers don't have cars like that!" he said. "That's just propaganda!" But he didn't really believe it was propaganda, nor did the Stakhanovites. I still remember them as the party broke up, talking eagerly about American workers and their cars.

I remember another evening on a mountain top near Djakarta, Indonesia, where our motion picture representative lives. Each Saturday night he puts up a bedsheet on his front lawn as a movie screen and invites the whole countryside to attend an American film.

I watched the audience arrive at sundown, women walking up the mountain with their babies on the shoulders, workers [573/574] from the local tea estates, soldiers from the nearby garrison. I was told that even the guerrilla fighters turned up for these shows, parking their guns outside along with the police. As long as the show lasts, a truce exists between guerrillas and police.

The movie that night was a rather antique but complicated Western, without subtitles. I doubted that the audience could make head or tail of it. But they cheered and responded in the right places and, afterward, a native priest came up to me.

"Americans believe as we do," he told me through an interpreter. "How do you mean?" I asked him. "Well," he said, "our religion tells us that good men prosper and evil men don't. From your fine movie, we see that you Americans believe this too!"

I remember other people, other places. I remember a breakfast with President Magsaysay, the late great leader of the Philippines. We'd been having difficulty negotiating currency exchanges with his government and my assistant observed that we might have to withdraw our films. "Oh, no!" the President told me. "We'd have a revolution here if you stopped your films. And besides, my wife would never stand for it!"

Looking back now, how does one weigh, how does one measure the influence of Hollywood? I would not attempt to analyze it in one afternoon but as I think out loud, certain impressions come clear.

Hollywood became and is today America's master salesman because it sells three concepts in which we deeply believe and in which men everywhere devoutly wish to believe. They are:

Hollywood sells the concept that man is an individual, not a mass.

Hollywood sells the concept that man can be and is meant to be free.

Hollywood sells the concept that man can remake his society as he wishes it to be.

In our own country, these concepts are respected but somewhat dated—the date, after all, goes back to our American revolution!

They have been part of our national fabric for almost two centuries, so long that we scarcely notice them any more. Because they are common to Americans, they are also common to Hollywood movies. As Hollywood successfully sells American production, it also successfully sells the concepts of our democracy—without deliberate intent, without an effort to sell anybody anything.

But these ancient concepts of ours—as reflected in our movies—are neither ancient nor commonplace elsewhere in the world. In Africa, in Asia, in many parts of the globe, they are as exciting, novel and challenging as the Bill of Rights was to our ancestors back in 1789.

And the way we shaped our American society, made it provide abundance for us all, is no less exciting and novel and challenging elsewhere. The farmer astride a mule in North Africa who sees in a film a fellow farmer aboard a tractor in Iowa is not likely to forget the experience. The communist peasant who saw "The Grapes of Wrath" remembers how even our dust bowl victims, when driven out of the labor camps, left in their own jalopies.

In such moments as these, I believe, Hollywood has made a lasting impression. It has shown that man can telescope his traditional slow growth from feudalism to free society. It has shown the new nations of the world, now engaged in a titanic struggle for economic freedom, that there *is* a basis for hope—a basis for energy, industry and faith. And with my friend Professor Brogan I say:

"What's wrong with that?"

What's right with it we will see more clearly in the decades to come. After all, Hollywood has been in business for only two generations. In less than a single life span, its mission of entertainment has made the motion picture the most popular art of this 20th century . . . the most popular art in the history of man. We will be just as true to this mission when Hollywood's centennial anniversary comes along.

Hollywood Faces the World*

RICHARD DYER MacCANN. For biographical data, see "The Problem Film in America," p. 51.

. . . .
"Drama is about extreme cases. Drama, from Sophocles to O'Neill, has seldom done a good public relations job for any country."

In these two sentences, Geoffrey Shurlock, administrator of Hollywood's Production Code, has summed up the fundamental problem underlying any ambassadorial function for American motion pictures.

Drama, most critics agree, is based upon conflict. The theatrical motion picture very often turns out to be simply conflict in motion. Film is essentially a physical medium, and it is not surprising that it turned, very early in its history, to the excitement of physical conflict. So long as conflict and shock are basic to drama— so long as twist endings and offbeat characterizations are interesting to audiences —these things will be more important to motion picture producers than precise truth or balanced reporting or even good will.

The question is not whether pictures like *On the Waterfront* or *The Defiant Ones* present a dramatized and therefore a distorted view of American problems. This is a question for students and critics of the film medium to [93/94] debate— and it is worth debating, case by case. The art of the film has a long way to go in learning how to cope with public issues. But the question for public policy is whether, on balance, foreign audiences see an excessive number of American films with the easy plot lines of violence and passion. And if there are too many, what can be done about it?

Federal censorship or even federal "guidance" is not likely to offer any special advantages, and the dangers run deep. A Washington official is no better prepared than a film producer to make decisions, pro or con, on scripts or on markets. Even the most gentle advice leads to the most surprising results.

A disturbing example of experimental censorship is already before us. The U.S. Information Agency has exerted firm pressure on choices of film titles in four countries whose opinions are important to the U.S.—Turkey, Yugoslavia, Poland, and Viet Nam. Under an American invention called the Informational Media Guaranty program, the federal government provides dollar exchange services at a favorable rate in these four blocked-currency countries. In effect, the United States pays the distributor his film rental until the frozen foreign funds become available.

This is a most useful and interesting way of encouraging international communication. But for several years there was an approved list of titles. This list included only films tending to show the U.S. in a favorable light. Granted that the emphasis was placed on promoting [94/95] "good" films—that is, "representative" ones—this was nevertheless clearly a case of censorship by the U.S. government of the films Yugoslavs, Poles, Turks, and Viet-Namese could see. It didn't even give them the opportunity to do their own censoring.

The producers most aggrieved by this

* Richard Dyer MacCann, from "Hollywood Faces the World," *Hollywood in Transition* (Boston: Houghton Mifflin, 1962), pp. 93-98.

USIA policy were the fly-by-night independents who thrive on crime and horror pictures. Nothing much was lost to civilization because these countries were not encouraged to see *Bottom of the Bottle, The Fly, Fort Massacre, Girls on the Loose, Guns, Girls, and Gangsters, Live Fast, Die Young, Love Me Tender,* or *Riot in Juvenile Hall.* But on the same 1958 list of films the USIA refused to help were *Anna Lucasta, Crime in the Streets, The Defiant Ones, A Hatful of Rain, I Want to Live, The Last Hurrah, No Down Payment, Paths of Glory, Pork Chop Hill,* and *Time Limit.* Most of these films were judged by various American critics to be among Hollywood's best.

It is true that a distributing company has the option of sending its picture into the country without benefit of the Media Guaranty program. But if this governmental "screening out" process were to be extended for a long period, or extended to other countries, it would unquestionably act as a brake on the making of certain kinds of films in this country—especially those films that call attention to evils in society.

In the era of the dominant foreign market, any kind of government pressure on world distribution, no matter how well intentioned, tends to have a marked effect on [95/96] production. Censorship abroad can no longer be separated from censorship at home.

The pressures from censors, theater managers, and co-production financiers overseas to devitalize—indeed to de-Americanize—the common run of films from Hollywood studios grows greater all the time. For the federal government to add to those pressures would make our pictures so bland and diplomatic and characterless that no healthy American individualist could recognize his countrymen on the screen. Samuel Goldwyn is certainly right when he warns of the distortions of "sweetness and light."

If the federal government wants films made in such a way as to separate the domestic and the foreign market, the obvious answer is some kind of subsidy. Every major film-producing country provides such support, through a box-office rebate or some other means. But it is extremely difficult to invent a system of subsidy which avoids the censoring function. And a proposal for government subsidy with no referencc to the content of films would seem meaningless to the congressmen who would have to vote on it.

The imposition of any effective system of restraints and values can come only through informal relationships within society itself. Restraints operate far more effectively when they are unofficial and integral to the social system. The important—and difficult—thing is for both Hollywood and American society to find new points of contact. [96/97]

Film trends are usually begun by individual decisions, by the stubbornly creative individual film maker. They are supported and continued by social response. A society which wants more vitamins in its screen fare will encourage film producers to want to be better and wiser—more deeply aware of the tangle of world issues.

During the 1960's, Hollywood film makers will be forced to be aware of the feelings of audiences abroad. The effects on the content of films will inevitably vary with the individual producer's sense of responsibility and with the quality of his information and background about foreign feelings and needs. A man with a strong sense of obligation may be meticulous—in a negative way—about such things as censorship problems and the representation of national types on the screen. He may even search hopefully for stories that might add in a positive way to world understanding. A producer, on the other hand, who is careless of such obligations will seek the shekels and let the duty go. He will pitch his appeal to the lowest common response of everyman everywhere, and his vested interest will be to keep that response low, undemanding, and unchanging.

Responsibility is a slippery word, and it carries no binding guarantees. It implies that finding new and better things to pour into the channels of communication is the most satisfying policy—the way to stay in business and be respected by society.

The burden of responsibility must rest, in the last analysis, not on governmental restrictions, but on Holly- [97/98] wood producers themselves. They have the daily decisions to make. Cecil B. deMille put the situation forcefully in a speech to the Screen Producers Guild three years before he died:

When leaders of nations tell us—as the highest officials of Egypt and Burma have told us—that as boys they derived their conceptions of the world, their ideas of right and wrong, from American motion pictures, they bring home to us our awe-inspiring responsibility. It is a sobering thought that the decisions we make at our desks in Hollywood may intimately affect the lives of human beings, men, women, and children throughout the world.

The main thing theatrical film makers can do, having already begun to face the economic facts of the world market, is to admit to themselves that there are positive duties involved in reaching a world audience—that they have a colossal amount to learn about the real world at home and abroad—that instinct and imitation and inbreeding are not enough. It is not pleasant to keep remembering this, nor easy to know what to do about it. But those who do will have far better prospects of competing in the long run, because their awareness of the world will help them reach the world audience with messages that lift the heart and open the pocketbook too.

· · · · · · · · · · · ·

The Cinema as a Moral Leveller*

GEORGE BERNARD SHAW (1856-1950)—political essayist, music and dramatic critic, commentator on the state of mankind, and probably the greatest playwright of the twentieth century (*Candida* [1898], *Caesar and Cleopatra* [1901], *Man and Superman* [1903], *Major Barbara* [1907], *Pygmalion* [1913], *Saint Joan* [1923])—had many hopes and doubts about the cinema. Some of these are expressed in the following paragraphs.

.   .   .   .
... the danger of the cinema is not the danger of immorality, but of morality. The cinema must be not merely ordinarily and locally moral, but extraordinarily and internationally moral. A film must go round the world unchallenged if the maximum of profit is to be made from it. . . .
.   .   .   .
... it is quite a mistake to suppose that conventional morality is all of one piece the world over. London cannot live on the morals of the Italian peasant or the Australian sheep-farmer. What is more, high civilization is not compatible with the romance of the pioneer communities of Canada. Yet commercialism forces such morals on the cinema.

The moral is, of course, that the State should endow the cinema, as it should endow all forms of art to the extent necessary to place its highest forms above the need for competition. The highest forms, like the lowest, are necessarily immoral because the morals of the community are simply its habits, good and bad; and the highest habits, like the lowest, are not attained by enough people to make them general and therefore moral. Morality, in fact, is only popularity; and popular notions of virtuous conduct will no more keep a nation in the front rank of humanity than [66/96] popular notions of science and art will keep it in the front rank of culture. Ragtimes are more moral than Beethoven's Symphonies; *The Marriage of Kitty* is more moral than any masterpiece of Euripides or Ibsen; Millais is more moral than Mantegna; that is why there is comparatively no money in Beethoven and Ibsen and Mantegna. The London boy can hear a little Beethoven occasionally from an L.C.C. band, and may see Mantegna's work in the National Gallery. Ibsen is to be heard cheaply (in Yiddish) at the Pavilion Theatre in Whitechapel. But the nameless exponents of a world-wide vulgarity (vulgarity is another of the names of morality) have complete possession of the cinema.

Already there is a cry, if not a very loud one, for educational films, meaning, as far as my experience goes, something ending with a fight between an octopus and a lobster. I suggest that what is wanted is the endowment, either public or private, of a cinema theatre devoted wholly to the castigation by ridicule of current morality. Otherwise the next generation of Englishmen will no longer be English: they will represent a world-average of character and conduct, which means that they will have rather less virtue than is needed to run Lapland. I shall be happy to contribute a few sample scenarios.

* George Bernard Shaw, from "The Cinema as a Moral Leveller," New Statesman, Special Supplement on the Modern Theatre, III (June 27, 1914), 1-2; reprinted in Sight and Sound, XXII (October-December, 1952), 66, 96. Reprinted by permission of the New Statesman, the Public Trustee, and The Society of Authors.

[The Internationalized Film]

WILLIAM R. ("BILLY") WILKERSON (1891-1962) was the founder (in 1930) and publisher of the *Hollywood Reporter*, the first daily trade paper in the movie capital. His enterprise and financial acumen used the power of advertising and journalism to influence the movies. His morning editorial was often wrathy, and the ones reprinted here appear to be contradictory; but they reflect Hollywood's own ambivalence on the subject of bowing to the foreign market.

"TRADEVIEWS" (October 28, 1955)*

Mr. Producer: If your picture hasn't an international flavor, you are losing lots of money you should be making.

The foreign market for Hollywood pictures continues to grow. Some say it represents 45 percent of the gross returns on their pictures; others report the take at 50 percent and over. The fact remains, however, that the picture-maker who designs his product for a world-wide appeal, instead of using material that will have little interest out of the U.S., is the producer who's grabbing the big, big money, using the jump in foreign coin to bolster the slowdown in U.S. attendance.

Too, a lot of pictures that are just so-so in our theatres are sensational successes abroad, such as MGM's "Rhapsody" that barely got off the ground here with a $900,-000 gross but rolled up a $4,000,000 foreign take. There have been many such pictures.

Twentieth-Fox so far this year has done $10,000,000 more in the foreign market than in the entire 1954 period. Currently this organization is collecting better than $1,000,000 in remittable dollars each week from its foreign exchanges. This because Zanuck has demanded stories and scripts that have more foreign appeal. You can't get that studio to even consider what might be termed a "typical American" yarn.

Every smart outfit must shoot for this foreign business, the returns of which are keeping Hollywood moving, without which there would be no Hollywood today. Each month better deals are being made to unfreeze the money in all foreign markets. Very little of Hollywood's profits are now resting in foreign clutches; this is resulting in each major and minor company not only shooting for the foreign market but building their organizations to better service that market. Spyros Skouras, who does more foreign traveling than all other company heads combined, sees the great need of more theatres for foreign operations, and he's currently planning to help create those needed houses; the first step, making CinemaScope production equipment available to a lot of foreign producers, to be paid for in their own currencies and out of their **profits**. He rightly figures more native production will spur the building of more native houses and create a greater exhibition spread for the product of 20th and other U.S. companies. [1]

* William R. Wilkerson, "Tradeviews" (editorial), *Hollywood Reporter*, October 28, 1955, p. 1. Reprinted by permission of the *Hollywood Reporter*.

"TRADEVIEWS" (March 23, 1956)*

We wonder, because of the great development of foreign business, if our picture-makers, through the designing of their product for world viewing, might be wiping out important story material of the type that made this picture business, not only in our domestic market and throughout most foreign fields?

We've heard recently of several stories being passed-up by major lots as being "too American." That's a dangerous appraisal and, we believe, a stupid analysis; for the reason that foreign audiences have been attracted, over the years, to our pictures because they ARE American pictures, American stories, depicting our lives, habits and mode of living. They have patronized our shows to get away from their own modes of existence and find in our product entertainments of greater cheer. Accordingly for studio heads and their producers to cause a switch away from pictures "too American," we believe, might eventually kill them off foreign markets as well as the domestic business.

It would be far better not to place too much emphasis on the production thinking for "foreign appeal" and continue selection of the type stories that made our pictures such great hits in theatres throughout the world and continue to give our domestic ticket buyers good solid American stories built around the American family. This would open up the story field that has been narrowing precariously since the "international angle" has been stressed in the search for yarns.

It's not that pictures that have great foreign appeal will not appeal to U.S. audiences, but the toss out of American yarns, generally, and for no good reason, narrows the production focus and is probably losing the studios quite a few good stories. Too, there is the possible hazard that our overseas customers might not like the switch away from tales of our peoples and their lands, business and pastimes. [1]

* William R. Wilkerson, "Tradeviews" (editorial), *Hollywood Reporter*, March 23, 1956, p. 1. Reprinted by permission of the *Hollywood Reporter*.

Universal Influences and Objectives of the Motion Pictures*

JEAN BENOIT-LEVY (1888-1959) produced an estimated 400 educational films in France, as well as the features *La Maternelle* and *Ballerina*. He was professor of visual education at the New School for Social Research in New York from 1941 to 1946, head of the United Nations film unit from 1946 to 1949, and director-general for UNESCO of the International Council of Cinema and Television.

. . . .

The basic idea contained in a film requires that the businessman be able to diffuse it as widely as possible. On the other hand, this diffusion cannot take place unless the idea takes into account the general laws of the motion picture and the psychology of the masses, and remains in touch with the constant evolution of the world. It follows that both the moral ideal and the commercial aim of every film tend to attain universality, that is, to reach every type of audience, made up of all the strata of human society.

Film producers and authors have all coveted universal appreciation for their works; very few have obtained it because they employed artificial means. On the pretext of making necessary concessions to internationalization, they went in for a perfect orgy of expenditures. Thus, they introduced artificial luxury, confusing it with good taste. They banned all local color, thereby obtaining films which had no nationality and which no country could recognize as its own, not even the country producing it. They tried to make "universal" films, which turned out to be films belonging nowhere, for they bore no mark of origin, expressed no conviction, had no soul of their own, and were nothing but lies.

We are lying when we try to express the feelings of others as our own and ape their manners in an attempt to please them. The lie is so obvious that it covers its authors with ridicule. For instance, a few years ago a European film, in order to tempt possible American purchasers, showed all businessmen signing checks with cigars in their mouths and their feet on the desk. Certainly, more than this is needed to make a film American.

We are also lying when we try to show ourselves, not as we are, but as other people see us, out of respect for them and out [220/221] of scorn for ourselves. Such a lie is worse than ridicule: it becomes a loss of dignity.

There are French films, designed for the international market, which have shown a France made up entirely of night clubs and bars in Montmartre and peopled solely by mannequins and apaches wearing caps and red scarves, a fantastic France, conforming exactly to those posters which traveling agencies stick on their doors: "Paris by night under reliable escort."

One day, a foreign buyer confided to me that the exhibitors in his own country would not dare to bill a film that did not contain at least one scene in a bar. If this were really true, the dilemma would be almost hopeless. Does the public really demand only that type of film which conceals the true face of a country under a grotesque mask? In other words, must we barter our dignity and our reputation? Must a film author be compelled to choose between love for his country and love for his occupation?

Fortunately, there is no truth in it, and we have seen countless examples proving the contrary. D. W. Griffith's *Birth of a Nation* (1915) showed the world an epic phase in a people's struggle to find a footing and how, in finding it, they created one of the greatest nations in the world. Much later, Jean Renoir's *La Marseillaise* was shown all over the world, bearing everywhere the eternal flame of the French Revolution and, at the same time, premonitory signs of the danger which once more was threatening Liberty.

Films such as Pagnol's *Harvest,* which, instead of bars and night clubs, showed the gradual resurrection of one of our ruined villages in the Lower Alps, were able to please, and consequently to "earn a living," though remaining specifically "native" products.

To please should never be a goal: he who aims only to please rarely succeeds and acquires a permanent dislike for his own work, since he does not believe in it. To please can only be the natural consequence of a sincere piece of work. All true expression has a magnetic power which exerts a spiritual attraction. Only that individual who expresses himself can be radiant [**221/222**] and vibrant. Likewise, everything sincere is strength while everything false is weakness. The truly universal film, far from being a film which belongs nowhere, is much more likely to be one about which a country can say, in all sincerity, "That is one of our own films."

In short, a film must obey the natural law that governs all productive effort. Here again, it is the earth which furnishes us with our greatest lesson. Fruits grow and ripen according to the nourishment they receive from the natal soil, and the best of them are the ones that are ex-ported. Only those artists who have learned this lesson in sincerity have produced great works. Every country has its own culture, its own writers; every country should have its own films. [**222/228**]

. . . .

My whole experience has led me to the conviction that, for a dramatic work to gain an international audience, it must above all be an essentially personal creation. Only then will it have some chance of taking a trip around the world.

A work should be stamped with its author's style. No one needs to be a specialist to recognize the work of Marcel L'Herbier, Julien Duvivier, Raymond Bernard, Jean Renoir, Jacques Feyder, René Clair, or the work of Frank Capra, William Wyler, Charlie Chaplin, D. W. Griffith, and countless others I could mention.

These films bear the imprint of the artist who created them, and the latter cheerfully accepts the imprint of his own country. An artist will do better creative work if he is on familiar ground and if he draws his inspiration from familiar sources. A film made in Paris will not become an international film merely because the author inserts a shot of Rockefeller Plaza, however fine a shot it may be; on the contrary, he must limit himself to translating his own thoughts, the natural aspirations of his own people.

A film author should take pride in saying: "Here is my country! This is what we think, this is how we live!" And the foreign spectator will say to himself: "There is France, there is Russia, there is America," or whatever country originated the film. In that case, the motion picture will have fulfilled its universal mission, for it will have introduced the people of the world to each other. It will have brought them face to face with each other's customs, cultures, daily actions and gestures, in all honesty and without deception. And for the first time, men will discover how much they resemble each other!

PART SEVEN

SHOULD FILMS FOR TELEVISION BE CONTROLLED?

Forgotten Clues to the TV Crisis*

JACK GOULD (1914-   ), after a five-year stint as a reporter on the New York *Herald Tribune*, joined the drama department of the New York *Times* in 1937, moving to the radio-television department in 1942. He has been the radio-television critic for the *Times* since 1944.

Television is at a crossroads. The sighs of disappointment over the fall of Charles Van Doren in a rigged quiz game have given way to a rising clamor for fundamental changes in the medium that enters 45,000,000 homes.

For the moment, video has a full-time job in merely tabulating the diversified indictments of its behavior. The aftermath of the hanky-panky in the isolation booth has taken on the proportions of a coast-to-coast morality play, involving the ethics of big business, the efficacy of American education and the solubility of aspirin.

Two governmental agencies, one branch of the Executive Department, innumerable Congressional committees, pedagogues, economists, industrialists and salesmen are examining the TV medium in varying depths. Moreover, the TV world itself is split over the most becoming posture to assume in its moment of crisis. The chaos of TV, in short, cannot be pictured in black and white; it comes in living color.

But there are two fundamental conditions governing television that have tended to become obscured in the welter of words over the future of an industry on which everyone is an expert.

First, the broadcaster receives free of charge a publicly owned channel that can be a veritable gold mine—a source of gross income running into millions of dollars a year. In exchange for this grant it is his responsibility to use that facility in the best interests of the people. Yet that responsibility has not been properly accepted.

Second, the Government, through the instrumentality of the Federal Communications Commission, should assure that television channels actually are employed as broadcasters, in order to obtain their licenses, promise they will be used. To give away a public treasure and then be indifferent to how it may be abused amounts to an abdication of government. Yet this is what has happened in TV.

Much of the growing argument over television's shortcomings and accomplishments suffers from a common weakness: too many people are speaking from prepared positions. The defenders of the status quo are erecting a wall of publicity handouts to conceal the problems which traditionally they have been loath to face; the reformers are convinced that a living-room poll of their intellectual acquaintances provides the answers for the medium's future. Not until the hard facts are spelled out dispassionately can one achieve a realistic assessment of television as it is and as it might be.

At the outset it should be noted that, while television is a business, it is not like any other business. Of course, video must make money but at the same time it must

* Jack Gould, "Forgotten Clues to the TV Crisis," New York *Times Magazine*, December 13, 1959, pp. 9, 88-89, 92. Reprinted by permission of the New York *Times* and the author.

perform a public service. Unless television rests on a firm and realistic economic foundation, it simply will be unable to offer the alternative types of programs that should accompany the more popular mass wares.

Inherent in an appraisal of television is the role of the American public. In this respect TV shares a problem common to all media catering to large segments of the population. Many people—a large majority—do not see the need for keeping abreast of the vital issues facing the world; unfortunate and undesirable as it may be socially, there are millions who do not yearn for education or uplift. Broadcasters often have been accused of underestimating the American intelligence; but reformers often have been just as guilty in overestimating it.

American television is not unusual in this respect. For many years in Great Britain there was only one television service —the non-commercial British Broadcasting Corporation. In terms of cultural objectives its performance was unique; free from the competitive pressures of the marketplace, it could pursue the loftiest [9/88] of goals. Three years ago there was inaugurated a commercial, advertising-sponsored TV network with a high proportion of typically American offerings. The popular wares have run away with the majority audience in the British Isles.

It is the same story in many another country—Japan, Canada, Italy, Australia. Most people most of the time do want to be entertained.

But where the television industry became sidetracked was in its decision to allow the doctrine of "giving the public what it wants" to obscure its companion duties and obligations to the viewing public.

Surely, television should be free to entertain and sell goods or the big shows enjoyed by many will become impossible. But, as part of its pledge in accepting a license, the television station must accept its share of the awesome job of elevating the public's awareness of major issues, of slowly inching forward toward a higher cultural level, of making sure neither the medium nor its audience succumbs to a state of stagnation.

In television's case this obligation to pursue balance is not theoretical. One of the engineering shortcomings of television has been that its place in the spectrum was restricted to a limited number of channels. There is not enough room on the air for all who might wish to try their hand at broadcasting; this explains, for instance, why New York does not have an educational channel. In short, the active broadcaster occupies space that is in scarce supply and may be sought by others.

Despite the uproar over quiz deceits, dubious commercials and the need for reforms, it should be recognized that TV has done good things. Edward R. Murrow's famed program on the late Senator Joseph R. McCarthy was a major aid in restoring national perspective in an era of hysteria; the Columbia Broadcasting System's recent study of birth control was a first-class illustration of arousing the public to think about a touchy issue.

One of the great services performed by television in the public affairs area, of course, is the medium's ability to provide a graphic and personalized view of major events, such as the recent trip of Premier Khrushchev to the United States. The power of the medium to make constructive contributions should not be minimized.

The criticism of television is that this power has not been used as it should be. The TV networks have not fully realized that their influence can be negative as easily as affirmative. To shield 100,000,000 people from the harsh realities of contemporary existence night after night can be a major cause of a most dangerous trend —national apathy.

As salesmen, sponsors may wish to bask in the warming radiance of happy programing that makes for coast-to-coast contentment. But if network broadcasters are to make their full contribution to the country's future, they must disturb, awaken and excite viewers to think for themselves. That is the acid test of citizenship in broadcasting. The current crisis of TV involves not so much what is on the air as what is not.

Responsibility for maintenance of balance rests in the first instance with the Federal Communications Commission, the agency established by Congress to license stations and see that the airwaves are used in the public interest.

In entertaining an application for a license, which runs three years, the F. C. C. examines the character and financial qualifications of the [88/89] would-be broadcaster. Detailed data on stock holdings in the station also must be listed. But when such factors are roughly equal for two applicants competing for a single license, the commission may give primary consideration to broad promises in programing.

In the broadcasting world the matter of promises is rather cynically regarded. A station owner can swear that he is going to flood his viewing area with nothing but cultural treats and news in unlimited volume and do a fine job reflecting local interests and problems. Once he receives his license, however, he can stop worrying, insert multiple commercials at every opportunity and just flick a switch and run movies, network quizzes or whatever makes the most money. Not all individual broadcasters do, of course; some station owners are conscientious community leaders. But the F. C. C. is notorious for not asking a broadcaster whether his performance matched his promise.

The caliber of the members of the F. C. C. admittedly is not as high as it should be. Few have the background—or have displayed much searching interest—in the broad social and philosophical aspects of administering a medium of enormous influence. The commission is overworked and undermanned, but Congress cannot escape its share of responsibility

for encouraging the existence of a weak commission. There has been too much political hanky-panky surrounding the F. C. C.

In the absence of minimum standards, the broadcasting industry has largely functioned in a vacuum where the strongest economic forces could make the ground rules. These forces have been the sponsors and their advertising agencies. By the power of their buying dollars, they have assumed control over the content of programming, even to dictat- [89/92] ing the types of plays that could be done, actively censoring scripts and avoiding the slightest hint of controversy. All too often their concept of competition has merely meant imitation.

With a weak government agency and strong sponsor influence the wonder is that TV did not encounter disaster long before now. Indeed, the joke is making the rounds of Madison Avenue that in generations to come Charles Van Doren may emerge as a historic figure. It was he, after all, who initiated the reform era in TV.

Plans for the improvement of television are a dime a dozen, most of them concerned with form rather than substance. Much has been made of the issue of control in TV, whether it rests with sponsors or networks. But in the last analysis the man who pays the bills always is going to exercise a high degree of control, whether he himself produces a show or someone else seeks to satisfy his taste.

Also in the present crisis of TV there has been the usual flurry of suggestions that either the White House or the broadcasting industry should appoint a citizens' committee to review TV, a neat way of using a bit of window-dressing to defer action on serious problems. Advertising-sponsored television in London also has been suggested as a model (but even the British have not elected to do away with the middle commercial).

It must be recognized that there always will be certain types of programs essential to a well-rounded schedule that may not appeal to advertisers. It is in this area that the networks have been primarily remiss. If sponsors are reluctant to offer penetrating news shows, plays of controversy and discussions that may offend, then it becomes the task of the broadcaster to take up the slack and assure the social validity of television's output.

The job confronting both the networks and the F. C. C. is to preserve what is good in the present system while laying the groundwork for continuing improvements.

Surely, the F. C. C. already has the legal authority to ask a broadcaster to demonstrate that he did on the air what he said he was going to do. If there is a wide gap between promise and performance, then renewal of his license should be held in abeyance until the situation is clarified. Once it was established that a broadcaster really risked his franchise if he did not keep his pledge to the Government, there would be a basis on which meaningful self-regulation could function.

Such a policy of weighing performance against promise would not involve censorship or dictation of television content. Programming needs never can be put in a bureaucratic straitjacket. All the F. C. C. would do is demand that a broadcaster actually meet those standards that he set up for himself.

The second step is to require the networks, as the primary sources of programming, to set forth in advance what they think is a desirable diversity of programs for their evening schedules. In other words, they should take it upon themselves to draw up a blueprint of programming intent that would be known and understood by sponsors, station affiliates and viewers.

It is a tradition of advertisers that, once they know what a medium's regulations are, they will conform. If the networks can summon up enough courage to let the world know who is boss in fact as well as publicity release, then sponsor dominance will begin to ebb.

But the networks at the same time must face up to an unpleasant yet important fact. If they are to perform a public service within the true meaning of the Federal Communications Act, then at some point there is going to be a limitation on how much profit they can make.

Actually, the future of television constitutes a genuine challenge to the resiliency of the free-enterprise system. The test that lies ahead is whether the profit motive can survive without compromising cultural values that are just as vital to a well-rounded society. What appears tomorrow on television's twenty-one-inch screen is not a narrow matter of electronics or show business; it also will be a reflection of democracy in action, one way or another.

Communications Act of 1934*

The Communications Act of 1934 was preceded, as most laws are, by public demand, presidential proposals, and committee hearings in Congress. The top officials of broadcasting urged its passage, in view of the inadequate powers of the Federal Radio Commission (established in 1927) to keep the frequencies of radio stations from conflicting. Recent amendments to the act have been concerned with such political problems as the obligation of TV stations to give equal time to all candidates for office.

An Act
To provide for the regulation of interstate and foreign communication by wire or radio, and for other purposes.

. . . .

TITLE I—GENERAL PROVISIONS

PURPOSES OF ACT: CREATION OF FEDERAL COMMUNICATIONS COMMISSION

Section 1. For the purpose of regulating interstate and foreign commerce in communication by wire and radio so as to make available, so far as possible, to all the people of the United States a rapid, efficient, Nation-wide, and world-wide wire and radio communication service with adequate facilities at reasonable charges, for the purpose of the national defense, for the purpose of promoting safety of life and property through the use of wire and radio communication, and for the purpose of securing a more effective execution of this policy by centralizing authority heretofore granted by law to several agencies and by granting additional authority with respect to interstate and foreign commerce in wire and radio communication, there is hereby created a commission to be known as the "Federal Communications Commission", which shall be constituted as hereinafter provided, and which shall execute and enforce the provisions of this Act.

. . . .

APPLICATION OF ACT

Section 2. (a) The provisions of this Act shall apply to all interstate and foreign communication by wire or radio and all interstate and foreign transmission of energy by radio, which originates and/or is received within the United States, and to all persons engaged within the United States in such communication or such transmission of energy by radio, and to the licensing and regulating of all [**1064/ 1065**] radio stations as hereinafter provided; . . . .

. . . .

DEFINITIONS

Section 3 . . . . (b) "Radio communication" or "communication by radio" means the transmission by radio of writing, signs, signals, pictures, and sounds of all kinds including all instrumentalities, facilities, apparatus, and services (among other things, the receipt, forwarding, and delivery of communications) incidental to such transmission. [**1065/1066**]

. . . .

* 48 U.S. Stat. 1064-1067, 1081-1084, 1091 (1934).

PROVISIONS RELATING TO THE COMMISSION

Section 4. (a) The Federal Communications Commission (in this Act referred to as the "Commission") shall be composed of seven commissioners appointed by the President, by and with the advice and consent of the Senate, one of whom the President shall designate as chairman.

(b) Each member of the Commission shall be a citizen of the United States. No member of the Commission or person in its employ shall be financially interested in the manufacture or sale of radio apparatus or of apparatus for wire or radio communication; in communication by wire or radio or in radio transmission of [**1066/ 1067**] energy; . . . . Not more than four commissioners shall be members of the same political party. [**1067/1081**]

. . . .

TITLE III—SPECIAL PROVISIONS RELATING TO RADIO LICENSE FOR RADIO COMMUNICATION OR TRANSMISSION OF ENERGY

Section 301. It is the purpose of this Act, among other things, to maintain the control of the United States over all the channels of interstate and foreign radio transmission; and to provide for the use of such channels, but not the ownership thereof, by persons for limited periods of time, under licenses granted by Federal authority, and no such license shall be construed to create any right, beyond the terms, conditions, and periods of the license. . . . [**1081/1082**]

. . . .

GENERAL POWERS OF COMMISSION

Section 303. Except as otherwise provided in this Act, the Commission from time to time, as public convenience, interest, or necessity requires, shall—

(a) Classify radio stations;

(b) Prescribe the nature of the service

to be rendered by each class of licensed stations and each station within any class;

(c) Assign bands of frequencies to the various classes of stations, and assign frequencies for each individual station and determine the power which each station shall use and the time during which it may operate;

(d) Determine the location of classes of stations or individual stations;

(e) Regulate the kind of apparatus to be used with respect to its external effects and the purity and sharpness of the emissions from each station and from the apparatus therein;

(f) Make such regulations not inconsistent with law as it may deem necessary to prevent interference between stations and to carry out the provisions of this Act: . . . .

(g) Study new uses for radio, provide for experimental uses of frequencies, and generally encourage the larger and more effective use of radio in the public interest;

(h) Have authority to establish areas or zones to be served by any station;

(i) Have authority to make special regulations applicable to radio stations engaged in chain broadcasting;

(j) Have authority to make general rules and regulations requiring stations to keep such records of programs, transmissions of energy, communications, or signals as it may deem desirable; [**1082/1083**]

. . . .

ALLOCATION OF FACILITIES; TERM OF LICENSES

Section 307. (a) The Commission, if public convenience, interest, or necessity will be served thereby, subject to the limitations of this Act, shall grant to any applicant therefor a station license provided for by this Act. [**1083/1084**]

. . . .

(d) No license granted for the operation of a broadcasting station shall be for a longer term than three years and no license so granted for any other class of station shall be for a longer term than five years, and any license granted may be revoked as hereinafter provided. Upon the expiration of any license, upon application therefor, a renewal of such license may be granted from time to time for a term of not to exceed three years in the case of broadcasting licenses and not to exceed five years in the case of other licenses; . . . .

(e) No renewal of an existing station license shall be granted more than thirty days prior to the expiration of the original license. . . . **[1084/1091]**

• • • • • • • • • • • • •

CENSORSHIP; INDECENT LANGUAGE

Section 326. Nothing in this Act shall be understood or construed to give the Commission the power of censorship over the radio communications or signals transmitted by any radio station, and no regulation or condition shall be promulgated or fixed by the Commission which shall interfere with the right of free speech by means of radio communication. . . .

• • • • • • • • • • • • •

"The People Own the Air"*

The toughest TV critic yet to appear in the U.S. last week dared the station and network operators and owners to sit down in front of their sets from sign-on to sign-off. They would see, he told them, "a vast wasteland—a procession of game shows, violence, audience participation shows, formula comedies about totally unbelievable families, blood and thunder, mayhem, violence, sadism, murder, western bad men, western good men, private eyes, gangsters, more violence, and cartoons. And, endlessly, commercials—many screaming, cajoling, and offending. And, most of all, boredom."

The critic was Newton N. Minow, 35, new chairman of the Federal Communications Commission, and his audience was the National Association of Broadcasters' convention in Washington. Accustomed to a mild FCC that never interfered with programing, the TV owners and operators were more deeply shaken by Minow's blast than they had been by the quiz scandals or anything else in TV history.

DEBTS TO BE PAID. Lawyer Minow refused to accept the broadcasters' argument that they are only giving the public what it wants. For one thing, there is some doubt as to what the public wants, and ratings are at best only "an indication of how many people saw what you gave them . . . I am not convinced that the people's taste is as low as some of you assume." Broadcasters, said Minow, ought to follow the example of the newspaper publishers, whose own polls consistently show that the two most popular items in the papers are the comics and the sob sisters. "But the news is still on the front pages of all newspapers, the editorials are not replaced by

more comics, the newspapers have not become one long collection of advice to the lovelorn."

Even if "people would more often prefer to be entertained than stimulated or informed," said Minow, "your obligations are not satisfied if you look only to popularity . . . It is not enough to cater to the nation's whims—you must also serve the nation's needs. The people own the air. They own it as much in prime evening time as they do at 6 o'clock Sunday morning. For every hour that the people give you, you owe them something. I intend to see that your debt is paid with service . . . Never have so few owed so much to so many."

HOW TO BRIDGE THE GAP. While promising that there would be no censorship, Minow announced that the FCC will no longer automatically renew the licenses of stations that insist on lowest-common-denominator programing. In the future, the agency will hold public hearings on stations whose performance has not measured up to their promise to offer a diversified output. "For those few of you who really believe that the public interest is merely what interests the public," said Minow, "I hope these hearings will arouse no little interest."

Minow's speech revealed both a first-rate legal mind and a deep personal conviction. Born in Milwaukee, where his father owned a chain of laundries, he is a graduate of Northwestern Law School ('50), where he edited the *Law Review*. In 1951 he was taken on as a law clerk by Supreme Court Chief Justice Fred Vinson; a year later he joined the staff of Illinois Governor Adlai Stevenson as an administrative

* "The People Own the Air," Time, LXXVII (May 19, 1961), 53. Courtesy Time; copyright Time Inc. 1961.

assistant. In 1955 Minow joined Stevenson's newly formed law firm, became a partner two years later. His personal taste in TV runs to public-service shows during Sunday's intellectual "ghetto" hours.

Minow's demand for better TV was seconded by:

Abraham Ribicoff, Secretary of Health, Education and Welfare, who gave the broadcasters a pretty tall order: "The national interest requires that we raise the cultural level of our country and that we bridge the gap between those of our citizens who have had the benefit of a great deal of formal education and those who have not."

Former Florida Governor Leroy Collins, who decried the low estate of broadcasters as compared with editors and publishers. As Governor of Florida, Collins recalled, he always turned to radio and TV if he wanted to reach a large audience, but only to the press "when I wanted help in carrying out my program, when it was influence I needed to help lead the thinking of the people." This situation can only change, said Collins, if TV, like the press, begins taking sides and editorializing, instead of being merely a "passive observer."

A HINT IN TIME. The buffeted broadcasters angrily replied that the Government was trying to control TV programing by using the FCC's licensing power as a club. "If you extend Minow's words, you get into tricky water," went a typical complaint. " 'I may not renew your license if I don't like your programing,' he says, and then in the next breath he insists there will be no censorship."

Among broadcasters, Minow's speech was hailed as "courageous"—which it certainly was—only by Leonard Goldenson, president of American Broadcasting-Paramount Theaters, Inc., parent corporation of the ABC network, which has risen to the top of the TV heap through its blood-and-thunder programing. NBC and CBS maintained official silence. But most broadcasters took the speech as a deliberate tactic to scare stations and networks into better programing, and as a hint that they should do something about it soon. [53]

The Bloodshot Eye*

ROY HUGGINS (1914-   ) studied political science at the University of California, graduating in 1939. From 1943 to 1946 he worked as an industrial engineer and wrote fiction in his spare time. He was offered screenwriting jobs as a result and became a TV film-maker at Warner Brothers, where he produced the *Maverick* series. At Twentieth Century-Fox, he was executive producer of *Bus Stop* and other series when the so-called Fabian episode was filmed. He joined Revue Productions (formerly a subsidiary of MCA, the artists' agency) in 1962, to produce the 90-minute series *The Virginian*. This selection is an excerpt from a speech given at San Francisco State College for the TV-Radio Guild.

The widely held belief that television experienced a golden age which was destroyed by the tyranny of ratings and the philistinism of a profit philosophy is one of the many myths of broadcasting.[1] There was a time in the early fifties when television was filled with a heady excitement, and recollections of it invite us to indulge ourselves in nostalgia. But that this brief period was television's apotheosis is denied not only by discerning critics but by the very men who were responsible for programming at the time. Television's impulse toward slow but steady improvement has never faltered, until today. Now, for the first time in that medium's brief history, a decline in quality and spirit is under way, and the abrupt reversal is largely the result of Newton Minow's policies as Chairman of the Federal Communications Commission. [6/7]

This premise is addressed to that group in our society whose first reaction will be one of swift and angry rejection. It is one of the mysteries of these disjunctive times that the liberal community gives impassioned support to governmental control of our greatest source of public art, information and orientation, thus putting itself on the dark side of a battle in which the stake is no less than America's tradition of free speech. The mystery is deepened by the fact that this fealty is granted to a seven-man regulatory agency made up of three lawyers, two engineers, one businessman, and a former member of the FBI. The mystery yields slightly to the inarguable: that no man of good will denies the worthiness of Minow's goals or fails to share his apprehensions concerning the trivial role assigned to this powerful medium by our society. But it should be one thing to share Minow's alarms and quite another to approve his policies. I agree with everything Newton Minow says, but I will oppose to the death his right to say it.

When Minow dropped his two-word bomb at the Sheraton Park Hotel in Washington, he said absolutely nothing new, but he said it as the representative of a new administration, and he said it to the National Association of Broadcasters. An implacable glut of words followed, but with the exception of network concessions

[1] Although Paddy Chayevsky, single-handedly, came close to making it a reality.

* Roy Huggins, from "The Bloodshot Eye," *Television Quarterly*, I (August, 1962), 6-22. Reprinted by permission of *Television Quarterly* and the author.

to UHF, no significantly original ideas emerged from the Minow phase of the debate, and no viable conclusion seems near. But if no new ideas emerged, a new program of action did, a program that threatens to produce a crisis in American television. I hope to document this statement with facts so manifest in the current experience of television, and rooted in causes which may be inferred with such certainty, that supporters of the FCC Chairman may at the very least consider a reassessment of his role in our culture.

Television's vulnerability is not entirely a question of quality, although one would assume so from reading the assaults upon it. Actually, most of its public problems have arisen out of simple facts of quantity and affective impact. Television drove from the market place such other mass media as pulp magazines, radio drama, the B motion picture as we once knew it, and numbers of large-circulation slick magazines such as *Collier's* and *American*. These displaced media had always been targets for criticism; but when many targets are reduced to one, the total amount of shooting appears to have grown enormously, and the concentrated uproar draws quite a crowd. It is in the nature of crowds to join the action, as witness the history of lynching. No subject, including politics, is today more widely discussed in the public prints than television, almost all of it malign. [7/8] In February 1962 an entire issue of *Cosmopolitan* was thrown into the breach, the cover carrying a banner reading "Televisionitis—Special Issue." All of which poses still another enigma. As W. Theodore Pierson, a member of the FCC bar, pointed out in *Television Quarterly*, the competitors in other media who support governmental control of broadcast programs should pause to consider "whether this is not really a cannibal's picnic—that while they may eat at this one, they might be eaten at the next."

There is no question that the FCC, the initials of which, the Commissioners are fond of saying, mean "from crisis to crisis," is charged by law with the duty to see that television channels are used "in the public interest, convenience and necessity." It is equally true that this is a phrase taken from public utilities legislation, and no public utility was ever confronted with a problem so complex, so fraught with social, political and moral overtones as programming. Nor are the broadcasters classified as public utilities. (Although Calvin Coolidge thought they ought to be.)

There is also no question that every broadcaster, in accepting his license, acknowledges the FCC's authority and promises faithfully to use that portion of the public air thus loaned to him in the public interest, convenience and necessity. But at no time in this basic contractual relationship is it acknowledged that the primary function of the public arts is to entertain.

Nearly 50 million Americans have purchased television sets, spending some 25 billion dollars in sets and service. Many researchers have asked them why they bought those sets, and no American has ever been known to reply that he did so out of devotion to the public interest, convenience and necessity. The vast majority simply replied: "For entertainment." When they were asked what television had done for them, "the great majority," reports Raymond Stewart, who surveyed the problem for the Division of Journalism at Emory University, "answered that it had entertained them." But the word "entertainment" does not appear in the Communications Act, and perhaps rightly so. The Congress was doubtless confident that entertainment would take care of itself, but feared that the public interest might not. However, the Act also failed to define the public interest,[2] avoided any language relating to the imponderables of programming for a mass audience, required the Commission to make judgments on program quality, but added a section (326) forbidding the Commission to censor or to interfere with freedom of speech.

The ambiguity of the Act probably re-

---

[2] A task which has, throughout history, proved too much for political philosophers.

sulted from the Congress's discovery of the impossibility of reducing to points of law the tenuous [8/9] relationship, if any, between the public interest and the public arts. The broadly stated Communications Act is evidently based on great faith in the democratic process and none at all in the contention of most intellectuals that mass culture is a corrupting and exploitive social force.

Minow plans to reach his goal of raising the aesthetic and public service levels of programming by following two divergent routes. He hopes to increase competition and variety through the expansion of television service. He has been one of the most effective chairmen in the history of the FCC in his efforts to enlarge limited markets, in his courageous fight for legislation to bring the dormant UHF channels into use, in his sponsorship of federal aid to educational television, and in clearing the way for the proponents of pay-TV to prove their contentions or to fail in the attempt. For these labors he richly deserves our esteem and our support.

It was along the second and, in his view, more direct and important route that the dangers lay, and Minow was acutely aware of those dangers from the start. In his initial appearance before the Senate Committee on Interstate and Foreign Commerce he carefully declared his distaste for censorship. Since that time he has not, in any important public appearance, failed to make this obeisance to the American tradition of freedom of speech. In his first public address he said, "There will be no suppression of programming which does not meet with bureaucratic tastes. Censorship strikes at the tap root of our free society."

But Minow came into government service with a mission: to bring all the power at his command to bear upon the broadcasters, to force them to program for the entire public and not merely for the lowest common denominator of that public, to force the broadcasters to lead the mass audience instead of slavishly catering to it, to raise the level of public taste instead

of debasing it. And since Newton Minow is a brilliant attorney who once served under the late Justice of the Supreme Court, Fred M. Vinson, he understood well the awesome limitations of the Act from which his authority stemmed. He was also aware that the Congress, over thirty of whose members have ownership interests in broadcasting stations, had never tolerated control of program content by the FCC. And since this was precisely what Minow intended to accomplish, his course of action demanded skill and audacity.

He began by making a painstaking study of FCC history, and one can infer that he learned much from the Commission's tactical error in issuing the "Blue Book," officially titled *Public Service Responsi-* [9/10] *bility of Broadcast Licensees* and containing specific guidelines to programming. That document well represents Minow's views on programming, and it has never been repudiated by the FCC; but Minow has made no effort to resurrect it. Its publication constituted a written, formal expression of the FCC's programming philosophy, and was therefore a vulnerable move, as was evidenced by the clamor inside Congress and out, for amendments to the Communications Act which followed the document's publication. The Act was not amended, but the "Blue Book" was quickly forgotten and was allowed to go out of print in 1960.

Approximately three months after the Senate confirmed Minow as Chairman of the FCC he had prepared his strategy. It soon became clear that it was based on the minimum formal use of his ambiguous authority and the maximum public use of the immense latent power of government, a power to be used obliquely in order to avoid challenge in the courts. The plan greatly heightened the historic problem of staying within the critical limits of Congressional tolerance, but that problem could be solved in the contemporary way: by winning broad public support.

On May 9, 1961, Minow launched his campaign to wrest control of programming from the broadcasters by indicting them for their past performance, choosing a time, a place and a manner calculated to arouse massive public interest and response. His success was astonishing, possibly even to Minow himself, although his famous phrase was not lightly chosen. It figured prominently in FCC publicity releases prepared prior to the delivery of the speech. Thus began that aspect of the Minow regime which is new in FCC history, but very much in keeping with the Kennedy administration's trend away from government by politicians and toward government by administrative personalities.

Having successfully laid the base for his program, Minow followed swiftly with further stinging censures combined with pointed reminders that the air belongs to the people, that broadcasters had better get used to the idea that their licenses are not property rights. "Spokesmen for the Commission" were allowed to make statements that, to quote *Broadcasting*, it was a "distinct possibility that one or more operating stations would lose their licenses in 1962." The old phrase from Chairman Fly's time about the "lifted eyebrow" was resurrected—no more true now than it was then. It is not the lifted eyebrow that terrifies the broadcasters, it is the lifted axe that Commissioner Durr once so bitterly complained of: "The Commission . . . has no power except the death sentence." [10/11]

Great numbers of broadcasters began to show up in Washington. "Station owners," reported *Broadcasting*, "even those with small outlets at a great distance from Washington, D. C., have been routing trips to include a stopover in the nation's capital this year. This increase in tourism is not necessarily due to cherry blossoms and the White House tour. It is more often so that station management can stop at the FCC to learn why they have been sent letters of inquiry on programming and what they can do to assure license renewal."

The kind of programming Minow held in low esteem became a matter of desperate interest to licensees. They learned that he did not care for "game shows, violence, audience participation shows, formula comedies about totally unbelievable families . . . Western bad-men, Western good men, private-eyes, gangsters, more violence, and cartoons." They also learned that he liked such shows as *The Bing Crosby Special, The Fred Astaire Show, Twilight Zone, Kraft Theatre* and *Peter Pan.* Puzzlingly, in the December 13, 1961 issue of *Daily Variety,* the comment was made that "Minow won't discuss his favorite programs or talk specifically about individual shows."

"If I did," *Variety* quoted Minow, "there would be justification in accusing me of being a censor."

As public approval persisted on Minow's side, and President Kennedy continued to hold him in high esteem—and to comment on the fact publicly—Minow became increasingly confident of his policy, which led to the inevitable: the public indictment of specific shows and specific series. This occurred dramatically and with dismaying license at the FCC hearings in Washington in February 1962.

A series called *The Untouchables* was brought before the Commission and was soon being dissected at such length that the questioning covered 67 pages of transcript. Minute details were probed, such as the meaning of a written request to the producer for "less dialogue and more action" in a particular script. The tone of the questioning indicated that the Commission suspected the instructions of being filled with guile. One of the basic principles of film technique is to tell stories through action, to the greatest possible exclusion of dialogue. But the issue here is not film technique but whether or not the Federal Communications Commission was acting in violation of the spirit, if not the content, of the Communications Act in so questioning a programming policy on a specific series, and in making public its disapproval of aspects of that series.

At these same hearings a single show was brought up for discussion, the so-called Fabian episode on *Bus Stop.* . . . [11/12]

The episode was based on a novel, an

allegory on the nature of evil, by Tom
Wicker. The premise of the novel was that
evil is insidious, not easy of recognition,
not subject to effortless defeat, and not in-
clined to vanish because we set up institutions to deal with it. The show was
shocking and disturbing. If it had not
been, it could not have been honest. But
its violence served an aesthetic purpose
and was not excessive, no adultery occurred, and the story did not touch upon,
even by inference, the subject of nympho-
mania. I say this because the show was
widely reported to have dealt with "murder, alcoholism, adultery and nymphoma-
nia." Ben Gross, of the *New York Daily
News,* a gentle and kind man who was
offended by the episode's subject matter,
made a point of the fact that the show was
not, "to be truthful," overly violent.

Then why was there such a strong emotional charge in the general reaction to the
show? In all private runnings before the
episode was aired the audience response
was enthusiastic. . . . But the agency representing the sponsors felt that the story
was so uncompromising, so stark, that their
clients' advertising would appear in an
"environment" that might negate the economic purpose of their sponsorship.

. . . .

When the episode was finally aired on
December 3, 1961, the possibilities for an
objective evaluation had become faint. The
show was extravagantly praised by some
reviewers and enthusiastically damned by
others more numerous, who appeared to
believe that it had been personally conceived, produced and publicized by Oliver
Treyz with the single, cynical purpose of
hiking the rating on *Bus* [12/13] *Stop.*
Mr. Treyz, former president of the American Broadcasting Company, is innocent
of any direct connection with the show beyond putting it on the air. The man who
produced it, Robert Blees, did so in the
conviction that Tom Wicker's premise
was worthy of being restated. The show
was finished before *Bus Stop* began the
season, at a time when the general feeling
was that the series would be successful
critically and statistically.

An important cause of the heavily emotional reaction probably lay in the fact
that the show attacked the cult of optimism, which once so fitly graced the American spirit. That cult still flourishes, with
understandable sensitivity to challenge. As
Dr. T. Earle Johnson, head of the Department of Speech at the University of Alabama, said recently to a meeting of radio
and television broadcasters, "We as a people must have a definite optimism concerning the future of mankind, and you in the
mass communications must give it to us."
[13/14]

. . . .

Thus far I have been unsuccessful in efforts to learn whether or not the FCC saw
the entire episode. I have been told that
they did not, but I choose to remain skeptical of that possibility. In any case, the
Commission discussed the show at length
in its questioning of Oliver Treyz, and
Mr. Minow left no doubt in Mr. Treyz's
mind or in the minds of the leaders of the
industry that he did not consider the show
to be in the public interest. In mid-Decem-
ber 1961, Minow had announced his satisfaction with the progress that was being
made in television. "The trends are pretty
good," he said. "Progress is being made
when 20-odd stations refused to clear
a network program they believed to be objectionable." On frequent other occasions
Minow has angrily protested this tendency
of licensees to air "sterile pap" and avoid
"the new, the creative, the daring." Minow
may have a few hobgoblins, but consistency is clearly not one of them.

It is quite possible that the Fabian episode was a bad show, and that its premise
was poorly stated, although William Wyler
has praised it highly, and novelist James
Jones, whose attitude toward television is
not calculated to warm the hearts of broadcasters, said after viewing it that he "had
just seen a show he thought . . . held some
hope for the future of TV in this country."[3] However, we need not be too concerned here with the quality, or lack of it,

[3] Reported by producer Mark Goodson to the
convention in Chicago of American Women in
Radio and TV.

of the Fabian episode. No charge of libel or of obscenity has ever been made against it. Therefore the point at issue is simply the propriety of the [14/15] FCC's public condemnation of the episode, the testimony on which occupies over 40 pages of transcript. The script of the show itself was hardly that long.

I would like to set aside for a moment the question of the propriety of Minow's policies in order to pursue a simpler inquiry. Assuming that present FCC policies are within the law and within the tradition of American freedom, are those policies in the best interests of American television? To put the question more pertinently, are those policies in the public interest, convenience and necessity? . . .

. . . .

In December of 1961, prior to the airing of the Fabian episode, a network program chief met with me to request that I avoid all "controversial" material henceforth because of growing apprehension among the affiliates. Three scripts were immediately taken off the schedule. This was my first experience with actual censorship as opposed to the normal restrictions of the television code. The network was reacting to its own well-founded fear of governmental regulation as well as to pressures from the beleagured [sic] licensees. Subsequently I learned that numbers of my colleagues were finding themselves subject to similar censorship pressures for the first time. [15/16]

. . . .

. . . Minow's dedication and zeal can only have sprung from a genuine desire to stimulate and to release, not to perpetuate what he honestly abhors: television's tendency to avoid the original and the controversial, its fear of the provocative and the shocking.

Where did Minow go wrong? He has been guilty of a number of errors stemming from his inexperience with the medium. His statements on violence are an example of a tendency to oversimplify a complex craft. Violence must always be interpreted in terms of the context in which it occurs. Slapstick comedy depends heavily on violence, where it has a meaning and effect quite different from the violence in melodrama, which in turn has a meaning and effect different from the violence in drama. Minow also seems to have aligned himself with those who naively regard television as a cause of various social ills. Television has been with us far too short a time to be, at present, anything but a symptom of those ills. He evidently assumes that television's aesthetic level has been fixed at its present low point by network executives who prefer it that way. Television has to provide well over 2000 hours of programming every season, and as Eric Sevareid once observed, "Considering the number of hours you have to fill, it's surprising there's enough mediocrity to go around." But Minow's major error was not one of inexperience but of miscalculation. He failed to understand that the single, compelling reaction among broadcasters to the enormous success of his program would be fear—fear of crippling regulation in the case of the networks, fear of renewal difficulties or actual license revocations in the case of licensees who have invested millions in plant and equipment and who have been told by Minow in his most baleful manner that "there is nothing permanent . . . about a broadcast license."

The public arts are created for a mass audience and for a profit; that is their essential nature. But they can at times achieve truth [16/17] and beauty, and given freedom they will achieve it more and more often. But imagination does not flourish in a climate of coercion. Television has steadily served to enlarge the range of our experience, but it will cease to do so in the atmosphere of panicked insecurity that pervades the medium today. A private enterprise devoted to the public arts cannot respond in health or vigor or courage to the actions of an enthusiastically supported government agency which has publicly declared its contempt for that enterprise and which can administer punishment only by execution.

Nothing affects our culture more deeply, or touches the spirit of the people more closely, than television. It therefore needs to be criticized, to be called to account, censured, threatened, on occasion publicly condemned, and on fewer occasions publicly praised. When this is done by Americans singly or in massive organizations, television can, and does, respond in a spirit of professionalism and public accountabil-

ity. But it also responds in a spirit of health and confidence, aware of its rights and its wider obligations.

I do not believe the Congress intended to grant the privilege of public censure to the FCC—an agency of government with coercive control—the power of life and death over broadcasting. . . .

Fabian Sole Survivor of "Bus Stop" Pileup*

HAL HUMPHREY (1912-   ), a native of Missouri, grew up in Montana and went to the University of Chicago and Northwestern University. He has written for the Chicago *Times*, *Time Magazine*, *Billboard*, the *Daily Journal of Commerce* in Seattle, the Los Angeles *Mirror*, and the Los Angeles *Times* (which absorbed the *Mirror* in 1962). Since 1951, Mr. Humphrey has written from Hollywood a syndicated television column, "Viewing TV with Hal Humphrey," which appears in many newspapers.

HOLLYWOOD—The one party who came out smelling like a rose from the recent Washington investigations into TV violence was 19-year-old Fabian.

As the star of an ABC "Bus Stop" drama last December, Fabian axed an old man to death and later buried a switch-blade knife into his attorney for insisting on a fee for getting Fabian acquitted of the axe murder.

This particular TV drama (it was subtitled "A Lion Walks Among Us") was held up by both the FCC and Dodd Committee as horrible example No. 1 for furthering juvenile delinquency.

Sponsors canceled the drama and ultimately the series. Several TV stations refused to carry the Fabian segment, and it is quite likely that the whole affair triggered the firing of ABC's president, Oliver Treyz.

"It's a shame it had to be something like this to get me recognition as an actor, but, man, this did it," says Fabian. "This whole town looks at me differently now—I feel it."

Pressed for some examples, Fabian (his friends call him "Fabe") cites phone calls from such glittering Hollywood notables as Howard Duff and Ida Lupino, and Carolyn Jones and her producer husband, Aaron Spelling.

"I got great notices from these people, and others," he says.

In Spelling's case, it turned into an offer to do a Dick Powell show, which Fabian was here to do last week. It goes on Powell's NBC series sometime in October.

"Tuesday Weld is in it with me. I like to work with her. We work well together. The story is called 'Run 'Til It's Dark,' and we meet in Las Vegas," Fabian explains.

This time, though, he plays a boy only slightly confused, and he doesn't kill anybody. In fact, he tries hard to save Miss Weld, who is the neurotic here, from going to the devil in a Jaguar. She goes anyway, but it happens so fast that even Sen. Dodd may not catch it.

"I had to go the other way with this one. Yeah! Did I ever!" says Fabian, reflecting on his role in "Bus Stop."

"It's a funny thing, though, about that show. I think if it had been one of Hitchcock's TV shows and with no big name in it, nobody would have heard of it," Fabian adds.

He is probably right. Much gorier TV dramas have been on TV than Fabian's

* Hal Humphrey, "Fabian Sole Survivor of 'Bus Stop' Pileup," Los Angeles *Times-Mirror* Syndicate press release, June 17-18, 1962. Reprinted by permission of the author.

"Bus Stop" show. But ABC's hassle with the sponsors and indecision about when to run it (at one point New Year's Eve was considered) opened the gates for lots of advance attention and speculation by the press and the FCC.

Fabian says that 20th Century-Fox, who produced "Bus Stop," wanted him to shoot some extra scenes around the TV version, so it could be released in Europe as a feature movie.

"I could see it being advertised over there as a wild kind of thing, and I didn't think it would do me any good, so we turned it down," Fabian explains.

He could have grabbed onto another chunk of dough for this movie rehash, but at 19 he has a long way to go before worrying about rainy days and Medicare.

There is a kind of poetic justice in all of this. A group of exploitation-minded impresarios (and the sponsors must be included) decide to take a teen-age idol and put him into what seems like a sure-fire piece of sensationalism. The only hitch is that timing, circumstances or plain Kismet fouls up their best-laid plans.

So what happens? Everybody gets burned except the kid they put out on the limb for bait.

Fabian says he learned this lesson well, and turning down 20th's offer to turn the TV show into a movie indicates he really has.

"I'm serious about acting, and that's why I'm going into summer theater after a short vacation with my parents in Philadelphia," says Fabian.

His first summer theater has Fabian as John in "John Loves Mary."

An Exclusive Interview ... E. William Henry*

E. WILLIAM HENRY (1929-   ), a native of Memphis, Tennessee, and a graduate of Yale and the Vanderbilt University Law School, became a member of the Federal Communications Commission August 30, 1962, and its chairman May 15, 1963, replacing Newton Minow. The questions are by Al Preiss, editor and publisher of *Telefilm International Magazine* in Hollywood.

Question: Chairman Henry, you have been in office as Chairman for about six months. Have you found any unexpected trouble spots in that time?

HENRY: I would say that I have found no unexpected trouble spots. I have found that I have earned my extra 500 dollars, however. There are a number of problem areas that I would like to discuss with this audience: I will mention some of the major problems that we have, just to alert the industry that we do consider them major problems. One of those is the problem of the networks' role in broadcasting.

Question: Chairman Henry, does the dominance by networks concern you particularly.

HENRY: It does indeed. Whenever you have only three outlets determining the major portion of what the American public sees on its television sets, there is cause for concern ... particularly if you see some manifestations of the fact that your fears are justified. In other words, if you see that the networks are going more and more into the production end or the licensing end.

.   .   .   .

Question: We have some things going on in Hartford, Connecticut and in Denver, Colorado, Los Angeles and San Francisco called Pay television. It has been of continuing interest to the Commission for years. Initial plans for pay-television were supposed to provide something we weren't getting from commercial television . . . looking at the Hartford programming schedule, we find that they are providing mainly motion pictures and sports. What are your feelings, Mr. Chairman?

HENRY: That is a big subject. It has developed to the point where the Commission is going to have to stay right on top of it. Pay television, even if it is conducted solely over wire, such as proposed in California, may eventually have such an impact on broadcasting that we will have to be concerned.

It is not really to that point yet. But it is developing in that direction and therefore we should be alert. I would agree that Pay television has the potential of providing some of the programs that commercial television will not provide. I think eventually it will be able to provide this to a minority audience that can pay for it—certain cultural programs that commercial television can't or will not for one reason or another sustain.

It is by no means a panacea in my opinion. It will never provide the public with what it really deserves in that respect, because there will always be a sizable segment of the public which will be interested in this so-called minority taste programming, but which will not be able to pay for it. [28/31]

. . . .

Question: This is more a philosophical question, Mr. Chairman. One of the great catch phrases in American broadcasting is a four letter word called, "free." And each man interprets this in light of his own particular interest, apparently. Usually it is cited that the Communications Act said that broadcasting be free. What the Act says is "it should not be regulated as a public utility." Without legal training, we find a wide divergence between these two interpretations. You are a believer in free broadcasting. What does free broadcasting mean to you?

HENRY: Well that is a good question. . . . [31/32] there are two things. One is the extent to which government can regulate broadcasting. And the other is the matter of which members of the public can receive it. Of course free TV, as far as the public is concerned is television that is sponsored by advertisers. It comes over the air free for all to see. And there is no levy by the government on an annual basis for the purchase of a television set, no licensing of sets. That is what it means to the public and I think that this is the road we have gone down in this country irretrievably and I am all for it. I am not at all interested in pressing for a government subsidized network. As far as government regulation of broadcasting is concerned, it is free in the sense that it is no public utility—its rates are not fixed. In other respects, regulation is the same.

I believe in other fields such as railroad, trucking and pipeline etc., those regulatory bodies get into authorizing borrowings and investments, the amount of money spent for a particular investment and they analyze the wisdom of that investment, etc.

The FCC doesn't get into any of that in broadcasting, so in that sense it is very different. But as far as the protection of

the public is concerned, the public's interest in the industry is the same.

. . . .

Question: We are all interested and stimulated by what you said as FCC Commissioner at the National Association of Broadcasters last spring. The thing that struck me the most—from your own studies, is that you have come to the conclusion that it was conformity that usually got broadcasters into trouble.

HENRY: With the FCC?

Question: What had led you to this conclusion, Mr. Chairman?

HENRY: What had led me to it was my study when I first came to the Commission of the question of censorship and just how a regulatory body, the FCC, could regulate the service provided, which is programs, and at the same time not censor. I came to the conclusion that what we would have to do is to express and reflect the needs and interests of the public as we have them told to us by the public—to make the broadcasters more aware of some of the things the public was telling us about.

But we would never get into the area of saying to a broadcaster that you can or cannot put on this or that particular program, or that on this program you can or cannot discuss this particular question.

Question: No advance blue penciling?

HENRY: Yes, no advance blue penciling and no efforts at after-the-fact censorship or censorship by innuendo or threat. What Newton Minow and myself, as Chairman of the FCC, have been concerned about and criticized the broadcasters for is the failure to get into areas of controversy and to [32/33] exercise the right of free speech. We have criticized them for conforming, for example, to advertisers' demands.

. . . .

Question: We don't want to leave this censorship question hanging because, as you know, there is a group in the Communications Bar Association that argues any fear of subsequent punishment, any fear that a license might be lost, is in itself censorship. You have had this argument before?

HENRY: Yes, and I don't dismiss it as frivolous. As a matter of fact, I can cite them an opinion, which I am sure many of them have seen, which speaks of censorship in exactly those terms. So it is a very real argument.

Question: You on the other hand sir, are charged with reviewing station performance and deciding whether the public interest has been served?

HENRY: While I recognize that argument and while I would be less than honest with them if I simply talked about prior restraint as being the only thing involved, I do feel that you have to analyze each effort that we make along these lines in context and under the circumstances in which we make the effort. My point is that all of our efforts where they have cried censorship, where they have cried threat etc., are instances in which we have in fact been encouraging more diversity and wider exercise of the right of free speech. [33/52]

. . . .

Question: Chairman Henry, can we say that the simple fact is when you do, for cause, take a look at the performance of a station or licensee . . . this does not constitute censorship?

HENRY: There is no doubt about that—absolutely. If a substantial segment of a listening or viewing audience complains about some aspect of a licensee's operation and in response to that, we examine it, we are only doing our job. If we didn't respond then there would be no point to our existence. The claim that the broadcaster may feel that his ability to operate is jeopardized by a Federal Communications Commission being critical of the industry in general is to me stretching a point beyond all validity. The claim that that constitutes censorship, and to say that we couldn't examine his overall performance, is simply stretching it beyond all reasonable bounds.

Question: Many people today are talking about the lack of creativity in the television business. Are you familiar with these charges of repetition?

HENRY: Not in the business but in the programs. There is a lot of creativity . . . it just doesn't seem to get to the tube.

Question: Do you feel with the restraints and with public policy background of the Communications Commission that a force can be exerted here by you as the Chairman?

HENRY: There is a force that can be exerted by me as Chairman—by continuing to talk publicly and continuing to have it aired and discussed; thereby creating a climate in which ideas and solutions will come. I think the Commission can take action in this field again by attempting, as it did in the option time proceedings, to loosen up the ground, so that seeds of creativity can come through. That is, so they can get by the vice presidents in charge of programming for the television networks.

Question: We are also in the midst of another television season. At your house the television set is turned on often. Have you any general reaction you would like to speak on?

HENRY: My reaction to television programs in general?

Question: What is coming out of the tube, that you just mentioned.

HENRY: My most usual reaction—the one that I keep coming back to is—I can go home and turn on the TV set, and if it is during the day most of the programs are of a similar type. They are panel shows, audience participation shows, quiz shows, and they are interrupted quite frequently by commercials. The programs are designed for the housewife primarily.

In the evening when you turn on the television set you get programs that appeal pretty much to the same audience level, pretty much to the same interest. And that is primarily to sit back and relax and be entertained on a very, very light scale. It makes very little difference as far as I can see if the program is a horse opera, a medical opus or an old movie or what have you. It is all at the same level. There is a dearth, except on special occasions, of other types of programming. Not only do I personally think this, but I think this feeling is representative of substantial segments of the viewing audience.

Question: There are multiple young Henrys at your house. What do you do about your children's viewing? Do you prescribe a schedule for them? What do you do?

HENRY: I do not prescribe a schedule for them, such as "this is the time they should watch television and this is a time they shouldn't." If they want to watch it and it is not bed time or meal time or play time outside to get some air, then they are perfectly free to look at television. We exercise some degree of control. I certainly wouldn't let my six year old stay up and look at a 10:00 o'clock [*sic*] program.

Question: Does Mrs. Henry act as a censor in your house? When she decides that there is something on that she doesn't want them to see?

HENRY: And so do I . . . There is often a conflict in the morning between one show and another. I try to exercise some jurisdiction over that—a father's prerogative.

Question: What about television re-runs?

HENRY: I mention very briefly the problem of summer re-runs. We have the networks on the one hand telling us that no one is able, including the networks, to satisfy the maw of television, and that, therefore, re-runs are necessary and enjoyable. On the other hand, many people in the production end, and the writing end, producing end, etc., say they are ready and willing and able to come up with a lot of new programs, but the networks will not let them. This is the direct conflict that we are going to have to consider.

.   .   .   .

Television and Juvenile Delinquency*

THE SUBCOMMITTEE TO INVESTIGATE JUVENILE DE-LINQUENCY. For additional information, see p. 121. The following interim report of the subcommittee to the Senate Committee on the Judiciary is based on hearings held in New York City on June 5, 1954, and in Washington, D.C., on October 19 and 20, 1954, and April 6 and 7, 1955.

A cursory view of program content shows clearly that a large amount of the crime and violence in television programs is from film. [27/29]

. . . .

Dr. Ralph S. Banay, a research psychiatrist from Columbia University, appeared before the subcommittee on April 6, 1955, and told of doing an analysis of the program themes for the week just before he testified as a witness. His statement read:

Dr. BANAY. Well, Hopalong Cassidy at 9 o'clock wipes out a gang.

The next program, Buffalo Bill, Jr., there is a false accusation of murder; at 11 there is a crooked insurance deal.

At 1 o'clock there is a story of kidnaping; at 1:30 there is a western story with cattle rustling; the sheriff is either shot in the back or is in cahoots with the gang.

At 2:15, 3 pirates, revenge; at 3 o'clock, a western story again with violence; at 5 o'clock, Roy Rogers; 2 desperadoes blow up the train; at 5:30, an orphan boy eludes the authorities.

Chairman KEFAUVER. Orphan boy does what?

Dr. BANAY. Eludes the authorities.

Chairman KEFAUVER. Yes.

Dr. BANAY. At 6 o'clock, a cowboy G-men story; at 6:30, the Black Phantom; at 7 o'clock, a vicious sabotage ring by Gene Autry.

At 8 p. m., a western, young man ruthlessly runs the cow country; then there is The Lineup, a crime story, safe robbery, and mugging.

At 10 o'clock there is International Police. I do not want to read it any further, because probably by that time most of the children are in bed.

Chairman KEFAUVER. Read a little further.

Dr. BANAY. All right; I will.

At 11:30, Man Behind the Badge, Mr. District Attorney; at 11, The Crooked Way; at 11:15, a western, with a lot of action and shooting; at 12 o'clock, Hit and Run, a man convicted and framed on a hit and run accident; Danger, several murder investigations. That was 1 day's programs.

The next day is Sunday, which is relatively free of crime stories.

At 10 o'clock western movies; at 11 o'clock a reluctant burglar, jilted rich girl plots revenge; at 1:30, Roy Rogers—a double-feature movie, western plus an ex-convict attempt to expose loan sharks.

Five-thirty, Captain Gallant, gang attacks a caravan; at 6 o'clock, Sky King, saboteur blows up a secret desert project; 7 o'clock, Big Town, crime drama; 7:30, steamship captain robs and deserts passengers; 9 o'clock, Watch Me Die, a man seeks a perfect method of murdering his wife, divorce won't do; he wants her money.

Nine-fifteen, Public Prosecutor, seeks out murderers and other criminals.

Nine-thirty, Front Page Detective; 10 o'clock, Ellery Queen, mystery; 10:30, Ellery Queen, mystery.

Do you wish to have a further recital?

Chairman KEFAUVER. Well, suppose we put it in the record.

Dr. BANAY. Should I read it?

Chairman KEFAUVER. No; do not read them now.

Dr. BANAY. I will turn it over to the reporter.

Chairman KEFAUVER. Let them be continued at this place in the record.

Dr. BANAY. Yes.

Monday: 4 p. m., Gene Autry, Law of the West, film; 4:30 p. m., Black Phantom, serial; 5:30 p. m., western film; 6 p. m., 5 westerns and Superman; 7 p. m., movie, chorus girl murdered. Ramar of the Jungle; 11 p. m., movie, murder;

* Staff of the Subcommittee to Investigate Juvenile Delinquency, Senate Committee on the Judiciary, 84th Congress, 1st Session, Television and Juvenile Delinquency, 27, 29-31, 34-35 (Committee Print 1955).

11:15 p. m., drama, gangsters shoot cops; 11:25 p. m., mystery, a young woman is charged with poisoning her husband.

Tuesday: 4 p. m., Gene Autry, Lone Shark; 4:30, Black Phantom, serial; 5:30, western; 6 p. m., 4 westerns and prison drama; 7 p. m., Superman, the Cisco Kid, western; 9:30 p. m., The Circle Theater, western, Mack [sic] Saber, and the Crime Man, and the Elgin Theater, a western with bigamy; 10 p. m., Danger, dueling; [29/30] 10:30 p. m., Badge 714, beating and robbing; 11:15 p. m., Danger, escape murder, et cetera, the Signet Theater, a woman leaves her crooked husband.

Wednesday: 4 p. m., Gene Autry and western film; 4:30 p. m., Black Phantom, serial; 5 p. m., Studio 7, drama, guide accuses boss of murder, and western; 5:30 p. m., western; 6 p. m., four westerns, movie, avenging a father's death; 7 p. m., Ramar of the Jungle, Superman; 10 p. m., Follow That Man, mystery; 10:30 p. m., Big Town; 11:15 p. m.[,] Signet Theater, suspense thriller about a murder epidemic; 11:25 p. m., western prison film.

Thursday: 4 p. m., Gene Autry, western movie; 4:30 p. m., the Black Phantom, serial; 5 p. m., western; 5:30 p. m., western; 6 p. m., three westerns; 7 p. m., Wild Bill Hickok; 7:45 p. m., movie, the Creeper, "serum turns people into cloying murderers"; 8:30 p. m., Justice, "wiretapping" and T-Men in Action; 9 p. m., Dragnet, Counterpoint, drama, "foolproof way to steal"; 10 p. m., the Public Defender; 10:30 p. m., Public Prosecutor, the Falcon, mystery, Paris Precinct, "a French dragnet"; 11 p. m., western.

Friday: 4 p. m., Gene Autry, and western; 4:30 p. m., the Black Phantom, serial; 5 p. m., Studio 7, drama, "doctor kills a patient," western; 5:30 p. m., western; 6 p. m., four westerns; 7 p. m., Badge 714, and two westerns; 9 p. m., the Big Story, "stealing and terrorizing"; 9:30 p. m., Paris Precinct, the Vise, drama; 10 p. m., the Line-Up, Mr. District Attorney; 10:30 p. m., mystery movie; 11:15 p. m., Signet Theater drama, "man discovers crime of his future father-in-law," crime movie.

Saturday: 95 TV hours; 23 hours of programs obviously having crimes, 24 percent.

Sunday: 110½ TV hours; 15¼ programs containing crime, violence, et cetera, 14 percent.

Monday, 4 p. m. to 10 p. m.: 48 TV hours; 8½ TV hours containing crime, et cetera, 18 percent.

Tuesday, 4 p. m. to 10 p[.] m[.]: 48 TV hours; 11½ TV hours with crime, violence, et cetera, 24 percent.

Wednesday, 4 p. m., to 10 p. m.: 48 TV hours; 8½ hours with crime or violence, 18 percent.

Thursday, 4 p. m. to 10 p. m.: 48 TV hours; 11¾ hours with crime or violence, 24 percent.

Friday, 4 p. m. to 10 p. m.: 48 TV hours; 12 hours with crime or violence, 25 percent.

. . . .

Dr. Banay dramatically stated that:

If the proverb is true that prison is college for crime, I believe for young disturbed adolescents, TV is a preparatory school for delinquency.[30]

Many social scientists . . . believe that the type of television program reported above has its most detrimental effect on emotionally disturbed children, or children with incipient delinquent proclivities. On the other hand, some industry spokesmen refer to this group as a very small part of the juvenile population and not within the purview of the industry as regards television programming or its effects. However, the subcommittee would like to refer at this point to the study of David Abrahamsen, Status of Mental Hygiene and Child Guidance Facilities in Public Schools in the United States, in the Journal of Pediatrics, volume 46, No. 1, January 1955. In that study a sample of the school popula- [30/31] tion of the United States was surveyed. Results in the study represented a total of 2,540,888 children. One of the purposes of the study was to determine the percentage of emotionally disturbed children in need of psychological help in the Nation's schools. It was found that in some schools as high as 60 percent of the pupils enrolled were experiencing some sort of emotional difficulty. The average shown for all schools was 10 percent. Projected onto the entire school population of the United States, there are approximately 2 million emotionally disturbed children in this age range. Needless to say this is a large group of children. . . .

. . . .

Several spokesmen for the television industry during the initial hearings testified to the effect that there is nothing wrong with television programs today and all

---

[30] Testimony of Dr. Ralph S. Banay in the hearings before the Subcommittee to Investigate Juvenile Delinquency, Television Programs, United States Senate, Washington, D. C., on April 6, 1955, pp. 79-86.

children may view them without harmful effects. [31/34]

. . . .

. . . Dr. Banay is consulting psychiatrist for the United States Bureau of Prisons and his testimony was based on his clinical experience with a great number of individuals who were delinquent or criminal. He was of the opinion that certain televisions programs do have a deleterious effect on a certain portion of the child audience, that is, the emotionally disturbed children. . . .

. . . .

Although not all returns from the members of the Academy of Forensic Sciences and the Medical Correctional Association have been [34/35] received, the majority have supported the statements made by Dr. Banay. . . . The subcommittee would like to point out that this is not positive proof, but does represent a well-thought-out, educated body of opinion of professionals who come into everyday contact with delinquents and criminals. It would also like to point out to the television industry and the National Association of Radio and Television Broadcasters, that there is a substantial body of opinion that is contrary to those they ordinarily present in defense of television programming.

. . . .

U.S. Television Abroad: Big New Business*

JOHN TEBBEL (1912-   ), chairman of the department of journalism at the New York University School of Commerce, is also a successful free-lance writer. He has done such biographical books as *The Marshall Fields* (1947), *George Horace Lorimer and the Saturday Evening Post* (1948), *The Life and Good Times of William Randolph Hearst* (1952). He has also written historical novels and many articles for magazines, especially for the *Saturday Review* communications section, from which this piece is taken.

LONDON.
While the debate over television's role in American culture is being argued on the playing fields of Washington, the entrepreneurs of the prerecorded small screen are quietly building themselves an international industry. With tape and film they have introduced the American wasteland, if indeed it is, into the programming of every country that has any television at all, and they are anticipating the needs of emerging nations that do not yet enjoy this blessing of civilization.

In little more than a half-dozen years, international television sales abroad have reached a total of more than $25 million. The center of the new industry is London, where the three major American networks and several producing organizations have sales offices busily selling United States television in Europe and on other continents.

London is the center for European, African, and Near Eastern distribution, but the networks and other distributors also have salesmen in Toronto, Mexico City (covering Central and South America), and Sydney, Australia, which is presently the distributing point for Asia.

There are sound business reasons for this expansion, which has only begun. One reason is the startling fact, little known outside the trade, that during this year the total of television sets owned outside the United States will surpass the American total. By the end of 1962, we will have fifty million sets; the remainder of the world will have fifty-three million, and this is one gap not likely to be closed. It will, in fact, tend to widen steadily as time goes on. As one might expect, the United Kingdom has more receivers, twelve million, than any other foreign country, but West Germany can boast four million in its rapidly expanding economy, while Italy has nearly three million and the Scandinavian countries nearly two million.

There is a tough competitive scramble to reach this juicy market. Of the American networks, NBC was first to realize and exploit the situation, and consequently has an impressive head start on the others as a supplier of television film. CBS has proceeded more cautiously, but it easily ranks second in sales, while ABC, a relative newcomer to the struggle, is third. Then there are the several large non-network suppliers: Revue (MCA), Screen Gems (Columbia), Ziv (United Artists), ITC (Independent Television Corporation of England, formerly an American-British company but now wholly British owned),

* John Tebbel, "U.S. Television Abroad: Big New Business," *Saturday Review*, XLV (July 14, 1962), 44-45. Reprinted by permission of *Saturday Review* and the author.

Desilu Productions, Warner Brothers, and Four Star. The BBC, too, is active all over the world; many of its shows are seen on American networks, who do not, however, distribute them through their international divisions. These strong competitors —producers and distributors—have one thing in common: they are big and getting bigger.

There is now some American television on every service in Europe, and it will be seen on the newest group of small TV services, just going on the air this summer in Sierra Leone, Kenya, and Gibraltar. For TV has become a status symbol. If a new nation wants status these days among the developing countries, it must first have an airline and then a television service, which will undoubtedly run at a substantial loss. In most of these countries, advertising revenue will be sought immediately to help offset the expense. The new African nations carry commercials on their services, as do some in the Middle East, but old established Western European countries like the Netherlands, Belgium, and France, along with some in Scandinavia, permit no commercialism.

The chief usefulness of television in every country is propaganda: it gives the government a means for communicating instantly with the people. While such usage does little for the quality of programming, it justifies a cost which few of these nations would otherwise consider worth meeting.

In spite of government propaganda, however, television remains an entertainment medium. This is particularly true in Britain, where the decision in 1955 to introduce commercial TV opened the way for American companies to establish their new industry. It was, in some ways, a painful introduction, accomplished through the Independent Television Act of 1954, which created the Independent Television Authority and ended the BBC's twenty-seven-year monopoly. This act was pushed through Parliament by a determined group of Conservative back-bench MPs, who later were accused of highpowered pressure tac-

tics on behalf of the "commercial interests," meaning industry and advertising agencies.

Having been created, the new Authority found itself confronted with the formidable task of filling the air in competition with the BBC's established programs. Fortunately for it, at about this time American television began to be available on film, especially the high-rating Western shows and crime thrillers in the usual thirteen-week and twenty-six-week series. This was exactly the kind of fare the Authority needed to create and reach the mass audience it believed was waiting in Britain. There were complicated questions of clearing rights to be solved, but the American networks were only too willing to help solve them, and on September 22, 1955, the new Authority put its first telecast on the air from a London station. By the end of last year, 95 per cent of Britain's population was within reach of ITA's operating stations.

Skeptics on both sides of the Atlantic who predicted that Britons would not like or understand American television films proved to be profoundly wrong. To experienced observers this was hardly surprising because the viewers were only looking at a condensation of something already thoroughly familiar to them, the American motion picture. Hollywood, in fact, has conditioned the whole world to easy acceptance of the rival medium. When the BBC, countering ITA's success, imported the Perry Como show on film, British intellectuals protested in the press and even in Parliament, but BBC audiences plainly enjoyed not only Como but the familiar motion picture and stage personalities who were his guests.

As America's TV film salesmen moved from Britain to the Continent, [44/45] they had to deal at once with the language barrier. Again the movies had broken trail, because American motion pictures had long been dubbed in French and other languages, besides employing English subtitles. Soon our TV films were being brought directly to France and dubbed there, although not without difficulties. "Lip synching," as dubbing is called, is a long and tedious process, and sometimes the French simply don't bother.

Not surprisingly, General De Gaulle has taken an austere view of dubbing. He believes French television ought to be French made, and there is a quota on American film coming into France. Quotas, in fact, exist nearly everywhere. In Britain, the independent companies have agreed on a quota of 14 per cent of total time for foreign film. The BBC, making its own rules, has a quota of 9 per cent. In Gibraltar, Kenya, and Sierra Leone, the quotas will be 50 per cent for the British, because that is the audience; 25 per cent from other countries, and 25 per cent live.

The West Germans have been exceptionally hospitable to the American film salesmen, and are already the second largest consumer. They can easily afford to buy the foreign product because of their substantial advertising revenue. After some early frostiness, the Bonn government has become much more receptive, and audiences have long been getting the benefits of expert German dubbing.

Germans have always loved the old-fashioned Western melodrama in books and motion pictures, and they love it no less on television film. This passion they share with the people of every country. Television sales executives say the most popular show in the world today is "Bonanza," which is telecast by every nation that has a TV service. The obvious reason for the Western's enormous popularity is the perfect escape it offers to an anxious world. Some television experts say the particular success of "Bonanza" rises from the fact there is no mother in the cast, thus offering a comprehensive psychological outlet to both men and women.

The pattern of popularity is almost exactly the same abroad as it is in America. Escape is the universal need. Dramatic suspense shows follow Westerns, succeeded by crime and mystery stories. Exact ratings, however, are virtually impossible to determine anywhere except in the United Kingdom, the only place which has ratings as we know them. Other countries make spot checks at the discretion of the program board or the buyer, but the resulting judgments are unavoidably subjective. Most boards and buyers display some sense of responsibility and try to maintain relatively high standards. American ratings mean nothing to the foreign buyer, however. He is always certain his audience is different—although he is likely to be uninformed about working-class preferences, because he so often judges his programming by talking to viewers who share his own interests.

In any case, the foreign buyers know they must depend on America for Westerns and crime stories. "We can do good dramatic shows of our own," says one, "but we cannot duplicate your gangsters and your cowboys and Indians."

Thus far, the tremendous supply of American film has guaranteed that the flow of business goes from West to East, but already there are indications that television film selling is not going to remain a one-way transatlantic street. There is increasing activity, most of it in Britain at the moment, directed toward developing shows for international export. Contrary to popular opinion, this summer's miracle of world-wide satellite transmission is not expected to alter present patterns. Most experts believe satellite TV will be used for spot news—what Europeans call "actualities." There is no foreseeable reason to use satellite transmission in place of far cheaper tape and film, particularly when time differences make live programming so difficult.

The reverse flow of international business is presently two pronged. One comprises the work of television producers who are making international shows, like the Inspector Maigret series based on Georges Simenon's novels, which is a British venture, and one-shot shows like the Jo Stafford special produced by Britain's ITC. The other prong is the formation of international producing companies like Intertel, conceived by Associated Rediffusion in Britain and involving Canada, Australia, and the United States as partners. Intertel's plan is to produce shows in all these countries and then circulate the product among themselves—a kind of television Common Market. This enterprise has been in business about a year and has already turned out "Decline of an Empire," made in Britain by an American producer; and a Canadian documentary, "Living With a Giant," about Canadian-American relations. TV's cooperative move to market an international product parallels the joint movie-making enterprises of Italian, French, British, and American producers.

Musical shows still offer a stumbling block to international television producers, because of the difficulties involved in clearing music rights and the legal tangles presented by personalities who are under contract to appear in participating countries. In the news field, by contrast, all countries draw on each other's resources, and television news is daily becoming more international.

International business is also branching out to include American participation in the ownership and management of foreign stations. Thus NBC has become a partner of the Nigerian government in setting up a new television chain. The network has sent key executives and technicians to assist in starting the service and to help maintain it for the next five years, during which time they will train Nigerians to take over the entire operation. Along with these developments, inevitably, an international advertising business is growing, based on such world-wide accounts as Coca-Cola and Lever Bros. Performers, too, are begining to think in terms of international audiences.

American television, having saturated time and priced itself to the top in this country, is on the way to conquering the Western Atlantic nations and Africa. Tomorrow, no doubt, the world.

Suggested Topics for Controlled Research

The Introduction should provide the interested student with a variety of subjects for his curiosity to pursue. The headings for each part of the book, phrased as questions, obviously suggest subjects that are debatable and require much weighing of arguments pro and con. Here are some further suggestions.

What is the difference between governmental censorship and the *Production Code* in Hollywood? The types of state and local censorship can be gleaned from the opening historical summary by Terry Ramsaye and from the history of American censors by Bosley Crowther. The whole story of *The Motion Picture Production Code* can hardly be told from material in this book, but the articles by Ramsaye and Crowther, plus the selection by Roger Manvell and the excerpt from the Kefauver subcommittee's report on *Motion Pictures and Juvenile Delinquency*, can give enough background to explain the differences between self-control and official control. The Supreme Court decision in the *Miracle* case also gives some insight into the way the New York state law worked up to that time.

How would you compare the Russian, the British, and the American systems of controlling film content? This topic is closely related to the preceding one, and might well be included in an overall study of censorship methods and purposes. The same selections from this book would be helpful for such a study. Which of the systems do you think puts the strongest restraint on the kinds of pictures that can be made? Which imposes the weakest restraint?

Should the states pass laws requiring certain kinds of films to be classified as "for adults only"? This question is debated, in effect, by Bosley Crowther, Joe Hyams, and the Kefauver subcommittee's report on *Motion Pictures and Juvenile Delinquency*. Note Crowther's implication that children should be allowed to see anything the theater shows, including *Two Women*. Compare the Kefauver subcommittee's assertion that movies should not be "hobbled by the mental and moral requirements of the immature." A longer paper would go into the whole question of the impact of the moving image on the attitudes of young people. For this paper the selection by Mortimer Adler about the Payne Fund study, together with the Kefauver subcommittee's descriptions of film content, would be helpful. What possibilities can you think of for "classifying" television programs?

Do you agree with Mortimer Adler's statement about the artist, "Moral instruction is not his task"? What other writers in this anthology would agree with him? Martin Quigley? Mervyn LeRoy? What appears to be the attitude of the Soviet Union? The Hollywood *Motion Picture Production Code?*

What is the difference between a "topical" film and a "problem" film? The article on the problem film suggests that a good many films of this kind have been made, but does not report on their financial success. (It is extremely difficult to get dependable statistics on box-office returns; in general, it can be said that pictures like these are not among the big money-makers.) Mervyn LeRoy seems to reject the notion that such films can ever be profitable. Does Irving Thalberg's praise for the "topical" film straddle this issue? Does he mean that he likes "message" pictures? What does he really seem to be saying? If a film reflects the times, does it necessarily concern itself with social problems? Were the gangster pictures "problem films" or entertainment?

Do you think it was a good or a bad

thing for *West Side Story* to be the most popular American film ever shown in Japan? Does the weight of the picture emphasize the excitement of gang fighting? Or does the violence in the story lead clearly to tragedy and sorrow? What kind of propaganda would you say this film represents overseas? Does it compare in any way with *Triumph of the Will,* which Siegfried Kracauer says seems to suggest that "life exists only in a state of transition"? What would Norman Cousins and Eric Johnston have to say about this? Would George Bernard Shaw or Jean Benoit-Levy say that a picture like this should be made with the world reaction in mind?

How much actual power over the content of television programs does the FCC have? Do you think Newton Minow was justified in trying to get the networks to improve their shows? What indirect effects does Roy Huggins really seem to be objecting to? What does the Communications Act say about censorship? Do you think the networks ought to give the audience what it wants? Or what it needs? Should anybody have the power to criticize the networks' performance? Should an agency of the government have that power? Or a Congressional investigating committee?

But some of these questions would profit from further reading and library work.

Suggested Topics for Library Research

Many of the selections reprinted in this anthology are taken from books. You have already seen the footnote citations on the first page of each selection and the occasional comments on them in the brief introductory notes. These works might well be your first list of outside sources if you plan to read beyond the limits of this volume. I must warn you, however, that film books are not always available in wide variety, even in big libraries, and that they also have a tendency to be out of print because the publisher didn't manufacture very many of them in the first place. My guess would be that you might find in a large university library the books by Seldes, Powdermaker, Agee, Kracauer, Adler, and MacCann. You are somewhat less likely to find the books by Grierson, LeRoy, Manvell, Nicoll, and Benoit-Levy or the world history of film by Rotha and Griffith.

If you wish to work on some aspect of the history of film, start with a recent book by Arthur Knight, *The Liveliest Art* (New York, 1957), which takes up the most important periods in foreign as well as American production. If you're curious about the silent era, try Joe Franklin, *Classics of the Silent Screen* (New York, 1955), or Arthur Jacobs, *The Rise of the American Film* (New York, 1939), which traces the American history up through the first ten years of sound. Bosley Crowther has written a history of one studio, Metro-Goldwyn-Mayer, in *The Lion's Share* (New York, 1957); and King Vidor, a world-famous director, has told his own story in *A Tree Is a Tree* (New York, 1952). Probably the best history of film in a single foreign country is Joseph Anderson and Donald Richie, *The Japanese Film: Art and Industry* (Rutland, Vermont, 1959).

Do you need, for background, simply an introduction to motion-picture technique? Try Ernest Lindgren, *The Art of the Film* (London, 1948), which is sometimes used as a textbook in introductory film courses; or W. R. Fulton, *Motion Pictures* (Norman, Oklahoma, 1960), which explains a good deal of technique and history along with a few key films.

Motion pictures themselves are source material, of course. The thoughtful student will look at them in a new light after reading some of the selections in this book and may want to use examples he has seen when he writes his research paper. The ones that relate most directly would be the problem films, including those referred to in Part Three. A careful criticism of two or three or even one outstanding film in the light of specific readings might result in a useful paper. You must avoid the temptation, of course, to write simply a personal reaction to the "great acting" and the "interesting story." A critical article is much more than that.

It may be possible to catch some of the older movies referred to in this book on daytime or evening television. Many universities also have campus film societies, affiliated with the American Federation of Film Societies, which offer weekly programs. A variety of features are available on 16 millimeter film for rental. Films, Inc., is the largest distributor of American movies. Contemporary Films and Brandon Films specialize in foreign pictures. Their New York addresses can be found in directories kept by any large library. Don't miss any opportunity you might get to compare American films with such permanent and universal foreign classics as Jean Renoir's *Grand Illusion* (Franco-German relationships in World War I) or Vittorio de Sica's *Umberto D* (the pensioner's predicament in Italy) or Akira Kurosawa's *Ikiru* (bureaucracy and ingratitude in Japan).

The documentary film, an area of film-making reluctantly excluded from this book except for the references in Kracauer and Grierson, presents a wide choice of problems. From Pare Lorentz' *The River* (conservation and flood control on the Mississippi) to John Huston's *The Battle of San Pietro* (American infantry in Italy), nonfiction has been a strong element in the American concern with visual communication. Study your contemporary television programs for continuing evidence of this. The inheritors of Edward R. Murrow's See It Now series have contributed richly to the tradition: Twentieth Century, CBS Reports, the NBC White Papers, Project 20, the Chet Huntley and David Brinkley specials, and the ABC Close-Ups.

For many students, specific films desired will not be available. A partially satisfactory substitute is to consult reviews. The more important pictures are reviewed in the New York *Times* and in magazines like *Time, Newsweek, Saturday Review, New Republic, Esquire, New Yorker, Show, Commonweal,* and *Commentary.* If you know the approximate year of release, it is fairly easy to locate the magazine reviews by looking them up under "motion pictures" in the *Readers' Guide to Periodical Literature.*

The *Readers' Guide* and the *International Index to Periodicals* are most helpful for research about any library project, but are particularly useful for a study of film and society because of the constant changes in this field. It is also true that many of the best things written about film and communication first appear in magazines, here and abroad.

The best film magazines in the English language are *Sight and Sound,* a quarterly supported in part by the British government and published by the British Film Institute in London, and *Film Quarterly,* published by the University of California at Berkeley. Monthlies with a more popular approach are the British *Films and Filming* and the American *Films in Review,* the latter published by the National Board of Review in New York.

In general, the reference books about movies are sketchy and inadequate. One exception is an early work edited by Harold Leonard, *The Film Index: Film as Art,* an exhaustive annotated bibliography of films, books, and articles, from the silent days through 1936 (New York, 1941). But it is long out of print and has never been followed by a later study. The annual *Yearbook* which comes with a subscription to *Film Daily* (New York) is in some libraries and is about the best American source for industry statistics. The *Motion Picture Almanac* and the *Television Almanac,* put out annually by the publishers of the monthly *Motion Picture Herald,* are also useful, especially for short biographies of film and TV people.

This sketchiness of reference books can be a hindrance in your research. If you wished, for example, to pursue the question of censorship in foreign countries, you would find it extremely difficult, since the sources are poor and the rules constantly changing. There is an early volume by Eugene Harley, *World Wide Influences of the Cinema* (Los Angeles, 1940), which has some early examples of films cut by the censor's scissors in foreign lands; but the latest policies must be found mostly in the *Film Daily Yearbook* or perhaps by writing to the Motion Picture Association in Washington, D.C. Certain countries recently the location for American film-making (Greece, Argentina, Spain, etc.) have been the subject of reports by the U.S. Department of Commerce, Office of Scientific, Motion Picture, and Photographic Products.

Are you interested in the kind of audience research the movie industry actually undertook at one time? See Leo Handel, *Hollywood Looks at Its Audience* (Urbana, 1950).

Would you like to read and criticize a psychological approach to love, crime, and the parent-child relationship as portrayed in American, British, and French films of the 1940's? Read Martha Wolfenstein and Nathan Leites, *Movies: A Psychological Study* (Glencoe, Illinois, 1950).

For one minority group's feelings about

film as a reflection of society, see Peter Noble, *The Negro in Films* (London, 1948).

For a statement of the Catholic position that morals and art are inseparable, see Frank Getlein and Harold C. Gardiner, *Movies, Morals, and Art* (New York, 1961).

Has the Hollywood *Production Code* been a protection for the American family or just a front for industry public relations? A good way to approach this touchy historical question, after the introduction this anthology affords, is to turn to Ruth Inglis, *Freedom of the Movies* (Chicago, 1947), for a critical approach. The final portions of Will Hays's own story, *The Memoirs of Will H. Hays* (Garden City, N.Y., 1955), provide a much more favorable view of the events concerning the code in which the first "czar" of the movies played such a prominent role.

For a detailed study of pressure by a Congressional committee on personnel policies in Hollywood, see John Cogley, *Report on Blacklisting: Movies* (New York, 1956). For several years after World War II, Hollywood was accused of yielding to Communist influences, and there were investigations by committees on un-American activities in the California state legislature and in the U.S. House of Representatives. Although Communist influence on film content was difficult to trace, it was found that certain writers and directors had joined the Communist party for various periods of time during and after the war. These, and many other suspected persons, were quietly blacklisted by the studios; they could not be employed again unless they made detailed "confessions" of their political sins. For a long time after the Congressional investigations, film-makers tended to avoid films of political and social controversy.

A second volume by John Cogley, *Report on Blacklisting: Radio and TV* (New York, 1956), is concerned with broadcasting. More recently, a decision by the FCC in the case of the Pacifica Foundation suggests that the Commission will take great care to avoid interfering with TV or radio stations on political grounds, especially if balanced programming is available to the community served. On the three FM stations operated by the Foundation in San Francisco, Los Angeles, and New York, a wide range of viewpoints have been heard, including the views of members of the Communist Party and the John Birch Society. The FCC specifically denied that it was the function of its regulation to prevent controversy or to encourage "bland" programming. (See "F.C.C. Sanctions Provocative TV," New York *Times,* January 23, 1964, pp. 1, 63.)

Many people in Hollywood still doubt the wisdom of the legal prosecutions by the U.S. government which divided theater companies from production-distribution companies. Since the rise of television, especially, production executives and union men alike have raised their voices against the anti-trust theory which lumped an art-industry with stockyards and steel mills. In Morris L. Ernst, *The First Freedom* (New York, 1946), is an impassioned statement of the case against monopoly and the "block-booking" of films, sight unseen, that went with it. Michael Conant has written a soberer economic analysis, *Anti-Trust in the Motion Picture Industry* (Berkeley, 1960). And if you should happen to have access to the old volumes of the *Hollywood Quarterly,* published by the University of California Press, you will find a defense of block-booking by Arthur Mayer ("An Exhibitor Begs for 'B's'," *Hollywood Quarterly,* III [Winter, 1947-48], 172-177).

If you are interested in the relationship between films and young people, look at Henry J. Forman, *Our Movie-Made Children* (New York, 1933), a summary of the Payne Fund reports that may lead you on to the whole series. J. P. Mayer collected some "personal documents" about reactions to films by young people in *Sociology of Film* (London, 1948), which finds echoes in the Kefauver report. Mary Field, on the other hand, successfully made movies specifically for children: her experiences in this British production program (1943-50) are told in *Good Company* (London, 1952).

If Gilbert Seldes' comments on the western myth in movies interest you, there is a new history of the western film by George N. Fenin and William K. Everson, *The Western* (New York, 1962), that might be useful for a research project. And in a book of essays from the *Partisan Review* and other sources, *The Immediate Experience* (New York, 1962), Robert Warshow has written an especially stimulating chapter on the role of the western film in American culture.

In the same book of essays Mr. Warshow also wrote about gangster films, in a chapter you might want to compare with the psychological insights of Wolfenstein and Leites and the historical comments of Griffith.

Perhaps some readers will be led into the whole question of mass communication and the mass audience in our time. Are we lulled by too much entertainment —or even too much information? Is the quality of communication leveled down to the lowest common denominator in order to get the widest buying audience? What should be the role of the editors and producers who choose what most of us shall read and see? Some recent books on this: Bernard Rosenberg and David Manning White, *Mass Culture: The Popular Arts in America* (New York, 1957); Wilbur Schramm, *Responsibility in Mass Communication* (New York, 1957); *Mass Culture and Mass Media* (Cambridge, Mass., 1960); Dwight MacDonald, *Against the American Grain* (New York, 1962).

By now you will have realized that there isn't much point in writing a paper about films in general. That would be like writing a paper about books in general. Motion pictures, whether they are projected from 8 millimeter film or on a Cinerama screen, are as wide as the whole world of discourse.